Educating Monks

Contemporary Buddhism

MARK M. ROWE, SERIES EDITOR

Architects of Buddhist Leisure: Socially Disengaged Buddhism in Asia's Museums, Monuments, and Amusement Parks
Justin Thomas McDaniel

Educating Monks: Minority Buddhism on China's Southwest Border
Thomas A. Borchert

Educating Monks

*Minority Buddhism on
China's Southwest Border*

Thomas A. Borchert

UNIVERSITY OF HAWAI'I PRESS
HONOLULU

Printed in the United States of America

24 23 22 21 20 19   6 5 4 3 2 1

Library of Congress Cataloging-in-Publication Data

Names: Borchert, Thomas A., author.
Title: Educating monks : minority Buddhism on China's southwest border /
    Thomas A. Borchert.
Other titles: Contemporary Buddhism.
Description: Honolulu : University of Hawai'i Press, [2017] | Series: Contemporary
    Buddhism | Includes bibliographical references and index.
Identifiers: LCCN 2016051213 | ISBN 9780824866488 (cloth ; alk. paper)
Subjects: LCSH: Buddhist monks—Education—China—Xishuangbanna Daizu
    Zizhizhou. | Buddhist monks—China—Xishuangbanna Daizu Zizhizhou. | Buddhist
    education—China—Xishuangbanna Daizu Zizhizhou. | Monastic and religious life
    (Buddhism)—China—Xishuangbanna Daizu Zizhizhou. | Buddhism and politics—
    China—Xishuangbanna Daizu Zizhizhou. | Xishuangbanna Daizu Zizhizhou
    (China)—Religion.
Classification: LCC BQ6160.C6 B67 2017 | DDC 294.3/657—dc23
    LC record available at https://lccn.loc.gov/2016051213

ISBN 978-0-8248-6649-5 (pbk.)

Contents

vii Series Editor's Preface

ix Acknowledgments

xiii Note on Languages, Pronunciation, and Names

xvii Abbreviations

1 INTRODUCTION
Buddhism and Monastic Education, within and across Borders in the New Millennium

PART 1: SHAPING BUDDHIST LIVES IN SIPSONGPANNĀ

27 **CHAPTER ONE**
LOCAL MONKS IN SIPSONGPANNĀ

52 **CHAPTER TWO**
FORTUNE-TELLING AND FALSE MONKS: Defining and Governing Religion

79 **CHAPTER THREE**
MONKS ON THE MOVE: Dai-Lue Monastic Networks

PART 2: EDUCATING THE MONKS OF SIPSONGPANNĀ

105 **CHAPTER FOUR**
LEARNING TO READ IN VILLAGE TEMPLES AND CHINESE PUBLIC SCHOOLS

127 **CHAPTER FIVE**
THE FRAGILITY OF AUTONOMY: Curricular Education at Dhamma Schools

152 **CHAPTER SIX**
TRANSNATIONAL BUDDHIST EDUCATION AND THE LIMITS OF THE BUDDHIST ETHNOSCAPE

172 Afterword

177 Notes

189 Glossary

193 References

203 Index

Series Editor's Preface

Thomas Borchert opens his remarkable ethnographic journey with a simple yet profound question: What makes a Buddhist monk? The answer, in all its complexity, provides exciting possibilities for contemporary Buddhist studies. Intimately tracing the education of Theravada monks from a minority ethnic group in southeast China, Borchert challenges traditional categorizations of Buddhism, identity, and nation. As the Dai-lue monks cross boundaries and forge identities in, through, and against various expressions of the State, he expertly expands geographic and conceptual scales to consider multiple frames in our studies of Buddhism today. Taking the education of these monks as a total phenomenon, Borchert invites us to approach Buddhism in both its concrete, localized forms and its imagined universals. He not only presents us with a specific Buddhism that is intimately tied to individual lives, but also charts national and international forces and flows that influence how all Buddhisms manifest in the world today.

Acknowledgments

THIS BOOK HAS BEEN A LONG TIME IN THE MAKING—more than twenty years if we go by my first research visit to Sipsongpannā in 1994. But it has also gone in fits and starts, as I've written myself into corners, or not understood what I was trying to say. While it has been too long in the making, I hope that the book has become clearer for all that. More than anything else, I have accrued many debts along the way. Indeed, I have relied on conversations, arguments, and laughter with many people. Their interventions have generally made it a better product; I have only myself to thank for the mistakes.

I have had many teachers—formal and informal—who have contributed to this book. When I was in college, Don Swearer suggested I look at Sipsongpannā as a place where I could combine my interests in China and Theravāda Buddhism, and in 1994 he set me up teaching English at a monastic high school in Chiang Mai. It was here that I first got a sense of the importance of education for understanding contemporary Buddhism. Much of what I valued in my time at the Divinity School at the University of Chicago was the experience of having people take my work seriously enough to critique it in its early stages. Frank Reynolds, Steve Collins, and Prasenjit Duara were exemplary mentors: encouraging, collegial, and critical. I am also deeply thankful for what I learned from Bruce Lincoln and the late Martin Riesebrodt. While they were not directly involved in this project, their teaching has stayed with me both in the questions I ask and in the tools that I have to try to answer them.

I have had the pleasure of being surrounded by good colleagues at a variety of institutions, without whom academic life would be much less enjoyable. At the University of Vermont for the last decade, I have benefited from conversations with Vicki Brennan, Anne Clark, Ilyse Morgenstein-Fuerst, Luther Martin, Abigail McGowan, Bill Paden, Richard Sugarman, Todne Thomas, Kevin Trainor, Erica Andrus, Mike Naparstak, and Cuong Mai. I also had the immense pleasure of spending a very productive and enjoyable six months in Singapore at the Nalanda-Sriwijaya Centre (NSC) at the Institute of Southeast Asian Studies (ISEAS). Many thanks to Tansen Sen and Geoff

Wade of NSC, Michael Montesano of ISEAS, and the reading group organized by Prasenjit Duara at the Asian Research Institute of the National University of Singapore.

Many friends and colleagues have listened to or read parts of this book through the years. I would like to thank (in no particular order): Jeffrey Samuels, Steven Collins, Kevin Trainor, Justin McDaniel, Alicia Turner, Loren Lybarger, Oona Paredes, Tracy Johnson, Carsten Vala, Gareth Fisher, Roger Casas, Fenggang Yang, Brian Nichols, the late Ian Harris, Juliane Schober, Amy Holmes-Tagchungdarpa, Cecily McCaffrey, Juliana Finucane, Wu Keping, Ng Zhiru, Kathleen Sullivan, Anne Hansen, Anne Blackburn, John Holt, and Phra-Khru Phisan.

Jeffrey Samuels, Steven Collins, Kevin Trainor, Catherine Borchert, John Sidel, and Alicia Turner all read full drafts of the manuscript. While not always easy to hear, their criticisms were invaluable in helping me cast and recast this book. I would also like to thank Alicia for sharing the manuscript in progress with some of her classes. I am grateful as well to Mark Rowe, the series editor, and Stephanie Chun of University of Hawai'i Press for their support in moving the manuscript forward, and to the two anonymous reviewers, who provided invaluable comments and criticisms. I also thank Emma Tait for correcting and improving my maps.

This project would not exist without the Buddhists of Sipsongpannā, particularly the monks and novices who were in residence at Wat Pājie in 2001–2002, and who have over the years continued to treat me as if I were still an active part of their community. Special thanks are due to Khūbā Meuang Jom and the senior monks of the Buddhist Association (BA) for permitting me to teach their novices and ask many questions over the years; to Dubi Samso, Dubi Ngen, the late Dubi Samlaw, and Khanān Bian for language help, teasing laughter, and friendship; to Khanān Samsaw for friendship and helping me to understand Buddhist institutions; and to Ai Ngen, Peng Yanqing, Yi Nang, Li Xiaoni, Li Xiaoye, and Su Youfa for great help in navigating Jing Hong. In Kunming, Yang Hui of the Visual Anthropology Department of Yunnan University kindly sponsored me in 2001, after just a last-minute e-mail introduction (and thanks to Sara Davis for that introduction). Yi Kaew of Yunnan Nationalities University (Yunnan Minzu Daxue; MinDa) provided a first valuable introduction to reading and speaking Dai-lue.

I am profoundly grateful to the many, many language teachers I have had over the years—teachers of Chinese, Thai, Sanskrit, Pāli, and Dai-lue. I have not usually lived up to their expectations but have often been able to make them laugh (at my pronunciation, if nothing else).

In closing, I offer thanks to my family, though the thanks I offer pales in comparison with what I have received over the years. My parents, Catherine and Frank Borchert, never did anything but assume that I could learn whatever I wanted to; my siblings, Anne and Terry, dragged me to Japan at age fifteen, only one of the many worlds that they have opened for me; my aunt and uncle, Sally and Ted Oldham, shared their love of travel and adventure with Rhonda and me. My children, Jasper, Kai, and Jing have all been my best research assistants, whether they knew it or not. Time with them has slowed down this book, but it has also made it better, and I will always treasure walking through China, Singapore, Thailand, and Vermont with them. And Rhonda, my partner ever since F class in Sapporo—it would not have been worth it without you.

With gratitude, love, and not a little relief, I dedicate this book to Rhonda.

Note on Languages, Pronunciation, and Names

SIPSONGPANNĀ IS A MULTILINGUAL PLACE. MANDARIN CHINESE is the language of the local government and local commerce, but because there are many different nationalities living there, it is possible to encounter a number of different languages and dialects. Most relevant here is the language spoken by the Dai-lue majority population of the region. In both Dai-lue and Chinese, this is referred to as the "speech of the Dai" (Dai: *gam dai;* Ch.: *dai yu*). Dai is closely related to other Tai languages of mainland Southeast Asia, particularly Shan, Lao, and Kham Muang of northern Thailand. While there are some minor differences between what is spoken in these places (and indeed, there is no standardized form of Dai-lue even in Sipsongpannā), they are largely mutually intelligible.

There is no Western academic standard for the romanization of the Dai-lue language, which, like both Thai and Chinese, is a tonal language. My practice in romanization and transliteration of Dai-lue has been to take the written language, transliterate it more or less following Thai, and then modify this according to the ways words are pronounced in and around Jing Hong. (For the same reason, I have generally chosen to use the Dai-lue pronunciation of a word rather than the Pāli. For example, I use *wihān* rather than *vihāra* to designate a worship hall in a monastery.) There are other complexities to contend with as well. The consonant vowel combination that would be written as "ra" in Thai (as in the word *rak* [love]) might be pronounced (and thus transliterated) using *l, r,* or *h,* depending on the word. (The Dai-lue in Sipsongpannā tend to say *"hak"* for love, though it is usually written with an *r.*) In both Thai and Dai-lue, there are several letters that are difficult for non-native speakers to say correctly. In particular, the first sound in the word "Dai" is something between a *t* and a *d* (like the *t* in "forty"). I have chosen to use "Dai-lue" rather than "Tai-lue" because it is a voiced dental, albeit a lightly voiced one. The other letter that causes difficulty is one that rests between *p* and *b* (this is the *p* in *panna* or in Wat Pājie). As in Thai, consonants at the end of words are not carried through, as, for example, the *t* at the end of "put" and the *k* in "book" when one quickly says, "Put the book down."

The pronunciation is mainly straightforward for speakers of English, but attention should be paid to the following:

Consonants

b	a soft *b* sound
c	as *j* in joke
d	a sound between *d* and *t,* as the *t* in "forty"
k	hard *g* sound (as in "go")
kh	aspirated, like the *ch* in Chanukah
p	a sound between *p* and *b*
ph	unaspirated, like the *p* in people
th	aspirated *t,* as in "tinker"

Vowels

a, ah	as in "ah"
ai, ay	as in "I"
ae	as in "cat"
ao	as in "ow"
aw	as in "flaw"
eu	as in the French *peut*
eua	as in "*peu*-ah"
ey	as in "eh"
i	inside a consonant combination, it has a short sound, as in "win"; standing alone (e.g., *dubi* [monk]), it has a long *e,* as in "sweet."
oy	as in boy
u	as in boon

I have generally used the Dai-lue version of names. Thus, I refer to Sipsongpannā rather than Xishuangbanna, which is the Chinese transliteration of the region. The one exception to my effort to use indigenous pronunciation as a guide to names is with the capital of the region, Jing Hong. I use the Chinese to avoid the confusion that might arise if I wrote it as "Jiang Hong." The Dai-lue do not have surnames. Most Dai-lue (both males and females) have a chosen given name or two and a prefix, not unlike "Mr." or "Mrs." The prefix for most laypeople is "Ai" for men and "I" for women. People who are of royal or noble descent (or claim to have such descent) might be referred to as "Cao" or "Dao." Ordination as a monk or novice also affects this. Novices use the title "Pha," fully ordained monks are referred to as "Du" or "Dubi," and very senior members of the sangha might be referred to as "Khūbā." When a man disrobes, he might receive another title. If he disrobes when still a novice, he is called a *jī noy,* but uses "Ai"; if he disrobes after having become a full monk, he takes the title "Khanān."

Throughout the book, I have changed the names of people and obscured the names of places. The one exception to this is the abbot of Wat Pājie, who is a public figure, and Wat Pājie itself.

Abbreviations

BA	Buddhist Association
BAC	Buddhist Association of China
BCS	Buddhist College of Singapore
BI	Buddhist institutes
CCP	Chinese Communist Party
Ch.	Chinese
Dai	Dai-lue
IABU	International Association of Buddhist Universities
IBC	International Buddhist College
Mahā-Chulā	Mahā-Chulālongkorn University
MinDa	Yunnan Minzu Daxue (Yunnan Nationalities University)
MinZhong	Nationalities Middle School/Minzu Zhongxue
MRAB	Minority and Religious Affairs Bureau
NRAB	National Religious Affairs Bureau
PLA	People's Liberation Army
PRC	People's Republic of China
PSB	Public Security Bureau
RAB	Religious Affairs Bureau
SBA	Buddhist Association of Sipsongpannā
TME	transnational monastic education
UNESCO	United Nations Educational, Scientific and Cultural Organization
YF	Yunnan Foxueyuan (Yunnan Buddhist Institute)

Introduction

Buddhism and Monastic Education, within and across Borders in the New Millennium

Making Monks

What makes a Buddhist monk? Is it a temporal matter, located in the moment when the monk makes the heroic decision to "leave home," to enter a life of homelessness? Is it a cognitive process, marked either by the attainment of Buddhist knowledge or the development of skills in Buddhist meditation? Should it be seen instead as an embodied phenomenon, marked by performance, visible in the practice of shaving the head, wearing robes, and keeping the Vinaya, the disciplinary codes of Buddhism? Or is it fundamentally a social process, that is, the result of institutional forces or the relationship between the monk and the laywomen and laymen who support him? Is it all of these things? If it is, are they all equally important? If not, how do we decide which is most important? Perhaps most intriguingly, what is a Buddhist monk in the contemporary moment? Is it different from what made a Buddhist monk in the past? And what, if anything, does this tell us about contemporary forms of Buddhism as a whole?

In the spring of 2010, I gave a lecture on the Dai-lue of Sipsongpannā at the Buddhist College of Singapore (BCS). The BCS is a school that was founded in 2005 by the abbot of one of the largest temples in Singapore as a location to train monks in Chinese Buddhism through an English-language medium. Almost all of the students at the BCS come from abroad, and the majority of these are monks from the People's Republic of China (PRC). The Dai-lue, the subject of my lecture that day and the primary subject of this book, are part of a Chinese minority, the Daizu, and they live primarily in Sipsongpannā, a small three-county region on China's border with Laos and Myanmar. The Dai-lue are well known within China because of their New Year celebration in April, known in Chinese as the "Water-Splashing Festival" (Ch.: Poshuijie; Dai: Song kān). The Dai-lue are also well known within Chinese Buddhist circles because unlike the vast majority of Chinese Buddhists, they practice Theravāda Buddhism, the form most common in mainland Southeast Asia. Thus, I presumed that most of my audience had heard of both Sipsong-pannā and the Daizu. This presumption was accurate, but not necessarily for the reason I expected, because when I asked the young monks if they knew anything about Sipsongpannā, they all immediately turned to one particular monk. While in outward appearance he was no different than his colleagues, it turned out that he was a Dai-lue from Sipsongpannā. Without going too deeply into the ironies of a white, nearly middle-aged American from Cleveland who lives and teaches in Vermont lecturing to a monk in English about his own community, it is perhaps worth noting that the title of my lecture was "Chinese Buddhists or Buddhists in China: The Case of the Theravāda Buddhists of Yunnan Province." While the monk-students at the school may not have agreed with everything I said, at the same time, they did not see my paper's interrogating the Dai-lue Buddhist relationship to China as an inappropriate one.

This encounter with a Dai-lue monk who was studying Buddhism as a Chinese monk wearing Chinese robes in modern Singapore was many worlds away from my first encounter with the education of Dai-lue monastics in 1994. At the time I was living in Chiang Mai, teaching English at a monastic high school. Needing to renew my Thai visa, I came to the PRC, and while waiting for approval, I traveled south to the small border region at the edge of this immense country. While Sipsongpannā (Ch.: Xishuangbanna) is very much a part of China, it is also an ethnically rich region with fourteen different nationalities (*minzu*). The Dai-lue are the most populous group within this region, and historically were the people at the head of a small Tai kingdom situated between and tributary to Burmese and Chinese empires. Like much of the Tai world of mainland Southeast Asia, Theravāda Buddhism has been a central institution within the Dai-lue communities of Sipsongpannā, and for many centuries young boys have become full members of the Dai-lue community by ordaining as novices for a period of time, ranging from a week or two to life. This link between being Buddhist and being Dai-lue was damaged during the Cultural Revolution when Buddhism was abolished in Sipsongpannā, as in the rest of China. By 1994, however, this link had been largely reestablished, though not without significant changes within the sangha. Indeed, what I found as I traveled around the region was young boys who had been ordained as novices, shaving their heads, wearing saffron, studying the classical language of the region, and not attending public school. What it looked like to me was the return of traditional forms of Buddhism.

On the surface, these moments of contact with young men training to be monks look very different. In 1994, we have traditional Buddhists located, learning how to be monks in very rooted ways. They were learning things that had been learned by their grandfathers, though not their fathers, in ways and locations that were very similar to their grandfathers. This is Buddhism that could easily be described as both local and traditional. In Singapore in 2010, we have a monk who traveled far beyond his original home. He was living in a society that might be thought of as "hypermodern," learning languages and Buddhist materials that were quite different from those of his ancestors, and being trained in how to be a very different kind of monk than they themselves were trained to be.

Probably the most obvious way to understand these moments is in terms of the expansion of transnational flows and increased levels of globalization. Despite the monks of 1994 and 2010 being linked through membership in the same ethnicity, in this reading, they exist at two ends of a conceptual divide. The monks of 1994 are located, immobile and traditional, whereas the monk of 2010 is an example of a transnational flow and is highly modern (despite his robes). His presence in Singapore is emblematic of the movement of peoples throughout the world during the late twentieth century, and he himself is perhaps an example of "modernity at large" (Appadurai 1996). While this opposition of tradition and modernity, between monks who remain in place and those that cross boundaries, is somewhat facile, it would also seem to be an undeniable difference between the monks of 1994 and those of 2010. Yet there is also a misleading diachronic aspect to the story as I have told it. In 1994, when I spoke with the novices in village temples, many of them knew of the temples of northern Thailand as possibilities for future study, and some of them spoke openly about a desire to pursue that possibility. While this kind of international travel for study had been going on for a decade in Sipsongpannā, there was even official support by the Chinese and Thai governments for it in 1994 (Hansen 1999; Wasan 2010). Moreover, in 2010, not only could one have gone to the villages of Sipsongpannā and met novices studying in ways similar to the one I found in 1994, but in 2011, I met this same monk in Sipsongpannā. He had returned from Singapore, deciding that he needed a break from studying in the school. In other words, the monks who inhabited specific locales were not as stationary as they seemed and the "mobile" were not as unrooted.

A second important, though largely obscured, aspect of both of the educational contexts is the role of the nation-state. Although it took place before my encounters, all of the monks I met would have been recognized by the state as having legitimate ordinations. This recognition in turn enabled their ability to travel. The Buddhist College of Singapore is not run by the Singaporean government, but it does work closely with the government to bring students from other countries, all of whom have passports. The monks and novices in Sipsongpannā in 1994 usually did not have passports, but they were shaped by the state in other ways. Their status as minorities, while not necessarily something that they had to think about at all moments, was a part of how they existed in society. Indeed, it was listed on their identity cards (*shenfen zheng*). It was a topic discussed in school, which the state required them to attend, although many of them ignored that requirement. In other words, while the state was (and is) not always an active participant in these monks' lives, in Singapore or Sipsongpannā it also lurks behind the scenes, in part creating the conditions that shape the educational experiences of these young men.

Beyond the narratives of modernity, tradition, and transnational flows that are implicit here, and the lurking shadow of the state, the first scene in particular raises some questions about Buddhism itself. How is it that a young monk trained in Theravāda traditions becomes a Mahayāna monk in other contexts? Is this a matter of conversion, or is something else at play? What enabled him to cross that barrier? Buddhism is most often described as having three main streams: Theravāda, Mahāyāna, and Vajrayāna. Of course, there are problems with this formulation. Where the boundaries between the different streams may lie is much less clear than early scholars of Buddhism thought. Justin McDaniel (2011, 100–109) and Kate Crosby (2013, 4) have argued forcefully that Theravāda communities have been pervaded with esoteric forms, despite the widespread understanding that tantra was primarily limited to Tibet. Indeed, recently Ajahn Brahm, an Australian monk, ordained within Thai lineages but expelled from (or perhaps just encouraged to leave) the Thai Sangha because of his support for female ordination, has suggested that the threefold division of Buddhism is simply a scholarly construction. And yet this tripartite division of Buddhism lives on in popular and scholarly representations of Buddhism either explicitly or implicitly, not because scholars are simply lazy but because there are real barriers between them. These barriers are both religious and practical, including different lineages and institutional structures, different philosophical concerns, and different languages (both scriptural and practical). That is to say, even as Buddhism is widely presumed to be a universal category, frictions prevent some Buddhists from associating with other Buddhists. It is at least curious, then, to find a Chinese minority member who is a Theravāda monk studying in English to be a Mahāyāna monk.

Beginning with these reflections, in this book I present two different propositions about the nature of Buddhist studies and how Buddhism works in the contemporary period. First, I believe that most studies of Buddhism have had too limited a geographical/conceptual scale. That is to say, most scholarship on contemporary Buddhism has either privileged the local, the national, or the transnational frames; instead, it is necessary to study all three of these together to understand contemporary Buddhist communities. The second point is about Buddhism and the state. The modern state, whether in China or elsewhere, has an enduring interest in regulating religious activity, but not in all spheres or at all times. Buddhism is governed locally by both local and national governance regimes, but the actions of these regimes are mitigated by how Buddhism is imagined within different contexts. While Buddhism and the ways that people have imagined the scope of their Buddhist communities have changed over time, its status as what we call a world religion gives it an appearance of being a stable subject.[1] Significantly, actors (Buddhists, states, non-Buddhists) treat it *as if* it were an unchanging subject. Partly because of this and partly because of other factors, the governing of Buddhism is uneven. States (and national discourses) are never completely absent in how they affect Buddhist communities, but I argue here that governance, local agendas and conditions, and the imagination of Buddhism both constrain and enable one another in the current practice of Buddhism.

These observations arise out of my experiences in Sipsongpannā, but the claim here is that they are more broadly relevant. To make sense of these observations, I would like to discuss the importance of monastic education, and then focus on Sipsongpannā, explaining why it is a productive place to consider the problem of monastic education.

Buddhist Education

In some ways, the importance of monastic education is—or should be—self-evident. Donald Swearer commented a number of years ago:

> Both the early Sutta material and the *Mahāvagga* depict the sangha with the Buddha at its head as fundamentally involved in the teaching enterprise. The Buddha is primarily a teacher who instructs both monks and laity and is only incidentally a yogic miracle worker. Furthermore, the importance of institutional Buddhism as a teaching center is reflected in the traditional division of monastic activities between study (*ganthadhura*) and meditation (*vipassanadhura*). In short, from the beginning, institutional Buddhism has been involved in education. (Swearer 1976, 63–64)

This is a perspective shared by the Venerable Khy Sovanratana, who begins a recent article about the current conditions of Buddhist education in Cambodia by stating flatly, "Education is a central component of Buddhism" (2008, 257), as well as by one of the monks I worked with in Sipsongpannā, who said to me clearly in one of our first conversations together that for monks, "It is not right not to study" (*bu xue, bu xing*). This particular monk has demonstrated this over the last two decades by studying in a village in Sipsongpannā; in Yangon, both at a monastery school and an English-language academy; at a *pirivena* (monastic school) in Sri Lanka; at a Chinese university; and in teaching novices in Jing Hong and in a Buddhist institute outside of Kunming.

Despite this centrality, or indeed perhaps because of it, there has not been a singular, straightforward narrative about the meaning of monastic education. Indeed, in some ways, scholars have really not paid much attention to monastic education. This second assertion is perhaps surprising given the importance asserted by Swearer, Sovanratana, and my colleague in Sipsongpannā, or indeed when one looks at the indexes of some of the classic (or not so classic) ethnographies of Buddhism in Southeast Asia. Most of these books (Tambiah, Spiro, Kingshill, Bunnag, Hayashi, etc.) have sections that are presumably devoted to the monks' daily lives, and also their training, but when one turns to the sections on monastic education, there is actually very little attention given to the education and training of monks. I would contend that Kingshill's 1960 ethnography of a village in northern Thailand, *Ku Daeng* (The Red Tomb), is exemplary of this. Kingshill refers to the need of young novices to memorize texts as well as to the fact that novices sometimes go to Buddhist schools to study the *nak-tham* (Dhamma student) curriculum (the subject of chapter 5 of this book). Roughly speaking, there is about a half paragraph that directly addresses the training of monks; by contrast, there are almost five pages describing the ordination of a novice. In other words, the first three days of a boy's life as a novice garner significantly more attention than the majority of time that he spends in robes. While the differentiated attention that Kingshill displays is perhaps extreme, it is not unique. Although Tambiah in *Buddhism and the Spirit Cults of Northeast Thailand* (1970) and Hayashi in *Practical Buddhism among the Thai-Lao* (2003) both spend significant space excavating the life of village Buddhism in northeast Thailand, neither really attend to the training of monks. Tambiah's attention, for example, is limited to questions of literacy, though he laterally refers to memorization. Save for a few paragraphs about the process of memorization (121, 123), however, Tambiah ignores processes of education.[2] Monastic education is essentially a part of the background noise of village life.

Beyond this background noise, attention to the education of monks (and to a lesser extent, nuns) has been dominated by two sometimes linked narratives: a political narrative related to processes of centralization, and a narrative focused on modernization and the development of modern forms of Buddhism. Much of the former has been directed at explaining the actions of the Thai state to reform the sangha in the nineteenth century. Craig Reynolds' (1972) dissertation, for example, shows how over the course of the nineteenth century, the modernizing kings of Thailand (in particular, kings Mongkut and

Chulalongkorn) used the development of monastic exams to rationalize the forms of knowledge that monks learned, through an emphasis on Pāli and what was articulated as canonical forms of knowledge. The system developed by the beginning of the twentieth century included two different curricula: one focused on the translation of specific Pāli texts and the *nak-tham* curriculum, including the study of Sutta, the Vinaya, and the life of the Buddha. Significantly, though, the information for this curriculum was largely based on textbooks written by the *sangha-rāja* (king of the sangha), Wachirayān, who was also Chulalongkorn's brother. The examination system, which was based in part on these textbooks, became an important mechanism for promotion within the sangha as well as a key mechanism for the centralization process over the course of the twentieth century. These points have generally been followed by scholars of Thailand since then (including Tambiah 1976 and Ishii 1986). We can see similar processes in French Indo-China. The French founded Buddhist institutes in both Laos and Cambodia to dissuade Lao and Khmer monks from going to Bangkok for an education and to encourage them to think of Indochina as the defining imagined community.[3] In each of these cases, we see different forms of the state (colonial, premodern, and modern) attempting to shape the nature of the sangha through education.

Of perhaps greater importance than the state's reform narrative has been the intellectual problem of Buddhist education and modernization. Many scholars have attempted to understand and define what constitutes modern forms of Buddhism, and the education of Buddhists, particularly monastics, has been an important part of this narrative. Many of these scholars have focused on the curriculum of Buddhist education, and how various actors, including states, monks, and lay Buddhists have all sought to "reform" Buddhism to make it relevant for modern times.[4] Emblematic of this were the efforts of the Chinese monk Taixu in the first half of the twentieth century to develop schools (*foxueyuan*) that would develop modern monks who could help the country reform itself (Welch 1968; Pittman 2001; Birnbaum 2003). There is an assumption here about the increasing irrelevance of "traditional" forms of education and Buddhism, and an increasing situation of crisis that is solved in part by monks learning subjects that we call secular, such as math, law, or history, English, and the literature of the national language, in addition to Buddhist subjects.[5] These curricular changes are developed in relation to "traditional" forms of education, which are perceived as being in danger of becoming irrelevant. This can manifest in a variety of ways. Ven. Dhammasami (2007), for example, talks about how the contemporary sangha in Thailand is no longer quite clear about what its role is or should be, while Julianne Schober (2007) argues that the Burmese Sangha's failure to incorporate secular/Western subjects in the late nineteenth century led to a decline in monastic education and the rise of avenues of Buddhist education for laypeople.

There are problems with these approaches. To begin, the phenomenon of education is somewhat underdetermined. Rather than paying attention to how monastics are educated and why, there is often a relatively narrow attention to curricula as a transparent source for understanding religious education. The more significant problem, however, is that the work in this scholarship mirrors the logic of the nation-state. This might not seem to be such a great problem; after all, the first type of scholarship is organized around showing how monastic education follows national political agendas, and this scholarship has tended to focus on how the state (of whatever form) has sought to organize, reorganize, and govern the sangha. Thus, it has focused on curricula and exams as mechanisms of control. Yet it remains unclear just how effective these states are at transforming the sangha. Justin McDaniel (2008) has argued forcefully that the Thai exam system seems to have had little effect, even in the long term, in transforming Thai Buddhism, nor does it seem that the Buddhist institutes of Laos or Cambodia ever accomplished very much. There is a danger, in other words, of assuming that the state actually accomplished what it sought to accomplish in implementing its reforms. What little scholarship there is has often failed to look at what local monks are doing educationally or the contexts of local Buddhist schools. This overdetermination of the nation-state also colors considerations of education and modernization, in which studies are generally organized around national communities, without much attention to how and when Buddhists cross borders for an education. In other words, much of the scholarship on Buddhist education does not do a very good job of explaining the kinds of cross-cultural experiences of the Buddhist College of Singapore, or, by contrast, the seemingly parochial experiences of the monks in the local temples in Sipsongpannā. I am not suggesting that the nation-state is not an important factor here. The question is, when are the lives of Buddhist monastics, and in particular their education, shaped by the politics of the nation-state and when are they not?

To understand the role that monastic education plays in the contemporary moment, it is necessary to look at the phenomenon much more comprehensively. To do so, there are three vectors of the study to which we need to pay attention. First, as is evident from the opening vignettes, there are a variety of contexts in which novices and monks are educated. Anne Blackburn has suggested that we understand monastic education as having two different modes, which she refers to as "apprentice" and "curricular" education (following a suggestion by Charles Hallisey; Blackburn 2001, 45). These modes should be understood as ideal types, emphasizing different pedagogical contexts and models of authority. Apprentice education occurs most frequently in village *wats,* and highlights the relationship between the novice/apprentice and the monk/master. Although there are consistent patterns within apprentice education, it relies more generally on local Buddhist cultures than curricular education and is marked by a variety of visions of what a monk needs to learn. Curricular education, on the other hand, takes place in locations that look like formal schools, with textbooks, novices seated at desks, and a greater degree of professionalization among the teachers and standardization within the materials learned.

Second, to make sense of monastic education as a phenomenon, it is necessary to have a clear sense of what kinds of novices/monks a given educational system seeks to create. Much of the scholarship cited above takes the goals of monastic training as self-evident (and therefore deems explication of them unnecessary), or alternatively, they simply mine this education as evidence of narratives of state power or modernization. Although monastic education is an important source of information for other questions of social theory with regard to Buddhism, there is a real danger in ignoring the perspectives of the various stakeholders within monastic education.[6] Among such stakeholders are the young monastics being trained, the lay and monastic actors who train them, the laity that supports the temples where this takes place, and both the local and national governments that regulate this training. Depending on whether one is focusing on apprentice or curricular education, the roles and opportunities of these stakeholders are going to be different, but this of course is one of the things that needs to be investigated. Justin McDaniel's (2008) study of monastic education in Laos and northern Thailand usefully divides the study of monastic education into three general frames: an attention to the nature of the institution, the curriculum taught in a given institution, and the pedagogical techniques in play there. All of these frames need to be examined to understand the goals of monastic training.

Third, it is necessary to see and understand the connections *between* different locations of monastic education. Much of the previous scholarship referring to the training of monks fails to take these connections into account. Or they refer to the fact that novices in a village temple travel regularly to a school in another town, without ever thinking through the consequences of this. The novices and young monks of Sipsongpannā in southwest China are first trained in contexts of apprentice education, but they have access to curricular education both within and outside of Sipsongpannā. They travel to schools in Jing Hong, Kunming, and Shanghai, to Bangkok, Yangon, Sri Lanka, and Singapore. They also study, as monks, in public schools and universities in China. Part of why this is important is that different locations of monastic education do not work in a vacuum, but are connected to greater and lesser degrees. Novices and young monks in village temples often know about other places where they might study, which shapes how they spend their time in their home *wat*. Similarly, their experiences in contexts of curricular education are profoundly conditioned by what they have done in their earlier educational experiences. Understanding monastic education in the contemporary moment necessarily examines not just particular locations, but the connections between them, across different kinds of borders and under different kinds of regulatory regimes, including political and religious ones.

Within this book, then, I will examine the education of the novices and monks of a specific community, the Dai-lue of Sipsongpannā. Dai-lue monks and novices experience curricular and apprentice education, as well as secular education, within and outside of Sipsongpannā. They are subject to a variety of different agendas, promulgated by laity, by Dai-lue monks, Thai monks, Chinese monks, and the Chinese and Thai states, among others. It should go without saying that while they are not immune to the projects these different actors seek to inscribe on the monks, nor are they without agency in their ability to shape their own experiences and identities as monks, as Dai-lue, as Chinese citizens, and as Buddhists. Indeed, I will argue that by attending to the variety of pedagogical contexts and agendas that the monastics of Sipsongpannā experience, we will begin to be able to answer the question of what makes a monk, and the complexity of the factors that go into the formation of monks.

Sipsongpannā as a Location to Study Monastic Education

Why Sipsongpannā? Indeed, where and what is Sipsongpannā? This is a region of southwest China, situated on the Chinese border with Burma/Myanmar and Laos, in close proximity to Thailand. It is where the Mekong River flows on its way out of China, and its topography is a combination of mountainous regions and valleys that have been the locations of small rice-producing states. There are thirteen Chinese ethnic minorities (*shaoshu minzu*[7]) that live in the region along with the Hanzu (the Han), and in the early twenty-first century it has a population of about one million. About one-third of the population is comprised of the Dai-lue people, referred to in Chinese as the Daizu. The Han, the majority population of China, also comprise one-third of the population, and the remaining third is a combination of a variety of upland minority people such as the Hani, the Bulang, and the Miao (most of whom have related communities in Southeast Asian nation-states). The Dai-lue are members of the Tai ethnolinguistic family that populates lowland areas of Southeast Asia from Vietnam to Assam, and from China down to Malaysia. While there are differences, their language is fairly close to that spoken in northern Thailand. Moreover, like many of the Tai peoples of mainland Southeast Asia, but unlike most other Chinese Buddhists, they practice Theravāda Buddhism.[8] The Lue as a subset of the Tai are not limited to Sipsongpannā; there are Lue communities in the Shan States of northeast Myanmar, as well as in northern Thailand. At the same time, the Dai-lue of Sipsongpannā comprise only part of the

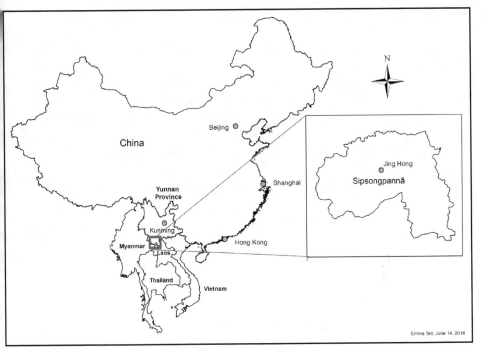

FIGURE I.1 Map of Sipsongpannā in China

Chinese minority, the Daizu. Other subgroups of the *minzu* are scattered around Yunnan Province, having been brought together conceptually into a single unit, the Daizu, during the *minzu shibie* (ethnic or national classification) project of the 1950s. While these facts are presented in fairly straightforward terms, this very straightforwardness hides much of what is interesting and important about a place such as Sipsongpannā and people such as the Dai-lue. It naturalizes their location within the Chinese "geo-body" (Thongchai 1994), and just as important, what it means for the Dai-lue to be both citizens of China and Chinese minorities. In the chapters that follow, these issues will be approached in a variety of ways.

There are three aspects of the context of the region that make it an important and useful place to think about monastic education in the contemporary moment. The first is the experiences of the Dai-lue in the post-Mao era. Like most religious communities in China, Dai-lue Buddhists did not fare well during the various movements of the communist revolution under Mao. Beginning in 1953, when the People's Liberation Army (PLA) entered the region and occupied Jing Hong, the capital of Sipsongpannā, until the end of the Cultural Revolution with the death of Mao in 1976, Buddhism was progressively eliminated from the public life of the region. From a society in the

1950s in which the vast majority of males ordained for at least a period of time, by 1976, there were no open temples and at most a handful of ordained men. The rest had either fled the region to live in mainland Southeast Asia or had disrobed (voluntarily or forcibly). With the beginning of political and economic reforms in the late 1970s and early 1980s, however, the practice of religion was again allowed. As part of a "religion fever" (*zongjiao re*) that swept through China, Sipsongpannā saw the reconstruction of village temples through-out the region (most of which had been converted to other uses during the Cultural Revolution), and the ordination (temporary and permanent) of large numbers of Dai-lue men as novices and fully ordained monks.[9] Training these novices and new monks to read Dai-lue and to have basic Buddhist knowledge was a pressing problem, exacerbated by the fact that a generation of men missed the previously widespread experience of ordination.[10] Along with rebuilding temples, monastic education, whether by monks imported from Thailand or former monks who had disrobed (*khanān*), became a focus of Buddhism in the region.

A second reason Sipsongpannā is a useful place for examining monastic education is the window it opens up to how the Chinese state works with regard to religion (an issue that I will explore more specifically in chapter 2). The ability to practice religion publicly in the early 1980s throughout China was in part a retreat from the active oppression of religion of the Maoist period. It was not a full liberalization by any stretch of the imagination, and the forty years of the Reform Era have been marked by moments of both liberalization and tightening of regulation by the Chinese state at its various levels (Potter 2003). Although all groups and institutions that the government recognizes as being part of a "religion" are subject to governance by the Chinese state, the state does not treat these various religions identically. Some religious groups, such as Protestants, Catholics, and Tibetan Buddhists, tend to receive greater levels of scrutiny by the state than do others, such as Daoists or Buddhists. Indeed, a number of scholars have recently shown how Han Chinese Buddhists as a whole interact effectively with the government and end up in development partnerships (Fisher 2008; Ji 2008; Nichols 2011). To account for these differences, I follow the lead of Yoshiko Ashiwa and David Wank in their analysis of the politics of religion in China (2006, 2009). They emphasize the need to analyze the institutional field in which a given religious community exists to understand both the possibilities and constraints on religious practices and communities.

In Sipsongpannā, the local Chinese state and Buddhists have had a relatively good relationship over the last several decades, certainly in comparison to other religious groups.[11] The local government has permitted the building or rebuilding of several important temples and has allowed the opening of formal schools (Ch. *foxueyuan;* Dai-lue: *hongheyn pha-pariyatti-tham*) at these temples (the largest of which is the subject of chapter 5). Government officials participate in important Dai-lue festivals with the Buddhists, even though as members of the Communist Party they are not legally allowed to be religious believers. Through the Minority and Religious Affairs Bureau (MRAB) and the Buddhist Association (BA; Ch. Fojiao Xiehui) of Yunnan, the local government has sponsored the travel of monks to Southeast Asian countries for an education (part of the subject of chapter 6), and has supported education based in Yunnan Province.[12] At the same time, these state–sangha relations are always complicated, and government regulations are as likely to cause problems for the Dai-lue as not.

An additional factor of complexity around the Dai-lue and Sipsongpannā is their status as minorities. China is a multiethnic state, comprised of fifty-five minorities and the Han (Hanzu). The minorities of China comprise some 10 percent of the population and live disproportionately in the border regions of the People's Republic. Being a minority of China, a *shaoshu minzu*, is to be enmeshed in a nexus of discursive and governmental structures that place minorities as central to the nation but also simultaneously external to it.[13] While many minority communities have had an existence somewhat distinct from the Han people for many centuries, we should understand the condition of being a minority in China as a particularly modern phenomenon, the result of the Chinese state's need to control its borderlands and population, and exemplified by the *minzu shibie* (ethnic classification) project of the 1950s.[14] During this period, the nascent PRC government sent ethnologists, folklore specialists, and anthropologists to classify the various communities of China, determining whether they should be understood as independent nationalities, fractions of the Han, or subsets of an independent nationality. This classification process ostensibly relied on scientific Marxist criteria as their basis, seeking to locate people along scales of development. Stalin's typology of a nation, that is, a people with common language, common territory, a common mode of production, and a common psychology that manifests in culture, was the foundation of the *minzu shibie* process, but as a number of scholars have pointed out, the process of classification and its consequences have been much more complicated.[15] The Stalinist formulations, for example, shared space with local understandings of ethnic difference, and also local political considerations (McKhann 1995; Harrell 1995b). The process had the appearance more than the substance of science (Keyes 2002), but it has been productive in shaping how China's minorities understand themselves. For example, the two largest groups comprising the Daizu, a group constructed through the *minzu shibie* process, are the Dai-lue of Sipsongpannā and the Dai-neua of Dehong. Dehong and Sipsongpannā are not far apart as the crow flies, but travel between the two regions was (and is) difficult without an airplane because of the mountainous nature of the region. As a consequence, the Dai-lue had very little contact with Dai-neua prior to the last several decades. Through governmental processes of education, however, as well as exposure to one another through bureaucratic institutions (such as the BA), the Dai-lue have come to understand themselves as part of the Daizu, and the Dai-neua as coethnics, and they have invited Dai-neua monks and novices to attend the Dhamma school at Wat Pājie in Sipsongpannā.

It is important not to overstate the completeness of this "ethnogenesis" (Gladney 1991), however. China's minorities have been subject to significant state attention over the decades, and there is a fairly large state academic-bureaucratic apparatus directed at creating and shaping knowledge of these populations. As I show in chapters 4 and 5, this has an impact on monastic education and the ways that monks and novices understand their place in Sipsongpannā, but it is also important to understand that state discourses on minorities are only one voice (albeit a powerful one). Stevan Harrell (1995a) has discussed this in terms of several different "languages" of ethnicity within the PRC, by which he means both the vocabulary used by various constituents and concerns embedded in the vocabulary. He distinguishes in this sense between the language of academics describing the history of a given group of people, the language of the state in classifying minorities for purposes of governance and control, and the language of China's ethnic minorities themselves. These languages are distinguishable, yet also have an impact on one another. The state's language and vocabulary was shaped in part by the local discourses, and over time, these local discourses have shifted as the state's vision has changed perceived realities. In a somewhat different way, Shih Chih-yu (2002) has highlighted variability of the experience of Chinese minorities. The state engages in projects that seek to create certain kinds of citizens, but this has a variable impact on people's lives, producing what Shih calls "China moments," that is, those experiences when the fact of being subject to the discourses and policies of the state is made more prominent in people's minds. Following Shih, I argue that an attention to monastic education shows there are times when the state's needs to govern either religious groups or minorities becomes pressing, and therefore makes people aware of its presence, and there are other moments when the state does not factor significantly into the day-to-day lives of religious or minority actors.

The third reason for focusing on monastic education in Sipsongpannā has to do with its location on China's border, or rather what the location on the Chinese border has meant for the development of both cultures and institutions within Sipsongpannā. Sipsongpannā, and the Dai-lue themselves, are betwixt and between the Chinese and Southeast Asian geopolitical contexts, and an old Dai-lue saying calls it a "kingdom under two skies" (*rāt song fayfā*). One narrative that could be told about the region is that it has essentially shifted from a focus on Southeast Asia to a focus on China. This is the point that Hsieh Shih-Chung makes when he suggests that "Lue" was once the most important part of the ethnoneme, but now "Dai" is (Hsieh 1995). This is also the narrative that the Chinese state (and Chinese academics) would tell, but the problem with this is that it tends to hide the ways that the Dai-lue continue to maintain and have vital contacts with both Lue and other Tai communities of Southeast Asia. C. Patterson Giersch (2006) has described the Tai communities of China in the imperial period as a "middle ground," that is, a contact zone between civilizational groups, none of which could attain lasting hegemony. Although Chinese armies would come in and (re)establish direct authority over the region, they were not able to maintain this rule over time due in part to malaria. This is no longer the case in a political context: Sipsongpannā was recognized as a part of China in treaties between the French and the British in 1896, and since the PLA entered Jing Hong in the early 1950s, the region has truly been incorporated into the political economy of China. Although Jing Hong might now be called a "Chinese" city (Evans 2000) and the capital of a Chinese "autonomous prefecture" (*zizhi zhou*), I would argue that it remains something of a "middle ground." The Dai-lue of Sipsongpannā speak a Southeast Asian language (along with Mandarin and Yunnan forms of Chinese), practice a Southeast Asian form of Buddhism (along with having ties to Chinese Buddhist institutions), and have relatives throughout Southeast Asia (and increasingly within China as well). As we shall see, the ties—in both directions—have been essential for understanding the conditions, possibilities, and limits of the education of novices and monks in Sipsongpannā. Indeed, it is not really possible to understand the Buddhism of the region if one does not examine it as part of China as well as a part of Southeast Asia.

Governing Buddhism and Moving Monks

Sipsongpannā is in the middle of what has come to be called "Zomia," a region that extends from the hills of mainland Southeast Asia up through the foothills of the Tibetan plateau, and encompasses parts of Vietnam, Laos, Thailand, Myanmar, Bangladesh, India, and the PRC. As discussed by James Scott (2010), it was a region marked by small-scale hill communities that engaged in consistent and regular interactions with the small states of the valleys but were able to escape their governance. Indeed, Scott's point is that the cultures of this region, which would include many of the minorities of Sipsongpannā (but not the Dai-lue) developed in ways precisely aimed at avoiding control by states. Scott argues that Zomia ceased to exist in the middle of the twentieth century when modern state technologies enabled greater control over space (with roads, airports, etc.), thus making escape more difficult. While he is correct to assert the greater ability of states to control space and limit escape, it is also clear that the border areas of China and Southeast Asia are marked as much by ineffective and inconsistent state control as they are by state development projects. States are centrally involved in the lives of people, but that involvement is not always uniform, and there remain many ways for people to circumvent state control. To put it differently, just because the states of the region have engaged in efforts to assert control over trade in the region does not mean that smuggling no longer exists. I would like to emphasize a vision of Buddhism in the contemporary world that is not dissimilar to the region as a whole: it is "emphatically marked" by the nation-state system—to use Anne Blackburn's description of the role of colonialism within nineteenth-century Lankan Buddhism—but not wholly subsumable by or to it.[16]

To make this point, it is useful to think about questions of governance. Although Buddhism is a world religion, its governance is decentralized. There is not, and never has been, a single institution that governs the actions of lay or monastic Buddhists. To state the obvious, there is no Buddhist Vatican, and there has never been a "Buddhendom."[17] Monastic actions are governed in part by the ideas within the Vinaya (the disciplinary codes); in part through the practices of a given lineage (which may be derived from local forms or in conversation with some of the ideas and ideals within the Vinaya, or both); and in part by local political forms. Today, and largely since the end of the Second World War, this has meant that Buddhists are governed by national regimes. To think of a somewhat prosaic example, Buddhist monks and nuns are citizens of particular nation-states, and while they travel (often easily), they do so while using papers (passports, ordination cards, etc.) given to them by the states of which they are citizens. Similarly, Buddhist institutions, practices of ordination, schools, and so forth are either inflected by national legal forms or governed by them directly. While there is significant variety across the Buddhist world, Buddhist institutions necessarily follow the rules of the local government in establishing their conditions. Thai Buddhist schools are regulated by the government, with the administration of the sangha housed within the Ministry of Education (Ishii 1986). Ordained and lay sangha officials determine issues of funding, the examination system, textbooks, and so forth. Thai police also have some responsibility for monastic discipline when monks are out in public (e.g., if they were to come across novices in video game parlors that were common before the widespread use of smart phones, the Thai police were supposed to remove them). In Singapore, by contrast, there is a very different regime governing all religious matters. At the Buddhist College of Singapore, the government has nothing to do with setting the curriculum or the pedagogy at the college. It does, however, interact with the sangha in different ways, such as in approving building construction (e.g., conversion of a retirement community into a school) and issuing visas for the students. These are prosaic matters, it is true, but they shape the possibilities for the practice of religion in Singapore (Eng 2003; Finnucane 2009). Arguing that the practice of Buddhism is "emphatically marked" by the nation-state does not mean that Buddhists follow the state slavishly; rather, they have agency that is limited and shaped within the context of regimes of governance. In this, Buddhist lives in general are conditioned by the institutional field, just as religion is within China (Ashiwa and Wank 2006, 2009). I address this most specifically in chapter 2, but throughout the book it should become clear how the Chinese state in its local, provincial, and national forms continually shapes the possibilities of the practice of Dai-lue Buddhism. This effect of national discourses and regimes of governance is not limited to the Dai-lue.

Although the nation-state is perhaps the biggest single actor or factor in the formation of Buddhist institutions in the modern period, even in a place where there is a strong state such as China, or where Buddhism has long been intrinsic to the nation, such as Thailand or Myanmar, Buddhism cannot be reduced simply to being a wing of the nation.[18] We see this most simply from the fact that monks and nuns travel across borders. Sometimes they do this for purposes of study, such as the Dai-lue monk in Singapore, or other examples of transnational Buddhist education (such as Nepali monks going to Thailand, or Taiwanese monks going to Sri Lanka); other times it is for pilgrimage, participation in rituals such as the dedication of stupas, or the ordination of female monastics; sometimes it is simply for tourism. Some of this travel is enabled by national connections, such as when Thai monks travel to Thai temples in Singapore (Pattana 2010) or in the United States, but much of it is not. Moreover, much of it is not even easily explained by lineage connections or ties of similar forms of Buddhism. For example, in June 2011, I was visiting a Mahāyāna temple in Shanghai, and a handful of Sinhala monks showed up to worship at the temple. These monks from Sri Lanka have no "natural" connection to the Shanghai temple: they do not share an obvious language, lineage, or form of Buddhism. How are we to explain such connections at a theoretical as opposed to an anecdotal level?

Just as political contexts vary in their effect on sanghas, similarly, there are patterns regarding how and where monks travel; we need to make sense of these. Indeed, Thomas Tweed has commented that a "translocative analysis" of religion needs to "follow the flows" and "notice all the figures crossing" (2011, 24). Steven Kemper has referred to the product of the movement of Buddhists in the colonial period as a Buddhist "ethnoscape." In doing so, he is drawing on the work of Arjun Appadurai, who defined an "ethnoscape" as a "landscape of persons who constitute the shifting world in which we live." This landscape is built on movement, and it is one of a number of "imagined worlds," deterritorialized imagined communities that may very well subvert the stabilities of communities as well as "the official mind" (Appadurai

1996, 33). Kemper uses this to make sense of the communities resulting from and reinforced by the movement of monks for missionary purposes and suggests that there are a variety of Buddhist ethnoscapes, such as a Thai Buddhist ethnoscape or a Sinhala Buddhist ethnoscape. "Extending beyond" these specific ethnoscapes defined by national communities, "and sometimes interacting with [them,] lies a broader Buddhist ethnoscape" (Kemper 2005, 23). Most of these ethnoscapes are shaped by sometimes overlapping vectors of identity, including locality, nationality, race/ethnicity, language, and sect. The last "broader" Buddhist ethnoscape that Kemper suggests would be one that relies on the conception of Buddhism as a universal beyond the effect of these different vectors of identity. In a sense, it is the *imagination* of a "Buddhendom"—an affiliation between Buddhists based solely on their ties to the religion—rather than a "Buddhendom" that is tied together by a robust transnational institution that has the ability to govern actors beyond the realm of national institutions. I would like to suggest that such a Buddhist ethnoscape shapes how Buddhists interact with one another across cultural and national borders.

Yet what is the material out of which such a Buddhist ethnoscape might be constructed? This is not an insignificant issue: Buddhism is not a single phenomenon. It has significant diversity within it in terms of languages, beliefs, practices, institutional formations, and so forth. Moreover, although Buddhists have traveled throughout history, there is little evidence that there was a practical sense of a unified "Buddhism" for most of the last two thousand years. There were linked regions such as Sri Lanka and mainland Southeast Asia that had intermittent interactions, or the linkages between lineages in China and Japan, but not a wider sense of the Buddhist world. At least since the middle of the nineteenth century, however, scholars, colonialists, and Buddhist intellectuals (lay and monastic) came to see more clearly that "Buddhism" was a single thing rather than multiple things, and that thing was a religion, analogous to Christianity. The story of how this viewpoint emerged is complicated and contested,[19] and my concern is not to make a point about whether Buddhism "really" is one phenomenon or multiple overlapping ones. The point is that Buddhists, and just as important, entities such as the Chinese state, treat Buddhism as if it were a single entity. They treat Buddhists as if they have natural connections simply because they are Buddhist. Although these actors understand that certain forms of Buddhism are naturally associated with certain regions due to their long histories, the idea of "Buddhism" as a universal category naturalizes the connections between Buddhists who might not otherwise have such connections through lineages or other historical links. It is this imagination of universality that provides the possibility of a Buddhist ethnoscape. However, perhaps because this has not been a strong force historically, and perhaps because Buddhism is perceived (rightly and wrongly) as a "peaceful religion," the imagined unity of Buddhists transnationally does not normally seem to threaten states in the region.

One consequence of the imagined universality is that it enables Buddhist movement across borders. The anthropologist of labor and the Chinese Diaspora Aihwa Ong has argued that in the current period of globalization, both individuals and governments utilize "flexible notions of citizenship and sovereignty to accumulate capital and power" (1999, 6; see also Ong 2006). She uses the idea of "flexible citizenship" to explain the mobility of elites within the Chinese Diaspora. This mobility was highly evident in the late 1990s when Hong Kong denizens gained citizenship outside of the erstwhile colony even as they retained residence there; it is based on the ability not only to accumulate capital but also to mobilize networks based on family, ethnicity, birthplace, and education. What is particularly useful about Ong's discussion is that she highlights flexibility in the context of state power. However, she does not recognize the cultural capital that is embedded in religion (or what might be more accurately described as the forms of religion that are seen as legitimate within society or by the state). As a number of the chapters below will show, the status of Buddhism as a legitimate world religion provides monastics in China with a degree of flexibility that nonmonastics do not possess. This is evident in the ability of the monks of Sipsongpannā to develop the sangha politically in ways that are surprising given the perception that the Chinese state is hostile to religion (which is not a wholly inaccurate assessment). In this context, both the perceived legitimacy of Buddhism as a legitimate and "normal" religion and the Dai-lue status as a recognized national minority of China provide cultural capital (or maybe cultural cover). In other words, Buddhism provides the monks with greater flexibility than they would otherwise have.

"Flexibility" here is not unlimited freedom. Instead, as articulated by Ong, it is the ability to mobilize networks and capital to move across borders and accumulate more capital. It enables an actor to move between social regimes and configurations of power. The nation-state, she argues, "along with its juridical-legislative systems, bureaucratic apparatuses, economic entities, modes of governmentality, and war-making capacities—continues to define, discipline, control, and regulate all kinds of populations, whether in movement or in resident" (1999, 15); it is not fading away. Indeed, when the monks and novices of Sipsongpannā travel to the Mahāyāna Buddhist institutes of China and the Dhamma schools of Thailand (see chapter 6), this is precisely what they are doing—moving from one set of power-laden relations to another. Thus, despite their greater ability to move and accumulate, the monks' activities are continually limited by the state (whether Thai or Chinese), as well as by the demands and possibilities of society.

As a concept, flexible citizenship helps us think through border crossings (and so is of real use with Sipsongpannā), but it is less helpful in making sense of globalization within a particular place. This is a problem when considering Buddhism from the frame of the local. Villagers would seem to have very little flexibility of the sort described by Ong. Their capital—cultural and otherwise—does not take them much beyond the local, and in Sipsongpannā, the local frame cannot be divorced from national or transnational realms. Moreover, these interactions can be both constraining and liberating. For example, as I will show in chapter 4, village monastic education in Sipsongpannā is inflected by Chinese public education (replete with nationalist discourse). At the same time, the legitimacy of Buddhism I referred to above filters down even to village monks, who can cross the border out of China with much greater ease than laypeople.

Nonetheless, the flexibility of connection is not limitless, or even untroubled; it is marked by "friction," to use Anna Lowenhaupt Tsing's (2005) metaphor. The purpose of talking about friction is to think about what happens to universals when they move from the global ether onto the ground. These "actually existing universals," she has suggested, are transient hybrids that must conform with the reality on the ground, even as an unchanging nature is assumed or claimed for it (2005, 9). Friction is a metaphor used to talk about globalization, not by focusing on flows and movement, but rather by focusing on the moments of connection. It focuses on the interaction between the universal concept and local conditions. Friction, as Tsing points out, is what enables movement. The concept directs one's attention not solely to where the "rubber meets the road," but also to how that connection inflects movement and gives it meaning ethnographically. Movement, whether within or across boundaries, depends on contingent and often supremely mundane factors (e.g., whether the bus is running, whether there is enough water in the river to run the ferries, and whether the visa-granting agent is feeling generous on a particular day). "Friction is not just about slowing things down. Friction is required to keep global power in motion. . . . Roads are a good image for conceptualizing how friction works: Roads create pathways that make motion easier and more efficient, but in doing so they limit where we go. The ease of travel they facilitate is also a structure of confinement. Friction inflects historical trajectories, enabling, excluding and particularizing" (2005, 6).

I would like to suggest that the idea of the force of Buddhism as a universal, as well as the idea of friction to describe transnational connections, give us a greater clarity for thinking about what enables and constrains the travel of the Buddhists of Sipsongpannā and elsewhere. While Buddhism is not a monolithic entity, and Buddhist communities are marked by national systems of governance, the idea of Buddhism as a universal cuts across these borders. Thus, in thinking about Buddhist communities, it is essential that we adopt a dual vision that takes into consideration not only the national community but also across and beyond it. This provides some degree of flexibility for monks and nuns in crossing borders, though as Ong points out with regard to Chinese diasporas, this flexibility is constrained by the structures of power within a given nation-state. Buddhist monks and nuns are still citizens of particular locations in all but the rarest of circumstances (such as the monks of the Tibetan diaspora in India) and are subject to the rules of national sanghas and legal regimes that govern religious actors. Because of this, we might identify a tension between the national and the transnational within Buddhism. Tsing's notion of friction helps us to think through this tension, allowing us to identify in a particular moment of connection the links between local, national, and transnational agendas for Buddhists.

Methodological Issues and the Organization of This Book

This book has several layers of concerns. In line with the questions that began this chapter, I am interested in understanding how Buddhist monks come to understand their place in the world, what their proper activities are, and the roles that they have within their community. I do this in the chapters that follow by paying attention to a specific community on the borders of China and Southeast Asia, and in particular how different actors within this community have chosen to train its young monastics. Answering these questions, however, entails attention to several other issues as well: how monks are governed, how and where they travel, and what enables them to travel. Thus, explaining what makes a monk allows us to understand how Buddhism works in the contemporary period.

Sipsongpannā provides the primary location of my research, and this book is primarily an ethnography of the monks of this region. Research for this book was conducted between 1994, when I first traveled to Sipsongpannā while renewing my Thai visa, and 2014, when I accidentally met a Dai-neua monk at a *wat* in Chiang Mai. In between those trips, I took eight trips of varying lengths to Sipsongpannā. The majority of my research took place during the longest one, which was a fifteen-month period in 2001–2002 when I lived in Jing Hong with my wife, Rhonda, and our then one-year-old son, Jasper. While conducting research, I visited temples throughout the region, but I also traveled most days to Wat Pājie, the central temple in the region, where I studied Dai-lue, and more important, also served as an English teacher at the monastic school. My status as a teacher at Wat Pājie had a significant impact on this project. Most of my research consisted of participant observation, and being a teacher allowed me to be at the temple every day. I learned a good deal simply by talking with students in the classroom. I also had the opportunity to travel to events around Sipsongpannā with the monks, and to ask nosy questions. I conducted very few formal interviews; most of my conversations took place iteratively with the monks, the novices, and the other people affiliated with Wat Pājie. My status as a teacher alleviated fears that the Public Security Bureau (PSB) might have had about my traveling to a temple every day for more than a year.[20] It is also important to acknowledge the value that my son, Jasper, played in my research. Far from being aloof, the novices and monks throughout the region played with him constantly, gave him small gifts, and even threw a birthday party for him when he turned one. Their interactions with Jasper taught me a good deal about how monks—or at least some monks—situate themselves in the world. Indeed, in many ways, they liked him better than they did me, and it remains the case that whenever I arrive in Jing Hong, the first thing monks or former monks ask me is, "How is Jasper? Does he remember me?" My other children have served equally important research assistant roles over the years.

Research for this book thus has been spread out over time, and took place in multiple locations.[21] In addition to the many trips I have taken to Sipsongpannā, I conducted research among Dai-lue novices in Shanghai, Kunming, various places in Thailand and Singapore, and even in Midway Airport in Chicago. I also visited temples and interviewed Han monks in Shanghai, Hong Kong, and Beijing, and Tibetan monks in northwest Yunnan Province, all of whom contributed to the argument in different ways.[22] This was thus something of a multi-sited ethnography, but only partially. Wat Pājie was my primary field site, and the work that I did outside of this "village" often relied on the connections I had established there and my own status as a teacher at the temple. The time factor becomes a complicated issue to deal with, because things change in Sipsongpannā, just as they do elsewhere. I often use the ethnographic present, because many of the dynamics I describe here seem to be exemplary of fundamental relations and ties within the Buddhism of the region; however, I do my best throughout to indicate when something may have taken place.

There are six chapters in this book, which are divided into two different sections of three chapters each: part 1, "Shaping Buddhist Lives in Sipsongpannā," and part 2, "Educating the Monks of Sipsongpannā." Part 1 provides a very particular ethnography of the region's Buddhism. While I focus to a certain extent on the Buddhist life within the region, here I am more interested in examining institutional organization within Sipsongpannā, the governance of religion there, and the movements of monks (revealing the "ethnoscapes" in which the monks of Sipsongpannā participate). The first chapter, "Local Monks in Sipsongpannā," explores the conditions of Buddhism in the post-Mao period. I examine the context of the religious field of Sipsongpannā and what "village Buddhism" looks like in the region. I also provide an explanation of both the organization of the sangha and the "life cycle" of monastics within the region. The second chapter, "Fortune-Telling and False Monks: Defining and Governing Religion" examines more explicitly the politics of religion in China and in Sipsongpannā. To explain a crisis that took place in 2001–2002 over a group of swindlers who dressed up as monks, I examine official discourse on the category of religion as well as structures of governance. I argue that religion in China and the institutions meant to regulate it are less repressive than productive in the Foucaultian sense, as exemplified in their encouragement of religious actors to align themselves with governmental norms regarding the proper place of religion in society. I then examine how the senior monks of the region locate themselves within this system in order to govern the Sangha of Sipsongpannā. Chapter 3, "Monks on the Move: Dai-Lue Monastic Networks," explores Buddhist networks both within and outside of Sipsongpannā. Using the monks of Wat Pājie as a starting point, I examine where the monks of Sipsongpannā travel, the relationships they cultivate, and to what ends they do so.

Part 2, "Educating the Monks of Sipsongpannā," examines the different contexts of monastic education in the region. Chapter 4, "Learning to Read in Village Temples and Chinese Public Schools," focuses on apprentice education in the region. Here I make an argument about "traditions" of Buddhism within Sipsongpannā. Although village education within the region remains Buddhist and traditional, contemporary training to become a monk within the villages has shifted in important ways because of the impact of education within Chinese public schools. Chapter 5, "The Fragility of Autonomy: Curricular Education at Dhamma Schools," focuses on curricular education at the Dhamma school in Jing Hong (at Wat Pājie, and then at Wat Long Meuang Lue after 2009). This chapter makes two points. First, I argue that much of the education that has taken place at the temple has been an effort to create a core group of locally produced intellectuals who might act as standard-bearers and protectors of Buddhism and Dai-lue culture. Second, however, I argue that the possibilities of achieving this in the long-term are significantly hindered by dynamics of Chinese economic development as much as by questions of governance. The last chapter, "Transnational Buddhist Education and the Limits of the Buddhist Ethnoscape" examines the phenomenon of monastics crossing borders and boundaries to become educated, and in particular the experiences of Dai-lue monastics in the Dhamma schools of Thailand and the Mahāyāna Buddhist institutes of China. This last chapter provides the clearest evidence of the dynamic of affiliation and Buddhist ethnoscapes discussed above. Yet at the same time that Buddhism provides a core mode of belonging enabling movement, I argue that it remains a weak force in the face of other modes of belonging, such as ethnicity, and especially, nationality. These dynamics of affiliation do not create a cosmopolitan identity, but enable, at best, cosmopolitan practices.

PART 1

**Shaping Buddhist Lives
in Sipsongpannā**

Local Monks in Sipsongpannā

AT THE END OF SEPTEMBER 2001, I RECEIVED a call from the vice-abbot of Wat Pājie, who was inviting me to join him at a ritual/festival at his *wat* (temple). Although I wanted to go, I apologized to him, telling him that one of the other (junior) monks of Wat Pājie had invited my family and me to go to his town to meet his parents. Despite declining the invitation, I was not too surprised to receive a knock on my door about an hour later, and to look out to find Ai Un Bian,[1] the Chinese teacher and part-time accountant at Wat Pājie waiting with the temple van to take us down to Meng Kham for the festival (a vice-abbot's invitation trumps that of a junior monk). Meng Kham is a small city about a half hour down the Mekong River from Jing Hong, and the village of the vice-abbot was one of a group of villages that had banded together to make a "nationality park" for Chinese tourists to visit. This might lead one to think that the Buddhism in the set of villages would be distorted as a result of this, but during a number of visits to them between 2001 and 2002, I rarely saw any tourists—foreign or domestic—outside of the main temple at Wat Manchuanman (one of the oldest temples in the region and one that the people in the area told me had somehow withstood the ravages of the Cultural Revolution).

This festival was taking place at a different *wat*, however, and when we got there, the main worship hall (*wihān*) was filled to the brim. With the exception of a three-by-twelve-foot platform at the side that was empty and reserved for the monks who had not yet entered, the rest of the hall was packed with people and the meritorious offerings (*dān*) they had brought to the ritual. The offerings, which spilled out into the covered porches outside the worship hall, were diverse, including food, buckets filled with items that monks could use in their daily lives (toothpaste, washcloths, toilet paper, etc.), small "trees" that had money (in small denominations) or short Buddhist texts hanging from them, and the occasional horse or elephant made of papier-mâché. Next to the empty platform, the *pu cān* (the lay ritual leader of the temple) sat by the dais, holding a microphone and reading out a long list of names of the people who had brought *dān* for the festival. No one was listening to him as they sat chatting and snacking. Indeed, as was normally the case at rituals, a 10 a.m. starting date was relatively flexible, and in fact, we went out into the courtyard and my not quite one-year-old son played in the mud by the worship hall, much to the delight of the elderly women of the village. The young men, most of whom were sitting by their motor scooters or gambling at the edge of the *wat* compound, paid us no attention.

The ritual/festival that we were waiting for (and we waited until well after lunch) was called a *salāt soy,* meaning a lottery, and it was an opportunity to make merit (*tham bun*) through a lottery. After the *pu cān* finished reciting the names, papers with individual names on them were rolled into bundles of banana leaves and put into a big pile. The *pu cān* and several other men picked up the papers and dropped them again, shouting "*Hoy!*" loudly each time they dropped the bundled names. These were then put into several bowls and placed in front of one of the monks who had come in and taken his place on the platform. This monk was one of the other vice-abbots of Wat Pājie, and though he was not from this part of Sipsongpannā, he had come to be the ritual leader. For the next twenty minutes or so, this monk led the other monks in a chanting of *paritta* from the *Mangala Sutta.* When he touched one of the bowls filled with bundled-up names with a fan that he held while chanting, the *pu cān* moved the other bowls over so that they were all touching one another, making a link between the merit (*bun*) being produced by the chanting monks and the names of the people who had made the offerings. After the monks finished, the *pu cān* took up the microphone again, leading the laypeople in another chant, at the end of which everyone poured water (*yat nām*) from small plastic bottles they had brought onto the ground, causing the merit accrued by offering the *dān* to be transferred to others (in most cases, it is dedicated to the spirits of family members who have died). And then the lottery began.

The monks all grabbed a handful of banana leaves, unwrapped them, and then they or a helper wandered around the worship hall looking for the donor or the family listed on the name. The vice-abbot grabbed Ai Un Bian and me, and gave us some of the leaves. As I was still only learning how to read Dai-lue letters at that point, I followed Un Bian around as we asked people who they were and whether they knew where the people we were looking for were. The people at the merit-making ritual were from several different villages, and so the monks and the men helping them often did not know whose *dān* they were seeking. As a result, it was a loud festive search, matching donor and monastic recipient. When we found a match, we took the offering back to the vice-abbot, who was also being helped by an older layman from his own village. There was no additional ritual involved in collecting the *dān* except if the offering was a dhamma text (i.e., the text hanging from the "money trees"), in which case the text had to be read as part of being received.

This ritual festival was both typical and atypical of Sipsongpannā. It was typical as a merit-making event in the region, as it was located in a village with members of several surrounding villages coming together. On the other hand, it was atypical because it was a lottery. In addition to being fun, this type of merit-making event is understood to be particularly efficacious because the donation is not consciously directed at a particular monk. The laypeople do not choose to whom they will give their offerings, and so there are no personal relations to taint the gift; it is outside of networks of reciprocity. Although this form of merit making is not uncommon in northern Thailand (I had attended several such events in Chiang Mai in 1994), this is the only place that it happens in Sipsongpannā. In other words, while this was a highly local affair, it was also one that implied at least a wider Tai Theravāda religiosity.

How to think about "the local" is a problem within Sipsongpannā, a region that is between two cultural spheres and is widely understood as being Theravāda. In part, this is because the idea of Theravāda, like Buddhism itself, has inherent translocal (not to mention transnational) aspects. Hence, whenever we speak of Theravāda, implicitly we are talking about a translocal form of religion. It is the type of Buddhism that is presumably the predominant form in mainland Southeast Asia and Sri Lanka and is sometimes claimed to be the original form (or at least the closest we have at this point to "what the Buddha taught"), and that is linked by and through the Pāli canon. In some ways, this assumption created the great problem of the study of Southeast Asian forms of Buddhism in the late 1960s through the early 1980s, epitomized by the work of Gombrich, Tambiah, and Spiro. For these scholars and many others, a key problem was the Redfieldian one of how to conceptualize the relationship between the "great" tradition of Theravāda and the "little" tradition epitomized by the national forms.[2] This is manifested in a variety of different frames, though the two major issues have been how to think about the various forms of magic practiced along with Buddhism, or indeed as part of it, in Southeast Asian countries, as well as the relationship between local spirit cults and Buddhism. Scholarly efforts have ranged broadly, seeing them as unrelated and diametrically opposed spheres, with magic/spirits serving as locations of corruption (Gombrich), to articulating a hierarchical relationship between them (Tambiah 1970), to highlighting the "local" (whether in regional or national terms; Tannenbaum 1995 and Southwold 1983). Some scholars presume there is a "real" translocal form of Buddhism, whereas others treat it as a logical idea that had no actual presence on the ground, such as the Pāli *imaginaire* (Collins 1998). However, whether real or imagined, or explicit or implicit, the study of Theravāda has long contained a hierarchical dichotomy between the "great," translocal form, and the "little," local form.

There have been a number of critiques of this dichotomy both within and outside of the study of Theravāda Buddhism. Justin McDaniel, for example, in his recent discussion of popular Thai Buddhism, *The Lovelorn Ghost and the Magical Monk,* forcefully argues against the binary framework articulated above. He does this by showing that for many, if not most, Thais, there is no clear distinction between what Spiro called "apotropaic" (magic) and "nibbanic" forms of Buddhism. Monks such as the late nineteenth-century prelate Somdet To (the "magical" monk of the title) were deeply immersed in the study of Pāli *and* magic. It is not that Thais cannot distinguish between what is *lokiya* (worldly) and what is *lokuttara* (otherworldly), it is that they do not distinguish between them in the ways that scholarship on Theravāda has tended to require (see McDaniel 2011 passim, but see especially 113–117). For McDaniel, then, the study of Buddhism should be about local forms, and the dichotomy between the great and little traditions simply misses the point.

While I am in sympathy with McDaniel's critique, I want to understand "local" in a somewhat different way. In his effort to shift the ways we study Buddhism away from the implicit dichotomy between the great and little traditions and towards the local and the lived, McDaniel tends to minimize the imagination of the translocal. While most Thai Buddhists may not spend most of their time thinking about Buddhism as a translocal or universal object, there are some who do. For example, Patrick Jory's (2002) discussion of Chulalongkorn's attitudes towards the *Jātakas* in the early twentieth century shows a very clear vision of the translocal (as well as a concern about using this strategically). Yet even for those Thais who are not focused on the "great" tradition, the translocal remains an implicit possibility. In 2009, I had a brief conversation about the political identity of monks with a Thai woman in a large temple in Bangkok. In the space of ten minutes, she asserted both that nationality did not matter for monks because all monks (at least all Therāvada monks) are the same in the robes, and that Burmese and Lao monks are "crazy [because of] communism." Even if my questions elicited these remarks (partially at least), within her views there is an implicit tension that arises from seeing monks as both universally the same and differentiable. In a critique of the anthropological turn to use "local" (to replace terms such as "primitive," "tribal," and "preliterate") and to qualify at least the notion of agency, Talal Asad noted that in a sense everyone ("modern" and "unmodern") is "local" because they are "attached to a place, rooted, circumscribed, limited," but that people have differing access to that which is "non-local" and cosmopolitan (1993, 7–9). Assuming this to be the case, the question is not whether Theravāda is local or translocal, but rather, when is the Buddhist form treated as local, translocal, or unmarked?

This begins to get at the sense of what I mean by "local" Buddhism in Sipsongpannā. As should be clear from the introduction, the monks of Sipsongpannā are highly connected to a variety of networks, some of which remain in Sipsongpannā (and therefore are local), some of which are national (meaning they have to do with an imagined China or directly with the Chinese government), and some of which are translocal, in that they extend beyond Sipsongpannā and their foundation is some form of Buddhism rather than an ethnic or national connection. Although the region is relatively underdeveloped, the monks of the region are also "modern."[3] By local, then, I mean neither unconnected, nor unmodern; rather I want to highlight the patterns that are visible in Sipsongpannā. Some of these are similar to other Theravāda locations, some not. They are the conditions on the ground as I have seen them, and as my informants have talked about them. They are not unchanging; the Buddhism of Sipsongpannā has been radically shaped by Chinese discourses and practices of governance, particularly in comparison to "local" Buddhism in Sipsongpannā prior to 1953, when the PLA entered Jing Hong and began the process of internal colonization. Indeed, as a result of these, it is not always easy to understand what counts as "local," which is a problem highlighted by the languages of Sipsongpannā.[4]

Approaching Knowledge of Local Buddhism

Buddhism in Sipsongpannā is a multilingual phenomenon. Nowhere is this more evident than at Wat Pājie Mahārāchatān, the *wat long* (central temple) of the region, on the outskirts of Jing Hong. Throughout the temple, signs and notices are written in Dai-lue, Chinese, and Thai.[5] These trilingual signs are most common in front of and attached to the sides of the major buildings on the monastery grounds. Most of these multilingual signs at Wat Pājie are marks of patronage: they mark who has given money to support the construction of a particular building (often sharing how much the person donated), and the language of the sign reflects the nationality or ethnicity of the donator.

Despite the equal way that these languages are represented on this (and other) signs, they do not exist in a vacuum. The three languages do not bear the same relation to political and coercive power, and they do not communicate the same thing to all people. Thai is far less common than either Chinese or Dai-lue, though where it does appear (in the main sign or in donation inscriptions), it is usually etched in stone. The carved wooden sign in front of the main worship hall and the sign painted on the back gate of the temple (which is the main one used) has both Chinese and Dai-lue, but no Thai. The lesser presence of Thai speaks to the fact that far fewer Thai people come to the temple than Chinese tourists or Dai-lue villagers. It is also reflective of the fact that Thai visitors already understand many of the rules of comportment for the temple. Signs by the door of the worship hall in Chinese and English request that foreigners take off their shoes; a sign in Thai is hardly necessary since Thais learn to do this from an early age.

There is both a public and private aspect to what we might think of as the semiotics of signs discernible in Sipsongpannā Buddhism more generally that is reflective of both authority and codes. This is evident in two different celebrations of new buildings: one in 2001 for the dedication of a new house for the abbot of Wat Pājie (see Borchert 2010 and chapter 3 of this volume), and the other in 2007 celebrating the opening of Wat Long Meuang Lue, a new temple built on the outskirts of the city. These events differed significantly in their public pronouncement. In 2001, for example, while the local government was involved in a variety of ways in the celebration and the head of the autonomous region was in attendance, it was largely an internal affair and the majority of guests were either local villagers or from around the greater Tai region of the Shan States, Laos, and northern Thailand. By comparison, in November 2007, Jing Hong was festooned with banners in both Chinese and Dai-lue celebrating the new *wat,* which relied heavily on the help of the Jing Hong government, as well as real estate developers from outside of Yunnan Province. The languages used on the signs revealed who the participants were, and some of the dynamics of the events. This is evident in other ways at Wat Pājie, where signs in Chinese, such as rules for cleaning, are for outsiders (i.e., tourists), whereas those in Dai-lue, such as a set of rules imposed on students at the Dhamma school at Wat Pājie in 2007, are only for the temple denizens. With rare exceptions, only monks, novices, and former monks can read the traditional script of the Dai-lue. In other words, this use of language can reveal how certain dynamics are local, or inflected with either national or transnational concerns. The context is important: the use of Dai-lue at the dedication of the abbot's house in 2001 signified links to other Tai sanghas outside of China; its use on a sign for students was a distinctly internal affair.

This dynamic also complicates how we understand both local Buddhism and local knowledge. When providing a background on what is happening in Sipsongpannā, we run into a particular kind of difficulty: what language is the most important to pay attention to, and moreover, what knowledge of the Dai-lue is authoritative? While the Buddhism of the Dai-lue is practiced principally in the Dai-lue language, one needs to be careful about assuming that it is the "local form." Historically, there was no single, standard form of the Dai-lue language. Although the different place-based dialects were largely mutually intelligible, the differences were as likely to divide as to unite the Sangha in Sipsongpannā. Moreover, other languages, mainly Thai and Chinese, enter into the practice of and knowledge about Buddhism. Thai Buddhism, for example, has been an important source of modern educational resources, such as textbooks that (re)shape the way some Dai-lue understand their traditions. The Chinese public schools and official policies have shaped the ways that many Dai-lue know their history, as well as the public language through which they sometimes talk about it. Indeed, while Dai-lue is most common in the village *wats* of Sipsongpannā, Chinese and Thai are often heard there as well. In other words, Dai-lue Buddhists neither reject these resources out of hand, nor do they accept them uncritically.

Knowledge about local Buddhism in Sipsongpannā is in part a problem of perspective, which is well illustrated by thinking about Sipsongpannā geographically. In the introduction, I referred to the fact that Sipsongpannā is in Yunnan Province, in the southwest corner of China. This is certainly true, but one might reasonably ask whether it is best to describe Sipsongpannā as being part of Southeast Asia or China. The region is within the borders of the Chinese nation-state, and has been since at least 1953 (and has had a political relationship with China for much longer). But it also remains the case that there is much exchange between people of Sipsongpannā (Dai-lue and others) and their kin in Southeast Asia. Moreover, while there are clearly geographical and political boundaries (e.g., the Mekong River, border posts), there is no great wall or fence separating China from Southeast Asia; it can therefore quite accurately be depicted as being part of both regions. Indeed, we might even say that the only accurate way to depict the region is from both sides. This conditions how we are able to know the region.

Perspective in this context is also a question of power and authority. Sipsongpannā is the subject of knowledge produced in several different locations, and this knowledge has different concerns as well as different relationships with state authorities. This knowledge is deeply conditioned by the context in which it is produced. That is, what we know and think about a particular subject and the aspects that we privilege when making authoritative statements about it are heavily inflected by the concerns of those around us, by our teachers and conversation partners, and what they find to be important (de Certeau [1975] 1988). It is also conditioned by relations of power and discourses that are at large in the society in which these "authoritative" statements are produced. This is not to say that we can know nothing (though no knowledge is final) or that academic discourse is at the service of the state or other institutions of power (though sometimes it is), but to acknowledge— indeed to highlight—that it cannot be unaffected by these institutions and the statements that they make.

Authoritative statements about the Dai-lue and Sipsongpannā are generally made in three different locations: China (outside of Sipsongpannā, mainly in Kunming), Thailand, and the "Western" academy. Each of these authoritative statements (and it should be acknowledged that they are differently authoritative) relies on certain assumptions. The Chinese, for example presume that Sipsongpannā is in China, and that even if Dai-lue culture has been influenced by the cultures of Southeast Asia, that was in the past. Thai publications on Sipsongpannā are often concerned with inscribing the Dai-lue as the siblings (*phi-nawng*) of the Thai, and Sipsongpannā is often spoken of as an ancestral home of the Thais, though a less civilized one. In these writings, Sipsongpannā is not a part of Thailand per se, but its portrayals are influenced by pan-Thai discourses (Thongchai 2008). Western scholarship is probably too often concerned with seeing the Dai-lue as victims of the Chinese state, or perhaps of the neoliberalization of the world economy. In all of this work, the statements of the Dai-lue themselves and their concerns are often absent, or at best, muted. We are all producing "knowledge of the local" rather than "local knowledge," as Asad rightly distinguished (1993, 10).

In thinking about this, it is important to acknowledge that most Dai-lue are multilingual, often with knowledge of Dai-lue (in one or two variants), Mandarin or Yunnan forms of Chinese, sometimes Thai, and perhaps a little English. Sometimes they even know a little Burmese. Their knowledge, particularly of written and spoken forms, and use of these languages is not uniform. Sometimes it is strategic, and sometimes, practical.

The Religious and Ethnic Field in Sipsongpannā in the Early Twenty-First Century

The smell of rice growing in Sipsongpannā is overwhelming. Throughout the 1990s, when I traveled to Sipsongpannā, I would take a twenty-four-hour bus ride from Kunming to Jing Hong, arriving somewhat dazed at the bus station, and wander around the city until I could find one of the two hotels that would take in a foreign tourist. By the early 2000s, however, I would fly down to Jing Hong, usually on a fleet of Boeing 737s, crammed with Chinese tourists, always wondering whether the stewardess' attempts to provide an English-language commentary on the rules of being on an airplane were for my benefit only (like some strange Zen koan: if no foreigners are there to hear the English on an airplane, does anyone hear them?). The Jing Hong airport is simply a terminal plopped down in the middle of rice paddies, and there are no gates. As a result, when one disembarks, you have to walk outside across the tarmac to go into the terminal. And it is at this point, going from the sterile environment of the plane to the middle of the rice paddies that I know I have come to Sipsongpannā, replete with the smell of sticky rice growing nearby.

Han Chinese scholars writing about the Dai-lue and Sipsongpannā often use stereotyped language, not unlike my sense of the smell of Sipsongpannā. One typical example is the following: "The Daizu, a minority who primarily practice rice-paddy agriculture, have their own written and spoken language and the whole people believe in Buddhism" (Zheng and Yu 1995, i). The truth of these statements can be seen readily throughout the region in a variety of ways. If one walks into villages, one quickly finds a temple (*wat*), sometimes in the center of town, sometimes on the edge. Depending on the time of day, it is not surprising to see young men, usually novices, walking around, hanging out at the *wat*, or perhaps doing chores or studying. At the same time, tourist industry images (at the airport, on signs around town, etc.) tend to have one of three images: young men, and particularly women, dressed in what the advertisers deem traditional Dai-lue clothing, splashing each other with water in the practice of the "Water-Splashing Festival" (Ch.: Poshui jie; Dai-lue: Song kān); young women with long black hair being portrayed as bathing in the river; and Buddhist monks, particularly young novices, walking around.[6]

As previously noted, the Buddhism of the region is Theravāda, having come to the region from either Lannā (i.e., northern Thailand) or the Shan States by the fourteenth century.[7] This is a fairly new way to refer to the Buddhism of the region, as indeed "Theravāda" as a way to refer to the Buddhism of the entire region is something of a neologism that emerged in the early decades of the twentieth century and was codified in the 1950s by the World Fellowship of Buddhists (Skilling et al. 2012). Different intellectual communities refer to the form of Buddhism in different ways. For both Dai-lue and Thai writers, the Buddhism of the region is unmarked as the "teachings of the Buddha" (*phra puttha sāsanā*), and the Dai-lue as "people of the Buddha" (*chao puttha; Wichā Puttha-bawatti* 2004, ii). Scholars writing in English are as wont as not to talk about the Buddhism of the region as "Theravāda,"[8] while Chinese scholars refer to it in a number of different ways. It is probably most commonly referred to as "Southern Tradition Buddhism" (Nanchuan Fojiao), but it is also not uncommon to see "Hīnayāna" Buddhism (Xiaocheng Fojiao; see, e.g., Li 1983). Less frequently, one might encounter Shangzuobu Fojiao, which is the Chinese term for Theravāda (see, e.g., Wang 2001, 367ff.), but this is fairly uncommon among Han Chinese scholars. (Indeed, most of the Han Chinese with whom I have spoken outside of Yunnan have never heard the term, whereas many have heard of "Hīnayāna.") I have been told by officers in the Yunnan Buddhist Association that "Southern Theravāda Buddhism" (Nanchuan Shangzuobu Fojiao) is the "proper" term, but almost no one uses it, either in print or in daily speech. The terms of Chinese and foreign scholars are, of course, meant to differentiate the Buddhism of the Dai-lue from that of the majority of China. While the latter Buddhism is usually referred to in Chinese as Mahāyāna (Dacheng Fojiao), the so-called greater vehicle is occasionally referred to as the Buddhism of the Han (Hanzu Fojiao; see Yang 1994, 27).

Nevertheless, in the eyes of many both inside and outside of Sipsongpannā, being Dai and being Buddhist are largely synonymous, and it is widely understood that Buddhism has played a central role in the life of the

Dai-lue people, at the very least as an institutional structure through which much of Dai-lue culture was maintained and transmitted. The Dai-lue have long practiced temporary ordination, as in Thailand and Laos, and while some men certainly remained monks for life, the majority of them did not. Indeed, in 1998 when I first began to do fieldwork in Sipsongpannā, scholars in Kunming as well as laymen spending time at temples in the villages around Jing Hong reported to me that in pre-Cultural Revolution society, it was necessary for men to ordain in order for them to get married. The temple, they told me, was the place where young Dai-lue men "got cooked," and became proper Dai-lue men. While it is no longer the case that this is the only place to learn how to be Dai-lue, it remains an important location of this training (as chapter 4 shows). It is in the temples—and largely only in the temples—that the Dai-lue learned and learn how to read and write the Dai-lue language.

It is also important to note that Buddhism in Sipsongpannā is highly gendered. Both men and women participate in the Buddhist world of the Dai-lue, but only men ordain as novices or monks, and thus only men learn how to read and write. Women take part in rituals and do things for monks and novices, but they do not "leave home." This is in contrast to some other Theravāda polities such as Thailand or Myanmar, which have vibrant female renunciant movements (Falk 2008; Kawanami 2013). This differentiation of male and female roles in Dai-lue Buddhism means that traditional knowledge among the Dai-lue is also gendered (traditional female knowledge is oral; male knowledge is written). One significant consequence of this has been a gendered division of pedagogical paths. Because they have not had the alternative of traditional education in the temples, girls have been far more likely to remain in the public schools than boys (Hansen 2001). This in turn can have an adverse effect on how being Dai-lue is perceived (Hansen 2001; Diana 2009).

Prior to the arrival of the PLA in Sipsongpannā in 1953, Buddhism seems to have been closely tied to the power structures of the region. Chinese scholars report that Sipsongpannā had a feudal structure, with a lord (cao) ruling over polities (meaung) of a variety of sizes. At the top of the society was a "lord of the earth" (cao phaendin) who presumably owned the region (Natchā 1998). Even as the premodern Sipsongpannā state appears not to have been a galactic polity as described by Tambiah (1976), it was still a hierarchical society, and the structure of the sangha reflected these hierarchies. There were seven ranks within the sangha, from a novice monk up to the sangha-rāt, that is, the "king" of the sangha. The first three (pha [novice], dubi [monk], and khūbā ["venerated teacher"]) were essentially open to anyone (though very few people ever achieved the rank of khūbā). The top four were only open to members of the aristocracy, and only close members of the cao phaendin's family could become the sangha-rāt (Li 1983, vol. 3; Yang 1994). Indeed, Chinese scholars generally note the close relationship between the sangha and the political structure: "The entire Buddhist temple system and the administrative system of a feudal system leadership by lords conform to one another" (Yang 1994, 82), and moreover that Buddhism was the "religion that protected the system of feudal leadership" (Ma 1988).

This is no longer the case since the feudal structure of society was removed in 1953 (LeMoines 1997, 172). The only ranks that continue to exist in Sipsongpannā are the bottom three: *pha, dubi,* and *khūbā.* At the beginning of the millennium, there were roughly 650 monks (a little more than one monk for each temple) and between 4,000 and 6,500 novices (Borchert 2006, 74). The majority of these were and are affiliated with their village temple. The head of the sangha, who is also the abbot of Wat Pājie, is no longer called the "king of the sangha," but rather the "head of the sangha" (*sangha-nayok*). In Chinese, he is referred to as the head of the Buddhist Association (*fojiao xiehui zhang*), and as of this writing, he is the only monk in Sipsongpannā who is currently recognized as a *khūbā* by the local government.[9]

Of course, the change to the sangha came during the Cultural Revolution. As in other parts of China, the Cultural Revolution in Sipsongpannā led to the effective destruction of Buddhist institutions. Most of the temples were closed and converted to other uses. Buddha images were destroyed, as were texts. Many were buried to hide them, but the effect was the same, and very few texts have been recovered. All but a handful of monks disrobed, willingly and unwillingly, or fled to Southeast Asia. The story of the Cultural Revolution in the region seems to be largely the same as in other parts of the People's Republic, though it is interesting to note that the Dai-lue tend not to want to delve too deeply into their own participation in the event (McCarthy 2001, 155).

The 1980s saw the return of Buddhism to the region. Like other parts of China, the pent-up religious energy resulted in a "religion fever" in the 1980s (Tan 1995), when many Dai-lue men took the opportunity to ordain, as noted in the introduction. For the most part, the energy and resources for rebuilding Buddhism in the region came from the Dai-lue communities themselves. They have poured their wealth into reconstructing village temples, and their young men have chosen to enter into the sangha. At the same time, the success of this rebuilding has relied on resources from both the sanghas of mainland Southeast Asia and the Chinese government. Buddhists of Thailand and the Shan States in particular have provided books, images, and money. Just as important, monks of these countries also traveled to Sipsongpannā, particularly in the 1980s and early 1990s, to serve as preceptors or abbots in village temples. These human resources were essential for the ability to conduct ordinations that would be recognized as legitimate outside of Sipsongpannā. The growth of Buddhism in the region, which was steady in the 1980s and 1990s, was also aided by the Chinese government, which, through the BA of Yunnan, provided financial aid for temple reconstruction (the ties between the local government and the Sangha of Sipsongpannā will be discussed more thoroughly in the next chapter). In other words, while Dai-lue Buddhism is a local affair, it is influenced directly and indirectly by Thai and Chinese notions about what Buddhism is, and who the Dai-lue are.

Most people, including both Dai-lue and Han, assume that all Dai-lue are Buddhist, thus naturalizing a Buddhist identity, but there are other religions in Sipsongpannā as well. Most significantly is spirit worship, similar to what one finds throughout mainland Southeast Asia. Historically, spirit worship would have been just as widespread as one sees in mainland Southeast Asia. During the high communist period, spirit worship practices, like Buddhism, were seen as part of feudal superstition and were therefore repressed. Furthermore, Tanabe Shigeharu argued almost three decades ago that the transformation of the social system (away from the traditional "feudal manorial system") starting in the 1950s led to vast transformations of the system of local spirit cults because a number of important rituals and sacrifices were sponsored by the local *cao* (1988). While there has been some recovery of spirit worship, it has been uneven throughout the region, due in part to the fact that such practices are at best understood as "folk beliefs" (*minjian xinyang*) or possibly "superstition" (*mixin*), rather than the more legitimate "religion" (*zongjiao*). I have had novices and young monks tell me that no one worships the spirits (*phi*) anymore, because it is not civilized to do so. This does not mean that spirit worship has disappeared in the region. On the contrary, it is still possible to find spirit houses throughout the region, as well as trees with ribbons wrapped around them and offerings to the *phi* housed in the trees. This was far more common in villages outside of the greater Jing Hong metropolitan region, and also seemed to be more common on small roads and paths approaching villages than on the main paved road leading to a village temple. It is also perhaps the case that other practices related to spirit worship, such as tattooing, have lost prestige in Sipsongpannā as well. Unlike conditions among the Shan in northern Thailand (Tannenbaum 1995), there seems to be very little tattooing being used for protective purposes in Sipsongpannā. Elderly men often have extensive tattoos in traditional letters as part of protective spells, but young men in their teens, twenties, and early thirties, often have very few tattoos. Moreover, when I asked them about what they did have (both at Wat Pājie and at the temples I visited on a regular basis), most of them told me that they had just been playing around when they got them. While I never encountered a campaign against spirit worship by the local government, the processes of modernization can be seen as undermining the practice of spirit worship in the region.

The other religions that the Dai-lue follow are Islam and Christianity. The ethnic compositions of these religions differ from that of the Buddhists that are the subject of this book. Muslims in the region, known colloquially as "Hui-Dai," are primarily the descendants of Muslim traders who worked the "southern Silk Road" in the centuries before the establishment of the PRC. For the most part, they lived in separate villages, and they remained fairly distinct from the "Theravāda" Dai. The Christians were not ethnically distinct, but rather comprised a number of ethnic groups (though when I attended several Sunday morning worship services in Jing Hong in 2002, most of those at the service were Dai-lue, at least as indicated by their clothing). Several of the minority groups in the region have much deeper Christian roots than the Dai-lue. There was (and is) in Jing Hong a Christian medical education nongovernmental organization (NGO) whose employees were the only permanent foreigners of European descent in the region in 2002 (beyond my family and me). These medical professionals told me that the number of Christians was increasing at a great pace, and that this scared the local government.[10] I never received independent corroboration of this, but it is consistent with the growth of Christianity in other parts of China. These three religions were the only ones the government officially recognized as present in Sipsongpannā in 2001–2002, and the Religious Affairs Bureau in the local government was organized to reflect this.

Village Buddhism in Sipsongpannā

In June 2007, I attended a meeting of a village *wat* committee that was concerned with the preservation of the village temple. The meeting was arranged by Roger Casas, who was working for a United Nations Educational, Scientific and Cultural Organization (UNESCO) project based at Wat Pājie that was focused on preserving and fostering traditional arts in Sipsongpannā. This particular meeting was the culmination of a number of conversations about how to restore the temple. This had become a significant issue because of the directions that temple restoration had taken in Sipsongpannā in recent years. During the 1980s, most villages in the region rebuilt or restored their *wats* in fairly traditional ways, using traditional materials (i.e., wood). The worship halls (*wihān*) were generally fairly plain on the outside, with murals on the walls and pillars inside. Since the late 1990s, however, temple renovations had changed, and it had become increasingly common for villages to rebuild their *wats* in a much fancier style, often resembling the temples of Thailand. Part of this was a function of deforestation and a need to use other materials such as concrete and bricks in the building of new *wihān,* but part of it also reflected the wealth that had come into the region as the result of rubber, the boom in cultivation of *pu'er* tea in the 2000s, and tourism. The UNESCO project thus was focused on trying to maintain and foster more traditional styles in *wihān* (re)construction. What was interesting about this particular meeting, and the lunch that followed it, was that the participation of the abbot, the resident monk of the *wat,* was marginal. The other members of the *wat* committee, such as the village headman and the *pu cān,* were the ones who did the talking. They were the ones who ran the meeting and seemed to be the decision makers.

The decision to rebuild a *wat* in part or in toto can originate from a number of different sources. It might come from the abbot of a *wat,* it might be the decision of a *wat* committee, or it might be the result of a development that is taking place in the village's environs as a whole, such as new road construction. In another village temple *wat* that I visited regularly in 2001–2002, a decision was made to repair the roof of the ordination hall (*bosot*). The committee made this decision collectively, but the abbot was clearly running the show, determining who was responsible for getting materials or organizing the labor for the reconstruction. He was also the one who made the decision to use the extra donated materials to build a new toilet for the *wat* (these buildings, the newly roofed ordination hall, and the new bathroom were dedicated during the same festival). In other words, village *wats* in Sipsongpannā are diverse places: some have strong abbots, some have weak ones; some are well maintained and are constantly being rebuilt, whereas others are falling into disrepair.

This diversity also characterizes the literal and figurative space of the *wat* in villages across Sipsongpannā. Almost all Dai-lue villages in the region have a *wat,* and they are usually easy to find. Up until the late 1990s, village *wats* looked very similar to the homes, except they were bigger and higher. They could be identified by a tall umbrella over the *wihān,* however, and they would be the one building in the village that was not on stilts. Rebuilt *wihān,* as noted above, look different, following an aesthetic pattern that is similar to the temples of Thailand. The location of the *wat* also varies: sometimes it is in the center of the village, sometimes it is on the edge; very occasionally it is a bit away from the cluster of houses that make up the village. The same can be said of Buddhism as a whole. Historically, *wats* were at the center of social life within Sipsongpannā; however, in the post-Mao period, conditions are more varied. There are *wats* that have an energetic abbot, a strong temple committee (usually made up of village headmen, the abbot, and the *pu cān,* as well as several other leaders), and active engagement from the village as a whole. In these villages, the *wat* is a local meeting place, the space of the temple grounds looks neat, well cared for, and regularly swept, and there are often novices (*pha*). At the same time, there are many *wats* that are run down and do not receive significant help from the village as a whole. Strong abbots—men who have energy and some knowledge (either in traditional forms such as medicine or tattooing, or through formal educational institutions)—are central to producing attractive *wats* that are supported by the denizens of the local village.

The people who actually spend time in most village *wats* in Sipsong-pannā are usually from the local village or one nearby. Any given *wat* will have a monk, and usually a handful of novices.[11] As elsewhere in the Ther-avāda world, there is a distinction between a monk (Dai-lue: *dubi*) who has undergone the "higher ordination" (*upasampadā*), and a novice (Dai-lue: *pha*), who has taken the ordination for "leaving home" (*pabbajjā*). Novices are boys under the age of twenty, and village abbots may be any age above twenty. Throughout Sipsongpannā since the return of religious practice in the early 1980s, it has been common for the abbot to be fairly young. Most men do not remain in robes for their entire lives, and never have in Sipsongpannā; it is therefore not uncommon for a monk to be abbot for five or ten years, and then disrobe. The village temple committee will either promote the oldest of the available novices to serve as abbot, or put out a call among nearby villages for a young, capable monk to be promoted into the position. This call is most likely to be answered by a young man from among the collection of temples where the monks perform the fortnightly recitation of the disciplinary codes (*pāṭimokkha*) together. In the first case, this has sometimes meant that the abbot of a temple is not yet twenty and so has not yet undergone the *upasam-padā* ritual. These are some of the cases where the abbot ends up being rather weak, and the authority of a *wat* lies with the older laymen on the *wat* com-mittee. I have asked both monks and laymen about the propriety of having an abbot under the age of twenty, and they have told me that it is not ideal, but I have heard a few different rationales. Some have said that they promote a young man to be abbot because they have a senior novice that they do not want to lose to disrobing. More commonly, they will just shrug and say that these are the conditions of Buddhism in post-Mao era Sipsongpannā.

Maintenance of the *wat* and its novices has the potential of being a unifying factor within a village and district. For example, sponsorship of a novice ordination has not generally been done by the parents or officials in a village. Thus, when a boy decides to ordain, the major sponsorship comes from a neighbor or a relative outside of the nuclear family. Bunchuay Sisawath, a Thai politician who visited Sipsongpannā in the 1950s, writes about how boys would go around to neighbors looking for a sponsor. Usually the boy could find someone who wished to repay the ordination of his or her own child (Bunchuay [1955], 2004, 2:132). Similarly, when there is a ritual such as the *salāt* merit-making ceremony that I discussed at the beginning of this chapter, the abbot or the wat committee invites monks from neighboring villages in part because there is greater merit in anonymous giving. The function of such invitations, though, is to wrap both villagers and monks in local economies of merit making. This is similar to what one finds in both village and urban Thailand (Bunnag 1973; Hayashi 2003).[12]

Other aspects of maintaining a wat and the monastics who live there are the responsibility of the village community, though sometimes the denizens of a wat end up having to handle them. In much of mainland Southeast Asia, monks, and sometimes novices, will go on the morning alms rounds, the *pindabāt*. While monastics may not go on the same routes every day, they usually have a set of lay supporters whose homes they regularly pass by. In this way, merit-making patronage networks are developed and maintained. In Sipsongpannā, however, there is no practice of *pindabāt,* except on a few festive occasions. Instead, villagers tend to bring food to the wat. This is particularly the case when they have a child or relative who is living as a novice. It is also the case, however, that monks will occasionally send novices to market to buy vegetables. Almost all of the *wats* that I went into had a kitchen in the dormitory building, although monks or novices do not cook every day. It is not uncommon for novices to go home for lunch. Bunchuay reports that the Dai-lue prefer that their novices ordain between the age of seven and ten years old (Bunchuay [1955], 2004, 129–130), because they believe this means that they are purer. This age remains common in the Reform Era (see below), and so it is rare that young novices fully "leave home," as they do in Sri Lanka (Samuels 2010). Like cooking, most of the physical labor at the temple is also performed by the monastics themselves (Borchert 2011), and not by lay villagers. While the villagers would certainly be engaged in major reconstruction projects (such as rebuilding the roof of an ordination hall [*bosot*]), novices in particular also do a significant amount of work. There is, in part, a pedagogical function to the labor, but it is also simply about the need to get work done around the *wat*.

In addition to the life of the *wats,* village Buddhism is marked by a variety of festivals, such as the *salāt soy*. There are three festivals that have a widespread celebration throughout the region: the Beginning of the Rains Retreat in late June or early July (Khao wasā); the End of the Rains Retreat roughly three months later (Auk wasā), and the biggest one of all, the Dai-lue New Year (Song kān pii ma). The Rains Retreat is the period when monks and novices are constrained from traveling, and the beginning and end of this period are marked by a variety of ritual activities that may last for several days. These include the construction of *ta* (reliquary mounds) made of sand; washing Buddha images; lay villagers making special offerings (*dān*) to the temple; and the water libation (*yat nām*), which marks the transference of merit (Tan 1995, 63–64). At Wat Pājie, Auk wasā was celebrated with a special performance of the giving of alms. People from five or six villages around the temple came, lining up around the courtyard, and the monks simulated the *pinda-bāt,* the daily alms round (see figures 1.2 and 1.3).

The Dai-lue New Year celebration is in many ways the same as the one that takes place in mainland Southeast Asia as well. Known in Chinese as

FIGURE 1.1 Novices and villagers repairing roof on ordination hall

the "Water-Throwing Festival," it is a three-day festival that climaxes with a chaotic day of people "blessing" one another with water. The official celebration in Jing Hong gets quite raucous, with the use of super loader cannons and people driving water trucks around the city dumping water on spectators. This event adheres to a regular schedule, taking place on April 13–15 every year, just as it does in Laos and Thailand. Once one leaves Jing Hong, however, the dates and the energy of the celebration are more variable. In some villages, the New Year celebration would only be one day, in others, two or three. Moreover, one could find Song kān celebrations taking place for most of the month of April. Tan Leshan reported that in the village where he did research, these three festivals (Khao wasā, Auk wasā, and Song kān) included five major parts: washing of the Buddha image with water brought by each household at the village temple; each family creating a stupa made of sand at the temple (all of which were linked by white thread); making offerings to deceased friends and relatives; making offerings to slaughtered animals (he did research in a village that specialized in butchering); and making offerings to the Buddha, the Dhamma, the sangha, the village pagoda, and the *pu cān* (Tan 1995, 79). There are a variety of other events that take place in villages, some that are regular, some not.[13]

FIGURE 1.2 Monks receiving alms at Auk wasā (End of the Rains Retreat) at Wat Pājie

FIGURE 1.3 Novices follow behind the monks and take bags of offerings to offices to be sorted and tallied

Monastic Careers in Contemporary Sipsongpannā

There are several different stages the monastics in Sipsongpannā go through during their careers (see table). At ordination, the *lūk kaew* (boy preparing for ordination as a novice) becomes a *pha noy* (junior novice), who is responsible for studying the Dai-lue alphabet (*akkhara*) and often also studies in elementary schools. Around the age of sixteen when the alphabet has been learned and the novice has learned a small collection of *suttas* to be chanted, he becomes known as a *pha long,* a senior novice, though there is no official ceremony celebrating this change. Usually by the time a novice has become a *pha long,* he will have finished his education in the Chinese educational system.[14] To the degree that he studies, it is usually on his own, though he is also often responsible for training the younger novices. The novice remains a *pha long* until he is at least twenty, when he will take the higher ordination and be referred to as a *du noy* or *dubi noy* (junior monk). While a *dubi noy,* he will have a preceptor, usually the abbot of a nearby village, who will serve as his guide. After he has been a fully ordained monk for a few years, the *noy* seems to be dropped from his title, and he is simply referred to as *dubi* (e.g., Dubi Kham or Monk Kham). Some twenty years after the *upasampadā,* a monk might become a *khūbā,* which is an honorific indicating both great knowledge and spiritual prestige.

These ranks are primarily determined as a matter of local traditions, but the Chinese government has had an influence, particularly at the top of this system. In addition to the ranks in the chart, prior to the incorporation of Sipsongpannā into the modern Chinese nation, there were four other positions above *khūbā,* including a *sangha-rāt* (Li 1983, 3:101). These positions, which were held by the *cao phaendin* prior to his ascension to the head of Sipsongpannā or by his family, were eliminated when the royal system of Sipsongpannā was changed. Of greater complexity is the position of the *khūbā* after the reestablishment of Buddhism in the early 1980s. Regulations promulgated by the Buddhist Association of Sipsongpannā and posted at *wats* around the region in the late 1990s note that to become a *khūbā,* monks need to have been fully ordained for twenty years, to have deep knowledge, to be supported by local people, and to have permission granted by the Buddhist Association. This rule seems to be an attempt to regulate the title, which has not been particularly successful. While the abbot of Wat Pājie has been the only monk officially recognized as a *khūbā* prior to 2016, there are a number of monks around the region who are referred to as *khūbā* by lay supporters.

When a monk's career path begins is not prescribed. Boys tend to ordain between the ages of nine and thirteen, though a few boys are younger and a few are older.[15] Chinese scholarship seems to understand that boys ordain between seven and eight years old, but in my experience at least, that

Educational and Career Cycle of Monks in Sipsongpannā

Title	Age	Responsibility	Pedagogical Tasks in the *Wat*
lūk kaew (precious child)	Usually under the age of 16	Attend school, spend time at *wat* (monastery/ temple)	Learn to chant, attend elementary school
pha noy (little novice)	Ordained, under the age of 16	Clean *wat*, follow orders of older novices and monks	Study *akkhara* (letters, alphabet), learn texts of morning and evening service, attend public school
pha long (senior novice)	16–20	Teach and supervise *pha noy*, clean *wat*, help abbot with rituals and ceremonies around *wat*	Independent study, attend middle school if desired, learn how to preach
dubi noy (junior monk)	20–24	Supervise *pha*, help run *wat*	Learn to be a ritual leader
dubi (monk)	25 and older	Same as above	Self-study, teach; may attend Dhamma school in Jing Hong or Kunming
dubi long (abbot)	19/20 and older (should have undertaken higher ordination)	Same as above	Same as above
Khūbā (venerated teacher)	At least 40, must have been *dubi* for twenty years	Spiritual and organizational leader of sangha	Well-versed in Buddhist knowledge

is less common.[16] At ordinations I observed, the ages ranged between eight and twelve, though most of the boys were closer to ten than to eight. As noted above, in the pre-Communist era, the ideal age for Dai-lue boys to ordain was thought to be between seven and ten. The boys of this age were seen as being pure, and if they had not ordained by their mid-teens, it was assumed that they would not ordain because they would be "wholly taken with the *kilesa* [defilements]: they have love, greed and infatuation and act without any concern for *bun* or *bāp*" (merit and wickedness; Bunchuay [1955] 2004, 2:130). National policy is that no one can ordain under the age of eighteen. This is in part to hinder the generational transmission of religion, and in part to ensure that no one will be coerced into a religious life. Perhaps for this reason, many of the boys and all of the parents with whom I spoke told me that the novice had decided himself (whatever the age) to ordain. A number of boys told me that their parents had participated in the decision, however, which seems reasonable since many were not yet teenagers. Nevertheless, all said that ordination is a path that the boys enter into freely. It is interesting to note that the age restriction noted above is more flexible when minority groups are under consideration.[17] The local government does not discourage the ordination of boys who are under the age of eighteen on the grounds that it is a traditional practice of the Dai-lue people, though novices are supposed to remain in elementary school. The regulations of the Buddhist Association of Sipsongpannā (SBA) state, "Novices must receive nine years of national compulsory education." Regardless of whether they do, from the SBA's point of view at least, ordaining as a novice and studying in temples is not meant to be a substitute for public school education.

At the other end of the spectrum, becoming an abbot (*du long*) of the village *wat* follows several different paths. Generally speaking, the abbot is the only monk in a village *wat* in contemporary Sipsongpannā, and most often, he was himself a novice in that *wat* or one nearby. When this monk disrobes or dies, a senior novice or junior monk will become the next abbot. If he is not quite yet twenty and hence unable to take the full ordination, the responsibilities that he cannot carry out are handled by the *pu cān* (who is usually a *khanān,* or former monk) or monks from surrounding villages. The Sipsongpannā BA regulations state that a young man must be a fully ordained monk for at least three years before he can become an abbot, though this is not observed strictly if the temple committee likes the senior novice/junior monk. If there are no monks that are available, they might invite a monk from outside of the district, the county, or even China, since there have been a number of monks from Thailand and the Shan States who have taken on the role of *du long* over the years.

There has been significant flux in the monastic population over the years, which is partly a function of the active effort to destroy religion during the Cultural Revolution, as well as modernization processes that have marginalized the historical role played by village *wats* in the education of Dai-lue boys to a certain extent. Over the course of the last thirty years, the monastic population increased steadily from less than 100 in 1980 to as many as 7,500 in the late 1990s. Since then, the population has declined somewhat to approximately 5,000 (as of 2007). Worth noting is that the population of monks has steadily increased, while the number of novices fluctuates. In comparison with premodern Sipsongpannā, the monastic population is roughly equivalent in absolute terms, but it is a much smaller percentage of the male population. Reliable statistics about the size of the contemporary monastic population are difficult to come by, and even more so for the mid-twentieth century. However, the monastic population in 1950 (before the PLA entered Jing Hong) was as much as 15 percent of the population, while it is currently probably only 4 to 5 percent (Borchert 2006).

Centralizing and Decentralizing Aspects of the Sangha Organization

The organization of the sangha has a variety of different facets, some of which will be discussed in the next two chapters with regard to governance and networks. It is important to consider such organization in relation to local concerns as well, however. Historically, Buddhism in the region was highly decentralized, and in this, it was similar to conditions in northern Thailand/ Lannā (Ratanaporn 2010). The entire region was ruled by the *cao phaendin,* but actual control within the region usually devolved to local *cao.* Buddhism in the region followed something of the same pattern. Promotion of monks to *du long* generally took place locally rather than from a centralized location. Influence and authority within the region was local.

There is an informal division of the region into districts that is distinct from the political division of the region. Sipsongpannā has been divided into three different counties (Meng Hai in the west, Meng La in the south and east, and Jing Hong in the center), which was itself a reordering of the twelve districts that were the traditional centers of authority in the region (and the source of the name "sipsong—pannā," i.e., twelve rice-growing districts). Local sanghas would have historically had some relation to the political authorities in these districts, but currently there is little direct contact between political authorities and most monks beyond village headmen. Instead, Buddhist districts within the region are established around ritual and merit making. For example, monks must recite the disciplinary rules of the *vinaya* (*pāṭimokkha*) twice a month on the full and new moons, and this recitation requires a group of monks to recite together. Thus, the monks of a handful of villages will usually gather in the ordination hall of a particular *wat* to perform this rite. This rite becomes a node in the local sangha network, and provides a natural way for monks to link up to other nearby *wats,* to serve as participants in ordinations in other villages, as the preceptors of the novices of nearby villages, and as guests in merit-making occasions such as the *salāt soy* I described at the beginning of this chapter. This informal organization, an economy of ritual and merit making, fosters the development of local sanghas, some of which are strong and well populated and others which are fairly small (Bunnag 1973, 60; Tan 1995, 83).

This fairly autonomous and local organization is layered over with the centralizing force of Wat Pājie and Wat Long Meuang Lue, the largest temples in the region, both of which are in Jing Hong. Wat Pājie was (re)established in 1994 on the outskirts of a park designed to display Dai-lue culture primarily to Chinese tourists. Referred to in Chinese as the "general temple" (zong fosi), it serves a number of different functions. With the largest single collection of monks in the region, Wat Pājie is the home of the Buddhist Association of Sipsongpannā, as well as the BA offices of Jing Hong City and Jing Hong County. The chief monk of the region (sangha-nayok), Khūbā Meuang Jom,[18] resides there, and from 1994 until 2010, Wat Pājie was the home of the Dhamma school that I discuss more fully in chapter 5. Wat Pājie was the sole large wat in Sipsongpannā until 2007, when the senior monks of Sipsongpannā dedicated a new major temple a few miles away, Wat Long Meuang Lue, the "major temple of the Lue state." This temple was constructed as part of a partnership between the senior monks of the region, the local government, and a real estate developer from northeast China who funded the operation in return for being able to manage it for ninety-nine years as a tourist destination. Although distinct, these two wats are run by the same monks and simply house different parts of a centralizing institution. They should be understood as two facets of a single entity.

This centralizing institution is layered in and around the local sanghas. In the eyes of the Chinese state, the BA is responsible for the rest of the monks of the region, but for most Dai-lue laypeople, the authority of the monks at Wat Pājie and Wat Long Meuang Lue is less about their ties to the Chinese government than it is to the fact that most of the monks affiliated with these temples have greater educational attainments than most other monks, and have spent significantly more time in robes. This allows them to participate in the ordination and merit-making networks referred to above. Most of the monks who have been associated with the BA and Wat Pājie have studied in Thailand or the Shan States, and they have also been ordained since the 1980s. Both of these factors—educational attainments and time in robes—tend to give them a high status throughout the region, and it is common for them to be invited to celebrations or ordinations around Sipsongpannā. They are also often consulted when there is a need to find a new abbot for a village wat. It is interesting to note that while many of the monks at Wat Pājie are abbots at wats throughout the region, Wat Pājie and Wat Long Meuang Lue are not directly affiliated with specific villages. Both wats can draw on the participation of several villages close by when there are rites or ceremonies, but this participation is not compulsory. Indeed, at several points in 2002 in preparation for celebrations, monks at Wat Pājie said to me somewhat ruefully that they had only themselves to rely on. This is, I would suggest, something of an overstatement, but it is also the case that monks at Wat Pājie can more easily draw on resources from their own wat and village than they can from the villages surrounding Wat Pājie or Wat Long Meuang Lue. These monks, then, have a status as regional monks while also being tied into their own local sanghas. From this, I would like to suggest that it is better to see the center of the contemporary Sangha of Sipsongpannā not so much as a center of power as a center of gravity. It is an institution with soft rather than hard power.

Conclusion: Thinking about Local Buddhism

At the end of the *salāt soy,* the lottery merit-making festival with which I started this chapter, the abbot of the temple where the merit making was taking place took me down the road to a nearby restaurant off the main road between Jing Hong and Meng La, which continues to Laos. As noted at the start of the chapter, in addition to being the local abbot, he was a vice-abbot of Wat Pājie and the head of the BA of the district we were in, Meng Kham. In other words, he had layered levels of authority in realms that were both "local" and outside of the district. I ate lunch with some friends from Wat Pājie while this monk sat with some local men while they ate. Grateful both for the opportunity to attend the *salāt soy* as well as for other kindnesses he had shown me, I thought it appropriate to try to pay for lunch for us all so this monk would not have to do so. This ended up being a complete failure. I did give the restaurant money for the food, but about ten minutes later, the young girl who had been waiting on us came back to me with my money and said that the guests of Dubi Kaew were the guests of the restaurant and they never accepted his money. In other words, without my knowing it, I had been incorporated into a local merit network, if only for the afternoon.

The use of the term "local" can sometimes seem to be a substitute for "traditional." It has an unchanging quality; it is located and not moving. This is not the way that I have been using "local." The Buddhism in contemporary Sipsongpannā has changed in important ways as a result of the processes of modernization. It has been incorporated into the political economy of China: while the authority based at Wat Pājie is largely the result of monks who are well educated and have been monks for a long time, in part the work and organization of the temple as well as its size are a function of it being the local version of the Buddhist Association. Moreover, even while Buddhism and ordination remain important in Sipsongpannā, it is no longer as central to Dai-lue culture, and indeed, ordination is no longer a requirement for marriage. On the other hand, transnational forces have also shaped post-Cultural Revolution Buddhism in the region. The sangha could not have been reconstituted without monks coming to Sipsongpannā from Thailand and the Shan States. The impact of this is not easy to measure, but at a bare minimum, it has made the novices and monks (the *pha* and *dubi*) of village *wats* in Sipsongpannā aware of other Buddhist polities to which they can travel and where they can study.

Yet at the same time, in many ways the daily world of the *pha* and *dubi* of Sipsongpannā remains a local affair. They interact with villagers from the local village or monks of the neighboring ones. This may seem a banal point, but the daily experience of Buddhism in Sipsongpannā is shaped by these close local interactions, which are both "traditional" and "modernizing."

2

Fortune-Telling and False Monks

Defining and Governing Religion

ONE MONDAY IN LATE SEPTEMBER 2001, I CAME to Wat Pājie to study Dai-lue with one of the monks only to find my Dai-lue-language teacher and friend in a state of extreme excitement. The monks of the temple had gone on an undercover mission and unmasked some false monks! The previous week, he told me, the monks at the BA of Sipsongpannā had learned that there were some "Theravāda monks" who were at a temple about three hours from Jing Hong who were charging exorbitant rates to cast people's fortunes. Telling fortunes is not uncommon in Chinese Buddhist temples, and indeed, there are fortune-telling practices at Wat Pājie, but the fortunes are standardized, and cost only about $1, which is understood as a donation not a fee. By contrast, the monks at this temple were said to be charging anywhere between 750 and 1,100 yuan (about $90 to $130 in 2001) for their activities. The monks from the BA told the Public Security Bureau (Gongan ju; PSB) about this problem and were told to get evidence. So the monks went about trying to get evidence. The only problem was that when the BA monks went to investigate, the alleged criminals kept disappearing. Apparently, someone in the village or in the temple was on the lookout and warned the fortune-tellers about the arrival of the governing monks. Finally, on their third attempt, the BA monks had managed to sneak up on the fortune-tellers by going a back way to the village. When they got to the worship hall where the alleged crimes were taking place, they found the "monks" and confronted them. It turned out that these were not Theravāda monks, or indeed even members of the Dai minority. They were Han Chinese who had come from somewhere outside of Yunnan Province. Even worse, it seemed that they might not even have been monks, since during the confrontation my friends of the BA apparently grabbed one of the monks, pulled aside his robes and revealed—to their shock—street clothes hidden underneath the robes of the monk. These fortune-tellers were revealed as "false monks"!

This should have effectively been the end of the matter, but it was not. In fact, the tale of the false monks kept popping up until the beginning of April the following year. When the monks went to the PSB, along with video-tape of the event filmed by a Central China Television crew that they had met by chance on their way to the great confrontation, the PSB took the information, and then failed to act on it. The BA monks tried to take matters into their own hands, summoning the village temple committee and holding a long meeting about the situation. They did this because it was clear that the false monks had been receiving support from the local villagers. Despite impassioned exhortations about needing to act for the good of the Dai people and the good of Buddhism, which amounts to the same thing in the eyes of the monks, these meetings achieved little (and in fact highlighted the monks' inability to resolve the situation). Even worse, the false monks reemerged several months after these meetings as "Mahāyāna Monks," doing the same thing. This made the situation worse from the perspective of the SBA: since these fortune-tellers were no longer Theravāda monks, the Sipsongpannā BA (which was specifically responsible for the monks of the Dai and Bulang minorities) no longer had even a modicum of jurisdiction over them (at least this is what they told me). In essence, there seemed to be a situation in which clear exploitation was taking place (on the part of the false monks), and the people who cared about it—the monks of the SBA—could not do anything about the matter, while those who could do something about it—the PSB and perhaps the village temple committee—would not.

This failure to act on the part of the local government is, on the face of it at least, surprising. The surprise has to do with the ways that the practice of religion in China tends to be represented in the international community, particularly the United States. For the most part, the US public tends to think of religion in China in rather stark terms. According to this viewpoint, the government tends to be rather brutish, and religious actors tend to be poor victims of this brutishness. This vision would seem to be confirmed by the examples of Christians being prevented from worshiping in their homes or teaching their children about Jesus, or Tibetan Buddhists whose entire world has been colonized by the Chinese state. Moreover, when the Chinese state attempts to vilify certain religious actors, such as saying that Xinjiang Muslim separatists are terrorists trained by Al Qaeda in Pakistan, or that the Falun Gong is an "evil cult" (and so the state's security apparatuses are crushing threats to society), this is widely understood to be simply the rationale of a Communist state.

While the scholarly community has tended to take a more balanced approach (at least in the last fifteen years), and is less likely to simply assume that the Chinese government hates religion, one of the dominant tropes in scholarship about the "post-Mao revival of religion" has been that the return of religion has taken place despite the Chinese state, and that to the degree that the government is involved in the practice of religion, its involvement is marked by the usage of the liberal language of rights masking a "belief"—indeed an obsession—with controlling religious activities (Potter 2003; Kindrop and Hamrin 2004). Given this attention to control, one might expect that the local government in Sipsongpannā would have had at least some interest in preventing borderline criminal activities using a false Buddhist identity to exploit "the People." However, these government entities did not seem to express much interest in doing so.

To begin to understand why this is the case, it would seem that a richer model for thinking about the politics of religion in contemporary China is necessary. Yoshiko Ashiwa and David Wank have suggested that scholarship on religion in China has had essentially two foci: either an attention to the state's efforts to define and control religion, or a close attention to the values, practices, and mentalities of specific religious communities in their efforts to rebuild religion in the wake of the Chinese reforms (Ashiwa and Wank 2006, 338). While both are important to the understanding of religion in contemporary China, the problem is that they tend to miss the degree to which religion takes place within a particular space. The Chinese state is an essential actor in religious life, but it does not control every action. Instead, religion should be understood as a series of interactions and relationships in institutions, some of which are established by and for the state, and some of which are less directly involved with the state. The politics of religion, they argue, "is constituted by ongoing negotiations, among multiple actors, including state officials, intellectuals, religious adherents, and businesspersons, to adapt religion to the modern state's definitions and rules even as they are continuously being transgressed" (Ashiwa and Wank 2009, 8). These negotiations take place within and between particular institutions and under the aegis of a particular discursive framework. Thus, understanding the conditions that provide the grounds for religious activity and action requires paying attention to the institutional and discursive frameworks in which actors and organizations engage in these negotiations and seek to maximize their interests (Wank 2009, 127; Koesel 2014).

I find their institutional model, and in particular Wank's attention to the "organizational field," to be a necessary and useful one for understanding not just what happened with the "false monks" in Sipsongpannā, but also to understanding how monastic education takes place within Sipsongpannā. In the last chapter's discussion of "local" forms of Buddhism in Sipsongpannā, state and national aspects entered into the discussion only briefly. This is because the practice of religion in Sipsongpannā is not always affected by politics, or at least not those of the Chinese state in its local and national forms. However, "China," that is, the imposition of the reality of the Chinese state and its vision of what China should be, is never really all that far away in Sipsongpannā, and the practice of Buddhism has been materially shaped by state definitions and policies of governance. The institutional field of religion in Sipsongpannā is that which has been established by the Communist Party of China (CCP), in its efforts to foster a particular type of citizenry within the PRC. This chapter is focused on explaining the organizational field in which Buddhism is practiced in Sipsongpannā. Doing so requires attention to three different topics: how the category of religion has been defined by the state in the Reform Era; the institutions of religious governance in China more generally, but particularly in Sipsongpannā; and the organization of the Sangha in Sipsongpannā. These topics cover the discursive field as well as the variety of institutions through which the Chinese state and Buddhists interact and shape the field in Sipsongpannā. In examining the discursive and institutional fields through which Buddhism is practiced, I demonstrate two different points. The first is to suggest that the politics of religion in China needs to be seen not in terms of Manichean conflict between religious and state actors, but rather as a dynamic and flexible system that the state has established to maximize its own flexibility in addressing what it recognizes as a challenge. The second, related to a central theme of the book, suggests that in creating this system, religious and state actors use national and transnational notions of "religion" to maximize the flexibility of their actions.

The Discursive Framework of "Religion" in the Early Twenty-First Century

One day in early 2002, I was at Wat Pājie to study Dai-lue and teach English to the novices at the Dhamma school there. I ran into one of the students, a sixteen-year-old novice from Meng La sitting on one of the benches reading a journal published by the Religious Affairs Bureau (RAB) of China, entitled *Zhongguo Zongjiao* (Religions in China; National Religious Affairs Bureau [NRAB] 2001). The presence of this journal was not particularly significant. Whenever I have been at Wat Pājie, I have seen copies of official journals lying around. Most of these are published by provincial BAs and sent to their counterparts in different parts of the country. This was unique, however, because it was the first time I had actually seen anyone reading one. It was also significant because it was focused on a single theme: the denunciation of the Falun Gong as a *xiejiao*, an "evil cult." The Falun Gong crisis had erupted in April 1999, and while it was not something that arose at Wat Pājie as a regular part of conversation, its effects were still being felt around the country. This particular journal was devoted to statements by the presidents of different religious associations of China that denounced the Falun Gong. The magazine included one from Zhu Depu, the late head of the Buddhist Association of China (BAC), which he gave "from his sick bed" in August 1999 and where he is quoted as having said:

> I strongly support the central provisions for dealing with the illegal organization Falun Gong. This is a really good thing: it is a chance for the people to eliminate a threat, for the state to eliminate a hidden danger, and for Buddhism to eliminate a clear threat. . . . The Chinese Buddhist Association was aware of the Falun Gong problem from an early point, because [Falun Gong] takes Buddhism as its guise and uses Buddhist terms to deceive society and hoodwink the masses. From the perspective of Buddhism, it is an evil cult (xie jiao). . . . [We are] convinced that Falun Gong isn't Buddhist law or an official religion, nor is it a proper form of qigong [breathing exercises], but truly an evil cult. (NRAB 2001, 4)

Zhu's statement, which is consistent with those from throughout the magazine, highlights the danger that Falun Gong was perceived to present, but also its deceptive and hidden nature. According to this viewpoint, it looks like Buddhism on the surface, but real Buddhists (i.e., the BAC) understand that this is a superficial resemblance (Goossaert and Palmer 2011, 339). These statements, being read by a minority novice in a remote corner of China in 2002, represent a fragment of what we might think of as the Chinese official discourse on religion.

"Religion" (zongjiao) is a commonplace word for speakers of contemporary Mandarin Chinese. When I have asked people about religion, they generally assume that it refers to one of the five religions officially recognized by the Chinese state: Buddhism, Daoism, Islam, Christianity, and Catholicism. Most also know that this does not exhaust the religions of the world, but assume that other "world" religions such as Judaism or Hinduism are not present in China. Some might also be aware of other kinds of categories of religions that are present in contemporary China, such as "primitive" religion (yuanshi zongjiao) or "minority" religions (minzu zongjiao). These tend to be viewed as religions that are practiced either by people in China's past, or perhaps by contemporary Chinese minorities. While Chinese scholars might think of these phenomena as different kinds of religions (see, e.g., Yang 1994, 1–5), nonacademics and state officials may be as likely to think of them as "superstition" (mixin), or even "evil cults" (xiejiao). Activities categorized as mixin are not thought to be merely practiced in the past or by minorities, however. Many Chinese believe that superstitious activities such as various kinds of divination and interactions with spirits are widespread in contemporary

China (Yang 2006). What is important is not that there are such practices, but that average Chinese people know—that is, have been taught—that certain practices and institutions are "religions" and others are "superstition."

This widespread knowledge about different kinds of *zongjiao*/religion was not always the case. Religion was a neologism within China, as it was throughout Asia, a point well-known among scholars (Reid 1998). The term *zongjiao* was borrowed from Japanese officials and scholars who had appropriated and repurposed a relatively minor Buddhist term (Yu 2005; Krämer 2015, 4). In both countries, the term for religion was part of the modernization process, as well as the effort to resist colonial encroachments. In China, it is worth noting that the meaning of *zongjiao,* particularly regarding its referents, was not settled for several decades. For example, it was not (and indeed in some ways still is not) clear whether the kinds of popular religious traditions that were widespread but not easily subsumed in Buddhism or Daoism should be called religion or something else. It was these kinds of popular traditions that were declared to be "superstition" and became the subject of repression by the Republican government during the 1920s (Duara 1995; Nedostup 2009). There are two observations about these categories that remain important for the issues that I am discussing a century later. The first emerges out of an observation by J. Z. Smith that "religion" is a "second-order category" (Smith 2004, 193), by which he means that religion is not a phenomenon found in the world; rather, it is a term people use to classify and describe the phenomena that they find. As such, the referent for religion can be quite flexible, if not quite empty: one man's religion is another woman's superstition, as it were. Deciding what does and does not count as religion thus becomes an issue of politics and governance.[1] The second is that since their inception in China, categories such as *zongjiao* and *mixin* have been embedded in power/knowledge frameworks that sought to reshape the nation and produce a modern citizenry. In other words, "religion" was not simply an innocent category for describing the world, but was instead embedded in the knowledge/power dynamic of the Chinese Republic. It became what we might think of as a "technology of control," that is, a tool of governance to shape the people—a job that it still has in the PRC.

To show this, and make sense of the Sipsongpannā government's response to the "fake monks," I examine how "religion" is defined and utilized in official ways in Yunnan in the early part of the twenty-first century. "Religion" (*zongjiao*) is not a stand-alone category, but rather part of a chain of related concepts that include "superstition" (*mixin*), "science" (*kexue*), and from the end of the twentieth century, "evil cults" (*xiejiao*).[2] These categories, and in particular *zongjiao* and *mixin,* have played a role in the governance of China since the beginning of the Reform Era when the CCP sought to step back from the oppressive policies towards religious communities and institutions that marked the Cultural Revolution. There, the party sought to clarify what it saw as the proper space for religion in Communist China in both internal party documents, such as that known as "Document 19," and in public outlets such as editorials on "Religion and Feudal Superstition" in the *People's Daily*.[3] Document 19 in particular articulated the foundation of the party's policy, which is that the government has ultimate authority over religion, but that citizens are guaranteed the freedom of religious belief (as well as the freedom not to believe). It emphasized that religion is a "private matter, one of individual free choice for citizens" (Document 19, 15; Goossaert and Palmer 2011, 323), and that as long as religion took place in circumscribed, registered locations outside of the public sphere, it had a certain legitimacy within society.

While this has largely remained the case for most of the Reform Era, the crisis precipitated by the Falun Gong brought into relief how these categories were not simply descriptive, but part of the governing structure. Special issues of journals such as *Zhongguo Zongjiao* were part of the official national response to Falun Gong, but these national efforts were supplemented by provincial and local work. In Yunnan, the Yunnan RAB, the PSB, and several ad hoc committees such as the Yunnan University Association to Oppose Evil Cults put together educational handbooks and policy statements that sought to provide cadres and others with a clear understanding of religion and related categories, in books with titles such as *Religion, Evil Cults, Feudal Superstition* (Chen 2000) and *Oppose Superstition, Oppose Evil Cults* (Xiang and Tao 2001). Locally produced but reliant on the official discourse from statements such as that of Document 19, these books articulate the crisis faced by China in terms similar to those used by Zhu Depu a few years earlier. They argue that despite the significant progress that society and humanity in general has made in recent years due to the "speedy advancement of the wheel of science and modernization," danger has recently emerged "unexpectedly as if an animal hibernating in winter came into summer." This danger, *mixin* and *xiejiao,* had been hiding behind the "flag of religion" and using the policies of freedom of religious belief "to make good, honest and innocent people unable to distinguish their true features" (Chen 2000, 1–2). Thus, part of solving the problem that groups such as Falun Gong created for society entailed articulating and propagating "scientific" and accurate definitions of "religion," "superstition," and "evil cults."

In discussing religion as a concept, there are several different facets that these handbooks highlight. Religion is generally understood as belief in and worship of supernatural forces (Lancashire 1981, 277; Chen 2000, 138; Xiang and Tao 2001, 1), and more specifically, those supernatural forces associated with the five religions that are fully and legally recognized within the governance structure of the PRC. These books treat religion in a way that might best be described as materialist phenomenology. They describe religion as an "objectively existing social phenomenon," which encompasses religious conduct and activities, organizations, and institutions. While from a strictly "scientific" sense these works see religion as a distortion and misinterpretation of reality, they emphasize that it is not "mysterious and unfathomable," but rather a comprehensible ideology whereby the "power of the human world has adopted the form of a supernatural power" (Xiang and Tao 2001, 1). Indeed, this helps to explain the continued presence of religion within a society that has advanced into scientific (atheist) modernity. Religion is old, and deeply embedded in the cultural systems of the people, such that religious thought and ethics "permeate the worldview, the perspectives on life and the daily conduct of numerous believers" (Xiang and Tao 2001, 2). In part because of this, government officials cannot simply remove religion by fiat. Indeed, "normal religious activities," that is, activities carried out "according to the religious scriptures, religious ritual patterns and the custom of the congregation organized by religious professionals," are legally permitted and even protected (Xiang and Tao 2001, 22). According to this viewpoint, religion has a positive effect on both social cohesion and the ethical heart of a people (Chen 2000, 42).

The same cannot be said of superstition and evil cults, however, which are both described primarily in relation to "normal religion" (*zheng-chang zongjiao*), though in different ways. The discussions of superstition emphasize both the ignorance of the people and the petty criminality of the practitioners. The category of "superstition" includes a wide variety of practices such as fortune-telling and various types of divination, as well as interactions with ghosts, fox spirits, and the like. These practices emerged in the feudal period and are techniques whereby the people sought to mitigate disasters and address the problems that they faced in everyday life. In a "modern socialist society," however, superstition exists because people use it to cheat others out of their money. Whereas religion has rich systematics that support ethical action, superstition is simply "techniques" used by individuals for the pursuit of graft, the "dregs of folk culture" (Xiang and Tao 2001, 6–7). These practices foster ignorance among the people, as well as rumor and slander, and as such, provide an insufficient foundation for a healthy society. This is a problem not just because people are cheated out of their money, but because when disasters do strike, superstition causes people to look away from the root causes of the problem, thus spreading ignorance (Xiang and Tao 2001, 17).

Whereas superstition is described in terms of low-level graft and the work of individuals, evil cults are presented as a perversion of normal religion. Evil cults are described as offshoots of folk religions that became twisted through a combination of wicked ambitions and ignorance. They often borrow external forms or names from "normal" religions, as Zhu pointed out, but where these normal religions are considered to provide the guidelines for ethical action or help the masses solve their problems, evil cults are described as rebelling against the truth of the text, spreading inappropriate and evil speech such as "propagating end of the world theories," which require participation in the evil cult for survival (Xiang and Tao 2001, 25). Characterized most clearly by the worship of the leader, they are also described in terms that might call to mind a funhouse mirror image of religions. Whereas religions have open dissemination of teachings in public places, evil cults are secret; their words and views are protected from outside people. They "say that they are religions," but they are really part of "dark societies" that are opposed to humanity and seek to control the spirits of their believers (Xiang and Tao 2001, 25; see also Chen 2000, 145–147). It should be clear that this description is filled with vague, morally freighted terms, rather than technical social scientific descriptions of what characterizes evil cults.

There are several aspects of this discourse that need to be highlighted. First, there is a desire to situate these terms in a context of international forms and norms. While there is an anxiety present in these documents about undue influence from outside of China that goes back to Document 19 (Xiang and Tao 2001, 4; Document 19 1989, 12), there is also an appeal to commonalities between China and international contexts to justify the need to govern what are deemed evil cults. They refer to scholarship and definitions (such as the nature of "new religions") from outside of China, and also discuss examples of new religions and "evil cults" both within and outside of China. Of greater significance, Xiang and Tao in particular discuss the strategies of foreign governments for handling such phenomena. Having detailed how to "correctly distinguish" legally protected *zongjiao* from illegal, "wicked" *xiejiao* and their occurrence in Yunnan, they detail the attitudes of the American, Japanese, French, and Ugandan governments towards *xiejiao* (Xiang and Tao 2001, 36–40). This shift suggests that "evil cults" are not simply a Chinese problem; they are a problem all over the world, one that the Chinese government deals with just as other governments do. This implies that despite what advocates of the Falun Gong might say internationally, China is dealing with an international problem, just as any other good government does, trying to protect its citizens (Goossaert and Palmer 2011, 341).

A second characteristic of this discourse is that while aspects of it are stable, its usage has varied across the thirty-five years of the Reform Era. Statements about religion from the first part of the Reform Era tend to focus on religion and superstition and do not reference *xiejiao*.[4] However, *xiejiao* was ubiquitous in official media at the start of the century, primarily because of the state's efforts to quell the Falun Gong. In mid-1999, there is a bifurcation of the category of *mixin*. Prior to 1999, activities that pertained to the worship of supernatural beings but were generally seen as legitimate were called *zongjiao* and those that were seen as socially negative were called *mixin*. The activities that were described as *mixin* were diverse, ranging from fortune-telling or praying for rain to actions by counterrevolutionary groups that use religion. However, in the wake of the Falun Gong crisis, *mixin* bifurcates into two—"(feudal) superstition" ([*fengjian*] *mixin*) and "evil cults" (*xiejiao*)—and both of these are placed in opposition to "religion" (sometimes "normal religion," *zhengchang zongjiao*). This bifurcation brought greater conceptual clarity with the extended number of categories regarding what society needed to be protected from: somewhat innocuous activities, such as geomancy or divination, fell into the category of *mixin,* and those deemed truly malign became *xiejiao* (Goossaert and Palmer 2011, 341–342). Indeed, it should be clear from this discussion that what the "fake monks" were doing in 2001 was a form of "superstition."

Rather than seeing this as a rationalization of academic vocabulary, however, these categories are doing a different kind of work, as is evident from another educational handbook published in Yunnan in 2006. This handbook, *Study Science, Break Superstition* (Wu 2006), is part of a series published by the Yunnan Technology Publisher with the support of the Yunnan government and focuses on the "quality of the New Peasants." Like the handbooks discussed above, it understands the proper defining and delimiting of "religion" to be an essential part of the job of building the new agricultural culture and citizen. However, rather than being concerned with marshalling evidence against "evil cults" to indirectly marginalize the Falun Gong, this handbook was concerned with the ignorance in the citizenry. By focusing on "religion," the book aims to "raise the quality of the moral thought of [Yunnan's] rural masses, the quality of their culture and science, and the quality of their health" (Wu 2006, 1). This is a handbook that participates in the official discourse about the "quality" (*suzhi*) of the Chinese populace, a Reform Era discourse widespread in the first decade of the millennium, focusing on the development of "high-quality" citizenry. It does this in part by legitimizing increased state intervention in some areas, but it also puts the responsibility for development onto the citizens themselves, "implicat[ing] every villager in the nation's quest for modernization" (Murphy 2004, 19). As such, and in contrast to the handbooks from a few years earlier, *xiejiao* only makes a small appearance in *Study Science, Break Superstition.* There are a few short sections devoted to explaining the emergence of "evil cults," but much more of the book addresses phenomena such as ghosts and weather patterns such as El Niño, which are described in terms of ignorance and superstition. To some extent, the difference in emphasis is because the handbooks address different problems. However, it also indicates that these categories do not refer to specific, universal phenomena, but are instead flexible tools to be used by the state according to its needs. Particularly in genres like these handbooks, produced by state and academic partners both for the use by cadres and available to the general public, categories such as "religion," "superstition," and "evil cults" are relational categories, defined in terms of one another rather than according to specific consistent criterion. These concepts and their official definitions are not "content driven" (Riesebrodt 2010, chap. 4); instead, they are empty categories waiting to have meaning poured into them, primarily (though not solely) by the state or the academic bureaucratic organizations it sponsors. Despite the state's efforts to mobilize academic and religious opinion on the problem, the knowledge that is produced about these categories is generally vague and without stable meanings. Indeed, the meaning shifts according to the needs of the Chinese state. This means (just to state the obvious) that they are political categories, not scientific ones.

The material here is very much a part of a discourse imposed from above.[5] It is the discourse of the Chinese state, even if it emerges from offices in Yunnan Province, but it was a discourse that was available and sometimes forced on the monks of Sipsongpannā. Monks regularly read newspapers, and were always watching the news at Wat Pājie (indeed, they were the ones who first told me about the events of September 11, 2001). The senior monks at the *wat* also had to travel to Kunming for official meetings with the provincial RAB, where they would learn about policy shifts and receive copies of magazines such as *Zhongguo Zongjiao,* which would then be available for novices to read. This does not mean that all the monks and novices of Sipsongpannā could fully articulate the official discourse on "religion" I have been discussing, but the sangha as a whole was responsible for knowing it.

Regulating Buddhist Communities

The discursive framework discussed above frames the meaning of different forms of religion in society, but at the same time, the categories of this framework condition the policies by which religion is governed. This is evident in reading a set of regulations for the governing of religion in the province and released by the Yunnan provincial government in 1997. These policies, the *Regulations for the Administration of Religious Work in Yunnan Province* (Department of Rules and Policies for the Religious Affairs Bureau 2000), precede the crisis of the Falun Gong, but otherwise rely on the same vocabulary and assumptions discussed above. According to these regulations, "religions" refer to the five religions (Regulation no. 2), and while citizens all have "freedom of religious belief," they have the freedom from being compelled to believe in either religion or nonreligion. Significantly, religious belief is located in the individual, and there is no distinction between religious and nonreligious citizens: all should have "mutual respect" and treat each other with equality (Regulation no. 3). Unsurprisingly, though, normal religious activities are circumbscribed by legal frameworks and entities (Regulation no. 1). While these normal religious activities are protected by law, they must also "comply with laws and regulations, accept the government's administration and organizations, and individuals may not make use of religion to engage in illegal activities" (Regulation no. 5). Moreover, these normal religious activities "must not harm national, social, or collective legitimate interests . . . or interfere with the state government, judiciary, education, or other public affairs . . . or family planning work" (Regulation no. 6). In other words, these regulations argue that normal religious activities are legitimate in society, as long as they are constrained and limited.

It is through this that we begin to see how the categorization of religion discussed above can be used as a technology of control. These regulations assert that freedom of religious belief is open to all citizens of China as long as they follow the rules, such as going to properly registered places at the right time (Document 19, 18). But because the definitions of religion are empty of content as discussed, there is significant uncertainty in how the rules will be implemented. If individuals or religious organizations do not follow the regulations, they might be subject to state surveillance or repression. However, the uncertainty makes it difficult to know what will trigger oversight, which depends on the concerns and demands of the local governing bodies at a given point in time. Definitions and policies then provide what we might think of as a bottleneck that provides the state with leverage. Carsten Vala (2009) has noted cases where Protestant churches have tried to register with the Religious Affairs Office of the local government, but are unable to complete the paperwork. He has suggested that this is not a matter of bureaucratic incompetence, but rather that the government keeps these groups from registering because this keeps them in a limbo status, and therefore vulnerable to state surveillance. This dynamic of registration, which is an example of what has been called "calibrated coercion" in Singapore (George 2005), is not limited to Christian congregations. Temples dedicated to local gods that are not obviously Daoist are also in an ambiguous position. Although they might be understood as "folk religion," this is not as yet officially recognized (Goosseart and Palmer 2011, 346), and during a period of heightened concern by either the local or national government, such temples could also be considered to be *mixin*. Adam Chau has shown how the officials of one such temple went to great efforts to have themselves reclassified and recognized by the local government as Daoist (a "normal" religion). Ironically, while the new association gave this temple a new social and legal legitimacy, thus serving as an insurance policy of sorts against official repression, it also opened the temple up to regulatory bodies to which it had not been hitherto beholden.[6]

There are primarily two organizations responsible for regulating and governing: the BAC and the RAB.[7] The former is categorized as a "patriotic, mass organization," which means that it is recognized (and often constituted) by the CCP as being a legitimate organization of the masses. It is not directly part of the CCP, but works in lockstep with it as part of the "United Front" for the building of "new China." The BAC was founded by Buddhists in the early 1950s who wanted to reform Chinese Buddhism to fit into the new order to preempt the inevitable efforts of the CCP to reform or abolish it.[8] In its current, post-Mao configuration, the BA has offices at the national, provincial, and local levels, and these offices are generally staffed by monks, nuns, and lay Buddhists. It serves a double function: on the one hand, it acts in the interests of the Chinese state by interpreting official policies and mobilizing Buddhists to comply with them; on the other hand, it also represents the interests of Buddhists to official organizations, helping Buddhists to mobilize resources to build or rebuild temples and other projects (Ji 2008; Wank 2009). Where the BA is made up of Buddhists who interact with the state, the RAB is a bureaucratic organ of the state. Its responsibilities are to "educate religious adherents about state ideology and policy, mobilize them to work towards state goals, censor foreign religious publications, monitor foreign religious visitors and give them the good impression that religions are protected and free in China" (Wank 2009, 130). In other words, the cadres in the RABs, who are often not well-trained in religion work (Vala 2009), are the ones who are responsible for making sure that religions fit into the state's vision of society.

These offices are key actors for making sense of the field of Buddhist relations and the politics of Buddhism in China. Relations between these two offices vary a great deal: they are staffed by different people (Buddhists and government officials), and as a result, often have different agendas. Sometimes they work well together; at other times, they seem to be in conflict with one another. Often, these conflicts revolve around the control of a space in a temple as well as the control of the money that comes in through admission fees. David Wank shows how monks, the BA, the RAB, and members of the temple administration commission at Nanputuo Temple in Xiamen engage in contestations over the control of the space of the temple (Wank 2009). There, monks and cadres used a variety of strategies to promote their respective, sometimes conflicting, agendas, including assertions of legitimacy in the control of the space, bullying, and appeals to both local authorities and national offices to shore up support for their activities.

This last point is an important one. Buddhists, particularly monks, seem to be very good at building *guanxi* (relationship networks) with government officials and party members. Building new temples or rebuilding old ones requires official permission and often the active aid of local politicians. Although they themselves are precluded from being publicly involved as religious believers, these politicians and party members are often willing to work with Buddhists to develop their temples. This is because these temples have an important impact on local economic development efforts. Buddhist temples, particularly famous ones with a long history, can bring in a lot of tourists, both domestic and foreign. They can become an important part of local development plans. Indeed, these officials sometimes refer to Buddhist temples as "factories without smokestacks" because of their ability to bring in tourist dollars.[9] Ji Zhe has referred to such cooperation as the "statization" of Chinese Buddhism. That is, for the first time in Chinese history, there is an organization that represents all Buddhists in China: the Buddhist Association. Ji argues that, paradoxically, this has meant that in creating this national organization and treating it as a legitimate actor, the CCP has created a group of people who are conversant with the language and institutions of the state. Ironically, this has also meant that the BAC is an organization that is capable of, and occasionally effective in, fostering the interests of Buddhists vis-à-vis the state (Ji 2008).

In other words, rather than seeing Buddhists or other religious actors as victims or oppressors, manipulators or stooges, the line of thinking is that we should see Buddhists as a class of actors, which, like other classes of actors, have certain attributes. Buddhist activities take place within a particular institutional field, and this field is productive. It usually provides clear channels for social action, though these channels might be blocked for political reasons, or they might be far from the religious actors' ultimate goals. Moreover, Buddhists as a class can be broken down into other subsets, and conflicts or negotiations might arise between monks and nuns (Qin 2000) or monks and laypeople (Fisher 2008). In these negotiations and conflicts, the institutional field, as well as the local and translocal cultural meanings of Buddhism, provide the tools by which these different groups engage in their negotiations. The question is, how do these dynamics work out in Sipsongpannā? And how does this help us make sense of the "false monks" of the beginning of this chapter? To answer these questions, and to understand religion and politics in the region, it is important to examine the organization of the Sangha in Sipsongpannā.

Wat Pājie, Sangha Organization, and State Relations

Understanding the institutional field in Sipsongpannā and how it shapes the politics of Buddhism is, in part, a matter of perspective. On paper and in organizational charts that the government might produce, conditions in Sipsongpannā match well with the system just described, but in terms of how this system functions in the governing of the sangha, the centralized system described above has its limits.

As noted in the previous chapter, Wat Pājie is the location of the Sipsongpannā BA. The Sipsongpannā BA is the regional office of the association, and structures the relationships between monks and the local government. It is affiliated with the national and provincial offices of the BA, and in theory at least, the SBA shares the same bureaucratic structure as the rest of the organization. Khūbā Meuang Jom, the *sangha-nayok,* is also the head of the BA (Xiehui Zhang) in the prefecture, as well as abbot of Wat Pājie and Wat Long Meuang Lue.[10] Officially, there are five BA offices in Sipsongpannā: the prefectural office, the Jing Hong City office, and one office each for the three regions of Sipsongpannā (Meng La, Meng Hai, and Jing Hong). Three of these are based at Wat Pājie (Prefecture, Jing Hong City, and Jing Hong District), while the other two are at temples in Meng La and Meng Hai. The monks at Wat Pājie have a variety of titles commensurate with these offices, but in reality, there seems to be only one office. The authority structure in the BA corresponds with the authority structure of the temple itself. That is to say, the abbot is the head of the BA, vice-abbots take on the "city office" head or the "district office" head. Moreover, when problems arise, all of the monks of the temple (and the handful of lay employees) regularly meet to discuss the issue without distinguishing between prefecture, city, and county. During my fieldwork in 2001–2002, there was no office open for Meng La County, and the Meng Hai office was presided over by a monk who lived in a temple three hours away from the office. This monk was a good friend of the monks at Wat Pājie and was as likely to be in Jing Hong as in his home temple. We should not see the organizational structure of the Sipsongpannā BA as simply a façade, however. The organization is real, but it also serves as the Chinese face of the Dai-lue Sangha. The local government must deal with some entity when its members need to communicate with or police the monks; the BA fulfills that role throughout China. In Sipsongpannā, the senior monks of Wat Pājie serve this liaison function.

The Buddhist Association and the Local Government

The nature of the relationship between the local government and the Sipsongpannā BA becomes clearer by considering the second day of the official celebration of Song kān, the Dai-lue New Year discussed in the previous chapter. In 2002, the day began with a procession of a Buddha image around Jing Hong, an event that ended with the formal washing of this image. Starting at Wat Pājie, the procession wound around over to what was then a new bypass to Man Ting Road (once the site of a thriving group of Dai-lue restaurants with traditional dance performances established for tourists). From there, the procession entered Jing Hong proper, going through the heart of the city by Peacock Lake, before returning along the main hotel road back to Wat Pājie.

FIGURE 2.1 The procession of monks and tourists returning to Wat Pājie during Song kān (Dai-lue New Year)

The procession was "led" by a Buddha image on a truck, followed by the monks of Wat Pājie. As the procession passed through Man Ting Road, it was joined by Dai-lue dance troupes from Bān Talāt and Bān Chiang Noi, and then tourists from the hotels. By the time the people returned to Wat Pājie, the neat procession had become a flood of people (see figure 2.1).

The local government figured into this event at two different points. The first was in the middle of the procession, when the Buddha image and the monks stopped in front of the compound of the People's Government. Nothing in particular seemed to happen when it stopped. No one joined the procession, and Khūbā Meuang Jom, the abbot, did not pull out his megaphone and start shouting at the government. Nonetheless, we were also clearly waiting by the offices of the prefectural government. The second point happened after the Buddha image and the procession of people returned to Wat Pājie for the washing of the Buddha. In both 2001 and 2002, the formal washing took place in the middle of the garden and was performed first by Khūbā Meuang *together with* the governor of the prefecture (*zhou zhang*), who in 2002 was a Dai-lue from Meng La named Ai Jom (see figure 2.2). After they washed the Buddha, one of the vice-abbots poured water over the image together with the mayor of Jing Hong. A number of lesser government officials took their turns, and then they all walked down to the lake in Chunhuan Park, where they released fish, turtles, and birds to make merit. This was in no way a quiet event. The park was absolutely packed, and hundreds of people, both Dai-lue villagers and Han Chinese tourists, witnessed the head of the government and the

FIGURE 2.2 Abbot and governor preparing to wash the Buddha

head of the sangha washing the Buddha and releasing fish. This was a striking moment of official participation in a religious ceremony in a country where Communist Party officials are members of the one class in society that is not guaranteed freedom of religious belief (Document 19, 14). While minority cadres are technically allowed to attend rites that are a part of their *minzu*'s culture in order to better govern, this participation is significant and exemplifies the cooperation and aligned interests evident between the Buddhist Association and the local government (Koesel 2014).

If the BA is the Dai-lue side of the official relationship, it generally interacts with two different offices within the local government: the MRAB and the PSB.[11] The MRAB in Sipsongpannā is rather small, staffed by just four men. In addition to the head of the office, each of the staff members specializes in one religion: Buddhism, Christianity, or Islam. All four men seem to be Daizu, though the one who works on Islam referred to himself as "Hui Dai," that is, a combination of the Dai and Hui nationalities.[12] The officer responsible for Buddhism, Ai Un Kham, in fact taught Chinese at the Buddhist institute at Wat Pājie for several years prior to my fieldwork, though he was never a monk. While he worked for the government, he also had good relationships with the monks of the temple. This positive relationship was not limited to Ai Un Kham, however. Although Ai Un Kham visited the temple the most, the head of the office and the officer who was responsible for Christianity also visited on a variety of official occasions. When the famous Tai monk Khūbā Bunchum visited in January 2002, these three officers came and had an audience with him. By contrast, the MRAB officer responsible for Muslims in Sipsongpannā never came to Wat Pājie.

While nationally the RABs serve primarily as regulators, in Sipsongpannā the MRAB serves as both regulator and facilitator. The MRAB is responsible for accrediting temples. Each temple needs to have a certificate that recognizes it as a legitimate site of worship, registered with the MRAB. It is also responsible for the behavior of the Buddhists of the region. If a monk commits a crime, for example, Ai Un Kham is involved with the process of forcing the monk to disrobe and his arrest. Ai Un Kham was also active in the efforts to resolve the "false monk" crisis. The MRAB's oversight also extends to the Dhamma school at Wat Pājie. Even though it is a school, the only educational project recognized by the state is a religious one, and it is therefore not under the purview of the Board of Education.[13] Thus, Ai Un Kham and the other officers of the MRAB made formal visits to the school at Wat Pājie throughout the year, such as during the *nak-tham* exams (see chapter 5). In his role as facilitator, Ai Un Kham also helped the Sipsongpannā BA deal with the problems caused by the large celebrations, such as that during Song kān, or the celebration for the dedication of the Wat Pājie abbot's *kuti* (monastic dormitory) in 2001 (made more complex by the vast number of foreign visitors; Borchert 2010). Indeed, perhaps because of his prior relationship with the temple, he often seemed to be as much in partnership with the monks as he was responsible for them. In conversations with him, it was clear that being Dai-lue was an important part of his life, and his partnership with the temple reflected that.

The Sipsongpannā BA's relationship with the PSB was also generally positive, which was in part the result of the monks' apparent efforts to follow the rules. During the preparations for the celebration for the new *kuti,* the monks went through the proper channels. They cleared all foreign visitors with the PSB and worked with the PSB on security for the event (which included such guests as the current and previous governors of the autonomous prefecture, as well as representatives from the Yunnan government). This was one of a number of positive interactions that the BA had had with the PSB and the police in Jing Hong. The PSB provided security (and oversaw the taking of entrance tickets) at the Song kān celebration, and had done so for a number of years. This cooperation helped the monks in other contexts. When a construction project caused a mess on the public road outside the temple, rather than harassing the monks, the PSB simply told them to clean it up (which the novices did). When the old prefectural governor saw that the temple was using a truck without a license plate (which was actually a gift from a Burmese monk), and told the PSB to make sure that Wat Pājie got rid of it, the PSB told the monks not to worry about it. This was because, as the monk who related it to me said, the PSB knew "we would not cause any trouble."

This relationship with the PSB, which was indicative of good government relations in general, was reflective of the monks' skill at managing their *guanxi* with the government. It is perhaps a cliché that *guanxi* is extremely important in getting anything done in China. As Andrew Kipnis points out, effective *guanxi* production and management goes beyond the instrumental, but there are nevertheless important instrumental aspects that inspire one to cultivate relationships with influential people (1997, 8–9). A clear example of the power of the abbot's good *guanxi* took place soon before the celebration of his new *kuti*. The temple put a garden in the front of the new building, which included a fishpond with a statue of an arhat in the middle of it. For the dedication *chalong* (celebration), the abbot (then titled *dubi long* rather than *khūbā meaung*) wanted the garden to look as if it had not been a construction site for the previous six months, and one way to do this was to have trees in the garden that were not saplings. He sent some young monks to find a big, older tree that would look good in a garden, which they were able to do in a village near the abbot's home village outside of Meng Ce. On their return to Wat Pājie from Meng Hai County, however, the monks got stopped at a border gate between the two counties. The guard told them that they could not transport older trees in the region without special permits. Despite the fact that it was after 11 p.m. on a Saturday night, the monks called Dubi Long Jom (all the monks at the BA had cell phones by 2001). Rather than waiting until morning, Dubi Long called the head of the district, who made calls that eventually resulted in the border guards letting the monks with their trees pass. It is particularly surprising that this happened very late at night, but it is indicative of the political connections that the senior monks of the BA possessed.

We might speculate on why there are good relations between the monks and the local government, false monks notwithstanding. *Guanxi* works when both sides have something to offer each other, and there is clearly a strategic relationship between the BA and the *zhou* government, revolving around money and development. It is fairly simple: the economy of Sipsongpannā relies very heavily on tourism, and most of the tourism in Sipsongpannā consists of domestic (i.e., Han Chinese) tourists coming to see their "exotic," ethnic conationals. The Buddhism of Sipsongpannā, which differs from the majority of Chinese Buddhism, is an important part of that exoticism. Buddhist temples, with their young boys in orange robes and shaven pates, provide a nice counterpart to the exuberance of the Water-Splashing Festival, which is reenacted daily in the various minority parks of the region. Buddhism, in other words, is a linchpin in the economy of Sipsongpannā—a "smokeless factory"—and this serves as a foundation of the relationship between the monks of Wat Pājie and the local government. This was perhaps best exemplified by the partnership of the local government and Wat Pājie in building Wat Long Meuang Lue as part of the economic development plan of Jing Hong.

Despite the strategic alliance and the good *guanxi* between the local government and the monks of Wat Pājie, there are also tense undertones in the relationship. Much of this tension has catalyzed around language policy. The SBA has been a strong advocate for greater use of the traditional Dai-lue script, as opposed to the "new" Dai-lue letters, developed in the 1960s by Dai-lue and Han linguists at the Nationalities Institute in Kunming (now Yunnan Nationalities University). The motivation behind this script was to enable more people (such as women) to learn to read Dai-lue, but it has never really caught on as a popular script. While the local government was greatly opposed to any use of the traditional script during the Mao era, since the mid-1980s its language policies have been inconsistent. For a short period in the mid-1990s, the local newspaper was published in the traditional script, though that policy was later reversed. Since the late 1990s, traditional script has been used in many signs throughout Jing Hong. While McCarthy suggests that this is something of a victory for Dai-lue cultural activists (2000, 110), the government agreement to the use of traditional script may very well be for aesthetic reasons. While the monks of the BA have advocated for the use of traditional Dai-lue script, and have even participated in the development of a Dai-Han dictionary in these characters, their advocacy has been met with grumbling by local politicians (Davis 2003, 195–196). Beyond language policy, monks are often suspicious of the political system as a whole, and conscious of their subaltern position. Once, when I asked one of the vice-abbots at Wat Pājie how the next abbot of Wat Pājie would be chosen (when Khūbā Meaung Jom either died or disrobed), he said somewhat disdainfully that it would be whomever the government wanted, noting that the agenda of the MRAB was not the same as that of the Sipsongpannā BA. Even more interesting, though, was the day that Khūbā Meuang Jom, quasi-governmental official that he is, told me that both the local government and the national government fear Dai unity (by this, he meant the Dai of Laos, northern Thailand, and the Shan States). This explained government support for the new Dai-lue script, since the old one could be read by Dai people across the region, not just in China. Language and religion could be the basis of a unified Dai nation in the Middle Mekong region (Keyes 1992; Cohen 2001).

However, this has not been the strategy pursued by the BA at Wat Pājie. They have generally decided that working within the Chinese system holds more benefits. Thus, they work with the local government to develop tourist resources, attend the required political meetings, and act as good patriots on study missions to Taiwan or as delegates to international meetings of Buddhists. In the same way that attendance in the public schools might be considered to be a trade-off for relative autonomy in apprentice education (Shih 2002, 194), this cooperation perhaps buys the monks of Wat Pājie the space to act as agents of Dai-lue cultural nationalism and preservation.

Leading and Governing the Regional Sangha

The Buddhist Association of Sipsongpannā is situated between two groups: the local government on the one hand and Buddhists on the other, particularly monks and novices. So the monks at Wat Pājie are responsible for communicating official policy to the Buddhists of the region, but they are also responsible for policing these Buddhists.[14] Unlike the government, however, which can (theoretically at least) always send police officers to arrest someone, the monks of Wat Pājie (i.e., the BA) do not have much direct control over the monks in the region. There are small things that the BA can compel, but for the most part, the monks of the SBA do not govern through direct control, but rather by whatever spiritual and moral authority that they are able to develop.

The centrality of Wat Pājie and the SBA are seen through their efforts to guide the sangha and foster Dai-lue culture. While each year the monks and lay Buddhists are supposed to come to Wat Pājie to pay their respects to the *sangha-nayok*, one is just as likely to see outreach efforts by the BA. In the late 1990s, the senior monks of the region took part in or sponsored a series of social projects, such as HIV-AIDS education, reforestation efforts, and flood relief (Hyde 2007; McCarthy 2009). They have also been deeply involved in efforts to preserve Dai-lue texts and foster knowledge and use of "traditional" Dai-lue. In addition to projects such as the Dai-lue-Han dictionary discussed above, they also sponsored the writing of a Dai-lue alphabet song and the creation of a video as part of an effort to popularize it. While it is difficult to measure the long-term impact of such efforts, it is easy to find Dai-lue textbooks and liturgies published at Wat Pājie at temples throughout the region. While some of this work has caused tension with local politicians as noted above, at the same time, it has allowed the monks of the BA to be seen as leaders of Dai-lue Buddhists. The effect of this can be seen when the monks at Wat Pājie are invited to take part in merit-making events around the region (not just in their home temples); when their advice is sought on the appointment of new abbots; and when Dai-lue laity donate money, rice, and labor to Wat Pājie, as they did when the abbot's new house was constructed.

Some of this leadership is visible to the local government, but some of it is not, primarily because it is in Dai-lue, the text of which is not known by local government officials, even those who are themselves Dai-lue. In the last chapter, I referred to regulations that were propagated by the BA in the late 1990s. These rules and regulations detail requirements for ordination, and guidelines for monastic life (such as when to shave one's head) and forbidden acts, such as stealing, killing, or lying. While distinct from the Vinaya, they are generally in consonance with it. The SBA printed up bilingual versions of these rules on metal posters in both Chinese and Dai-lue, and required that they be hung up on temple walls throughout the region. In large part, these rules are similar in both Chinese and Dai-lue, but there are some differences in tone, particularly in the prefatory statement between the two versions. The Chinese-language statement is relatively bland and straightforward. It says:

> We lay down these rules to standardize the conduct of the sangha of our prefecture; to strictly hold the Vinaya; to strengthen the building of Buddhism; to protect [Buddhism] and make clear the laws administering Buddhist affairs; [and] to foster the development of Buddhist causes and enterprises in our prefecture according to the precepts and ideals of Buddhism, as well as the relevant national laws and the situation in our prefecture.

The Dai-lue version is as follows:

> Under the auspices of the Buddhist Association of the Dai domain of Sipsongpannā, a group of leaders met and determined a set of regulations and prohibitions for the monks and novices in our *meuang* Sipsongpannā. This is because not every monk lives in the midst of a large group of monks that can help him be attractive,[15] nor is there a system to ensure being polite. There is regular behavior that is not proper or composed, which leads to a lack of respect for morality and the Dhamma, according to a strict Dhamma-Vinaya. Since this is the case, and [since] we wish for the words and appearance [of the monks] to be lovely; to add strength to building and repairing the business of the polity, the village, and *meuang,* as well as the work of spreading the teachings of the Buddha; and to contribute to the flourishing of the polity (*prades baan-mueang*) and religion, then we send out this set of regulations to be followed by the head of temples in our *meuang* Sipsongpannā. [It] allows them to make arrangements to act according to these rules and prohibitions, thus causing monks and novices to help protect our religion so that it will then reach five thousand *wasā* into the future!

There are three important differences here between these two statements. To begin with, the Dai-lue version identifies the monks themselves as the actors. This is a set of regulations that the monks of the region themselves are promulgating, for religious and cultural reasons. Moreover, it is not a text that is simply imposed on the wider sangha; it is used to support village abbots in their efforts to create a healthy Buddhism. In addition to identifying Dai-lue actors as agents, this text also identifies a religious and cultural problem that the regulations are being promulgated to solve: to wit, monks are not acting properly in an "attractive" way, in no small measure because they are alone and not surrounded by other monks who know how to act properly. While it does not state this explicitly, it is not difficult to imagine these problems being attributed to the effects of the Chinese Revolution. Finally, where the Chinese-language version ends with a bland statement about fostering a healthy stable Buddhism, which supports the "relevant national laws and the reality" of Sipsongpannā, the Dai-lue version ends with the hope that making these changes will protect Buddhism so that it might reach five thousand years (*wasā*) into the future. Or rather, it will allow "our religion" (*sāsanā khowng hao*) to survive that long. Obviously, "our religion" is Buddhism, but the ownership in the use of the word "our" is important. While this poster does nothing to promote sedition, it does assert the authority and centrality of the monks of Sipsongpannā as the leaders of Buddhism in ways that are only partially visible to the Chinese-reading populace or government.

While the monks of the BA seek in these ways to lead, and indeed to govern, the sangha, there are limits to its authority and its ability to access resources or discipline monks beyond the walls of Wat Pājie. The significant status of the senior monks of Wat Pājie within Sipsongpannā did not mean they were always successful in their efforts in the Dai-lue community. In a series of construction projects in 2001–2002, senior monks of Wat Pājie put out a request for donations to the region as a whole. They sent out younger monks to canvas different parts of Sipsongpannā, but they were largely unsuccessful. Indeed, the case of the trees that showed the abbot's ability to cultivate the local government, also demonstrated the limits of his ability to draw on the resources of lay Buddhists. When the younger monks traveled around Sipsongpannā asking villagers for trees to donate to the garden adorning the new *kuti,* they found a number of trees between ten and twenty years old that would do, but wherever they went, the Dai-lue villagers refused to give them the tree (apparently some *dān* is more valuable than the merit it produces). While they were ultimately successful in this endeavor, it proved to be a more difficult project than the abbot had originally thought it would be.

A similar thing happened a few months later when Khūbā Bunchum, a Tai charismatic monk, came on a pilgrimage tour to Sipsongpannā.[16] Since Khūbā Bunchum was an important patron of Wat Pājie over the years, and had spent the 1990s traveling around the "golden triangle," the monks of Wat Pājie wanted to refurbish a cave in the southern part of Sipsongpannā where he would stay. Again, these younger monks went out to collect funds, but came back empty-handed. The funds they collected were minimal, and the plan to refurbish the cave was scrapped. Even if part of their failure was because they were junior rather than senior monks, it is clear that there are limits to the BA's ability to marshal grassroots support for some of its projects.

Their ability to govern is also evident in the limit to their disciplinary reach. While the BA was able to mandate that the rules and regulations be posted throughout the region, they have not always been able to fully enact the rules on this list. The decentralized aspect to running village *wats* discussed in the last chapter is evident here as well, and it is generally understood to be the responsibility of temple committees (usually comprised of the abbot, the lay leader of the *wat* [usually a *khanān*], and the village headman, among others) to address disciplinary problems, though there were some moments when the monks of the BA could intervene. If a monk clearly committed an illegal act, then the BA could effectively resolve the matter, as in one case where it ensured that a monk caught smoking marijuana disrobed.[17] Yet even in situations where there is clarity about what was done and what should happen as a result, the BA's ability to act is limited. The monks have to know about the illegal act, which can be surprisingly difficult even in such a small region. An American college student who visited Wat Pājie told me about a young monk trying to chat her up in a bar in the Meng Long region. When I told some of my friends at Wat Pājie about what she told me, they tried to find out the details, to determine whether they needed to try to have this young monastic disrobe. Just as with the "false monks," it is likely that some people in the region knew that this monk (or *pha long*) was acting inappropriately, but they did not believe it was necessary to pass the information on. Without having more proof of the details of this alleged infraction, the monks of Wat Pājie were helpless to enforce the disciplinary standards.

Conclusion: False Monks and Models of Power and Authority in Sipsongpannā

Buddhism and politics have long been intertwined, perhaps universally within Buddhism. The ways in which Buddhists have interacted with states has varied in time and space. What I have sought to highlight here is that Buddhism in Sipsongpannā during the Reform Era has been marked in some ways by older forms of power and influence married to the conditions established by the CCP in its efforts to control religions after the Cultural Revolution. Religion in post-Mao China is shaped by a discourse on "religion" that highlights certain kinds of activities and that the state uses to its own ends. The impact of this discourse can be muted or magnified by the particular relationships between governmental and quasi-governmental entities such as the MRAB and the BA, as well as local conditions and traditions. In Sipsongpannā, these national frameworks have been fused into a context where there has long been a tradition of superficial central control and significant actual autonomy. Chinese scholarship has tended to view the sangha as acting as the handmaiden of a highly centralized "feudal political" system, with the *khūbā meaung* or the *sangha-nayok* "exercising jurisdiction" directly over village temples (Li 1983, 3:101). But just as the traditional government was centralized more in name than in fact (Hill 1998, 65), authority in *wats* in Sipsongpannā has long been in the hands of village abbots and headmen. It is in this tradition that we should see conditions at the head of the contemporary Sangha of Sipsong-pannā: formally centralized as the local form of the Buddhist Association, its status relies on different bases of authority such as educational attainments. As noted above, the senior monks of the sangha exercise indirect authority rather than direct control; Wat Pājie and Wat Long Meuang Lue are a center of gravity, rather than a base of power.

How does this help us understand the case of the false monks, then, and the government's failure to act? Discursively, the false monks did not demand action. Their activities—exploitative divination—fit easily within the frame of "feudal superstition." They were scamming tourists, but in the eyes of the state, this is what "feudal superstition" does. At worst, these false monks were petty criminals; they caused an annoyance, but not necessarily anything else (despite the feelings of the monks of Wat Pājie). This is particularly true when we think that 2001 is still a period of heightened concern about the Falun Gong, and a period when the power of the categories of "evil cults" is at its most prevalent. What these "false monks" were doing was not "evil" or "cultish" but simply low-level graft.

To a certain extent, the Chinese state's goals in governing religion are about maintaining stability and social control. I suggested above that the system is set up to maximize the state's ability to act when it feels threatened. In this case, the state was not particularly threatened. The local villagers near the temple were not concerned; indeed, they seemed to be supporting the false monks by warning when the monks of the Buddhist Association would arrive to unmask them. This meant that the villagers or monk associated with the particular temple did not complain. The only complaints were coming from the Buddhist Association (whose members were not local stakeholders), and since the false monks were not a threat to society, the security apparatus was not activated. Indeed, one of the things this incident reveals is the weakness of the BA locally, and perhaps nationally as well. It is an official organization, and one with both national and local presence. Moreover, as Ji argues, this has meant that it is in a position to advocate for the concerns of Buddhists. But it has little power of its own. It can only appeal to the state, that is, to encourage the state to follow its own rules. If the state does not want to (for whatever reason), then the BA is hamstrung in its ability to act—at least in the immediate situation. We see this in Sipsongpannā where the monks of Wat Pājie have a good bit of authority among the Dai-lue, but they have little direct power. It is worth noting that the government did finally deal with these false monks, arresting them and kicking them out of the region. I was told that the reason was that tourists complained about the costs of divination. At the point at which the false monks became a threat to the local government's bread and butter, the situation was resolved. The point is not that religion is irrelevant to the issue, but rather that whether something is defined as "religious" or not is a point of control on the part of the state (at whatever level). Buddhist monks, like other religious actors, are not powerless, but they have a weak hand, and must work within a system that was established to maximize the state's power to act, and not on behalf of the rights of religious actors and institutions.

This raises another interesting dynamic. When scholars discuss state–sangha relations within Theravāda Buddhism, they often do so within the context of the paradigm of legitimation and galactic polities that emerged during the 1970s. This model emphasized the structural symbiosis of the sangha and kings within premodern Theravāda polities, whereby the king or state would help preserve the *Buddha sāsana* (Buddhist religion) by maintaining the sangha. In doing so, the monks would bestow legitimacy upon the king, allowing him to be seen as a *dhamma-rāja* (a king marked by and ruling with Dhamma). This model's apogee was in the "galactic" or "mandalic" polities of Southeast Asia, such as Ayutthaya or Pagan, which brought together a "Brahmanical" ritual complex and military power under the rubric of Theravāda Buddhism in what John Holt has referred to as an "ethics of power" (2009). In more recent times, this was a role that modern states have sought to take on (Tambiah 1976; Seneviratne 1999). This relationship allows monks to maintain their purity—remaining above the fray—while the king performs the dirty work of politics. While this relationship between sangha and state was always assuredly more complicated than this structural formulation allows (Blackburn 2001, 90n18), at the same time, as an ideal type of history and a heuristic model for understanding how fundamental religious-political relationships have been structured within Theravāda Buddhist polities, it is quite useful.

However, this discussion misses the fundamental conditions of Buddhism and politics in Sipsongpannā. While the preceding discussion should make clear that the contemporary Chinese state is very involved in defining and governing religion nationally and locally, unlike the Theravāda states of Southeast Asia, the Chinese state's legitimacy does not rest on its support of Buddhism in particular or religion more broadly. This does not mean that the state gains nothing in its association with religious communities. Indeed, at least some of the conceptual tolerance of "normal religions" discussed above derives from the international standards of freedom of religion. At a bare minimum, by permitting the proper practice of religion, the PRC avoids international censure.[18] As a result, the relationship between religion and politics in China is generally not symbolic, as Tambiah describes the "galactic polities" of Thailand, Burma, or Sri Lanka; instead, it is focused on proper social actions and social stability, embedded in discourses of the nation. It is interesting to note, however, that the Chinese state's emphasis on religion remaining outside the political sphere means that it is just as likely to ignore the ways that monks and other religious actors act politically, as long as their actions remain outside the institutions of power.

Perhaps the very fact that the Chinese state is not as deeply engaged in maintaining a certain image of Buddhism reveals some of the ways the monks do engage in politics. Moreover, what we see within Sipsongpannā with the Buddhist Association seems to be a grafting of new forms of state power onto older types of relationships, also embedded in structures of authority. In the contemporary form of state power, the monks are constrained by the rules of the Chinese state to act within certain frames. They can engage in politics, and interact with political actors, but only in spheres that the state understands as properly "religious."

Monks on the Move

Dai-Lue Monastic Networks

IN NOVEMBER 2001, AFTER MONTHS OF PREPARATION, THE Sangha of Sipsongpannā celebrated the opening of a new office building and home for the abbot of Wat Pājie, the Wannasiri Kuti (so named because it is the dormitory, or *kuti,* of the Dubi Long [now Khūbā Meuang] Jom whose Pāli name is Wannasiri). Aside from the months of construction time that had been required to put up the building, the denizens of Wat Pājie, monks, novices, and lay workers had all worked for months to prepare for the event. Indeed, in the two weeks before the event, the Dhamma school at Wat Pājie ceased classes, while the novices were directed towards a variety of tasks for the management of the event. These included things such as preparing for guests by setting up beds in extra offices, cleaning the grounds and constructing booths for villagers to come and make merit (*tham bun* or *heu dān*), or preparing signs and setting up a stage where the festivities would take place. It also included tasks outside of the temple that were more likely to be handled by the junior monks at the temple. In the last chapter, I discussed the search for a tree to adorn the garden of the *kuti*. That particular trip was only one of a number of trips that the junior monks and lay workers at the temple had taken around Sipsongpannā, to Thailand and to a town in Myanmar called Xiao Meng La. This place, something like a Myanmar version of Tijuana, had been set up by Chinese business interests to give Chinese tourists a chance to go to Myanmar in relative safety. It was also a convenient place to go to get tiles and other materials for temples from Thailand that could not be easily purchased in Sipsongpannā. Beyond the hunt for materials, one of the junior monks spent most of a week traveling back and forth between the PSB and Wat Pājie, registering the foreign guests who were going to attend the event.

The actual celebration took place over three days and included a diverse number of activities. The first day was taken up with the official celebrations and included the formal arrival of guests and welcoming speeches. The rest of the first day and the entirety of the second day was filled with traditional Dai-lue dances by dance troupes from around Sipsongpannā and a performance by a Dai-lue pop band. The third day included more overtly religious activities, being comprised of a formal merit-making ceremony; several sermons by monks visiting from the Shan States; and the formal transference of merit (*yat nām*), the pouring of water while the monks chant, which closes most merit-making activities in Sipsongpannā (and elsewhere). This event could be examined in terms of the political relationships that are evident in the activities and speeches of the first day, which reveal the kinds of relationships I discussed in the last chapter (see also Borchert 2010), but here I would like to pay more attention to who attended the event, how, and why.

Broadly speaking, there were three groups of people at the celebration: local monks and Dai-lue villagers who had come from around the region, though in particular from the villages near Meng Ce; Tais from outside of Sipsongpannā, including some Dai-neua monks from Dehong, Shans from Meng Yong and Tachilek in northeast Myanmar, and some Thai nationals; and official guests and representatives of the government, the Buddhist Association of Yunnan, or Religious Affairs Bureaus, who were a variety of nationalities (*minzu*). After the speeches and blessings at the dedication, a formal photo was taken of the dignitaries who attended the opening of the Wannasiri Kuti. This group was also roughly reflective of the second and third groups listed above. In the first row were monks who mainly came from the Shan States. Of particular note here was Khūbā Siang Lā, a monk who grew up in Sipsongpannā and fled to Myanmar sometime after the Communist takeover. In the second row were the first two governors of Sipsongpannā under the Communists, as well as the mayor of Jing Hong; right behind them was a representative of the Religious Affairs Bureau of Yunnan (a letter from a vice-president of the Buddhist Association of China was read at the event, but he could not attend). Behind the politicians were a Tibetan Buddhist monk from Yunnan and several Mahāyāna monks, all of whom came from Yunnan according to my Dai-lue friends (one novice said that the Han monks were from "Shaolin Temple," but this was corrected by his friends, who said they were from Kunming).

In the introduction, I suggested that the movement of monks is based on interlinking imaginations of connections through Buddhism, and that the notion of Buddhism provides "flexibility" to move across borders, just as capital provides overseas Chinese businessmen the same flexibility (Ong 1999). In this chapter, using the monks that attended the dedication of the Wannasiri Kuti as a point of departure, I want to explore this idea in more detail. If we look at all of the types of monks that were at the celebration, we see several different interlinking sources of connection and flexibility. In particular, connection is based on Chinese Buddhist ethnoscapes, to use the language of Steven Kemper (and Appadurai), as well as Theravāda ethnoscapes. Working together, they provide a Buddhist ethnoscape that is recognized as legitimate by the Chinese government and not as a threat that would trigger the security apparatus. Moreover, while state discourses and institutions about citizenship, ethnicity, and Buddhism provide flexibility, they also provide the frictions that both enable and hinder connections between different kinds of Buddhists. To make these points, I will examine local, national, and translocal networks in which the senior monks of Sipsongpannā participate.

Considering Networks

Buddhist monks—Dai-lue and otherwise—travel a good deal. This has probably always been true, but at least in my experiences in Sipsongpannā and in Thailand, with the exception of the rainy season when Theravāda monks at least are constrained, one is as likely to find monks traveling as staying in place. In *wats* that I have visited regularly in Sipsongpannā, it was not uncommon to come looking for a monk only to find that he was not around. Normally, he would simply be visiting villagers, or *wats* in neighboring villages. However, it was not uncommon for certain monks to be traveling: to far away parts of the autonomous region; to Kunming, Shanghai, or Xiamen in eastern China; or out of the country, to the Shan States, Thailand, Sri Lanka, or even the United States. Much of this travel was and is prosaic: to visit patrons, see friends, or purchase goods. It is no different than the travel of nonmonks (though as will be clear, being a monk sometimes facilitates this travel). While it might be interesting to think about when and why Theravāda monks go to stores to buy things, what is of more interest here are the patterns of interactions that occur, and what these networks reveal about how the Dai-lue imagine themselves as Buddhists, as Chinese Buddhists, and as Tai Buddhists.

First, some basic terminology will help make sense of these patterns. In their discussion of Muslim networks, Cooke and Lawrence refer to them as "phenomena that are similar to institutionalized social relations, such as tribal affiliations and political dynasties but also distinct from them, because to be networked entails making a choice to be connected across recognized boundaries" (2005, 1). Yet at the same time, as they also point out, following Charles Kurtzman in the same volume, the networks themselves are not reality, but rather a metaphor "representing human relations as a structure of nodes connected by spokes" (Kurtzman 2005, 69). This does not mean that they simply reside in the minds of the scholar, but rather that the scholar "privilege[s] certain aspects of reality that are deemed to be of theoretical importance" (ibid., 70). This means that networks are a reflection of the interests of scholars or religious actors, who identify certain institutions or patterns of interaction as networks. In making this point, Kurtzman is highlighting the perspectival aspect of our descriptions: a network viewed from other angles may be simply a trip to the store.

The "nodes," "spokes," and "structures" referred to above are simply ways of identifying aspects of connection. Nodes are the social units of the network, and they may be any size: a person can be a node, as can a school or a *wat*. Certain monks, for example, are well known, not just to people in their village, but to monks in the BA, people in the government, and Buddhists in a variety of locations. As should be clear from what has already been discussed in previous chapters, Khūbā Meaung Jom is a node, in part because of his social location, but in part because of his ability and desire to foster relationships that allow him to pursue his agendas for building Buddhism in Sipsongpannā (and bigger houses). Spokes are the relations that connect nodes on the networks, and they include economic exchange, friendship, and information flow. Celebrations such as the dedication of the Wannasiri Kuti and merit economies are important spokes within the Buddhist networks within which the monks of Sipsongpannā move. Finally, the structure is the pattern that is formed by the nodes and the spokes, and like these, they might be described in a variety of ways: centralized or not; dense, diffuse, or intensive; homogeneous or heterogeneous (Kurtzman 2005, 69–70).

Wat Pājie is a primary node in the Buddhist networks of Sipsongpannā, or perhaps more accurately in the networks that the Buddhist monks of Sipsongpannā construct and participate in. This is in part because of the concentration of well-educated monks who have been in robes for many years (see chapter 1), and in part because of the institutional field provided by the Chinese state's policies on governing religion (see chapter 2). Regardless, Wat Pājie participates in local, national and transnational networks. In all of them, Wat Pājie and the monks there play an important role either in gathering monks or connecting them. One of the implications of this is to highlight that there is a temporal frame to the networks I describe here. Some of the local and transnational flows have very deep roots (Davis 2003), but Wat Pājie was only (re)founded in the early 1990s. The national policies that shape the structure of these networks are specific to Reform Era China, and these policies (e.g., on travel and on the ability of religious actors to set up schools) have changed since the beginning of the Reform Era, affecting the shape of the network structure. As Kurtzman points out: "Networks must constantly be built and rebuilt. Nodes, spokes and structures only form a network so long as people maintain them through ongoing interaction" (2005, 82). As will be evident both here and in the discussion of transnational education in chapter 6, novices and monks make choices about where to go for an education, though those choices do not occur in a vacuum. As Tsing points out, the frictions along certain paths, such as cost, need for a formal invitation, a passport, or a visa, and so forth, encourage Buddhists to travel along certain spokes rather than others. The attractiveness of a given node shapes the structures in which they participate. Finally, it should also be noted that while the networks I discuss below are "real," they are also shaped by my location at Wat Pājie and the timing of my trips there. Wat Pājie is *a* central node, but it is not the only node in Sipsongpannā; had I been located in a different place, such as Meng Ce in the northwestern part of the autonomous prefecture, or Meng La, near Laos but with a relatively small concentration of monks, different networks would have been evident. This is not to render my observations pointless; rather, it is to acknowledge that these observations are the product of a specific location.

Local Networks

There are a number of different local Buddhist networks within Sipsongpannā, including the movement of images, the economy of merit, the appointment of abbots, and education. An economy of merit is a network where festivals, celebrations, and dedications (such as the *salāt soy* of chapter 1) make up the key nodes to which monks circulate, while merit making is the spoke for such circulations. Economies of merit are common throughout the Theravāda world, and are important within Sipsongpannā, as I discussed in chapter 1 (see note 12). They can, like the material culture discussed above, move beyond the local context, but their structures are usually densest at the local level. While any donation to the sangha makes merit, there are ways to maximize merit in the Theravāda world more broadly. Monks who are seen as particularly "holy," either because they are recognized as good meditators with spiritual attainments, good teachers, or because they have been in robes for many years, are considered to be more productive "fields of merit." While monastic education can buttress such a view, in and of itself it is not usually enough to make a monk or nun a significant object of veneration. Another vector of effective merit is to give to monks who are not a part of the local community or *wat*. It is important at festivals, for example, that there be monks from outside the village, and preferably outside of the district, so that the benefit of the donations does not return to the giver (Ohnuma 2005, 119). As a result, merit-making events in the Theravāda world, especially those that are more public (as opposed to individuals forging a merit relationship with a particular monk), will always include monks from inside and outside the immediate community.

The monks of Wat Pājie are deeply tied into a variety of local economies of merit, and the dynamics that make a particular monk effective as a field of merit tend to work in the favor of these monks. They are among the oldest and best-educated monks in the region. During my fieldwork in 2001–2002, there were ten monks who comprised the leadership of the BA and regularly lived at Wat Pājie. Six of them were in their midthirties to midforties (including the abbot, then titled Dubi Long Jom), and eight of the ten had spent time studying in monastic schools in Thailand and the Shan States. During this period of research, while I often traveled to festivals and rituals with these monks, I also made it a point to go to temples separately from them, and so would learn about events taking place that would be part of different economies of merit. Regardless of where I went in Sipsongpannā, one, two, or more of the monks of Wat Pājie were already there, participating in the local merit network. It was impossible to avoid them! They were invited as guests, of course, because they were old, well-educated monks, and they often served as the outsider whose presence made for a more meritorious event.

Participation in this flow of monks via merit brought these monks to *wats* around the region, which allowed them to be participants in a different spoke: headhunter for abbots. The average *wat* in Sipsongpannā has only one monk, and this has long been the case, though the number is increasing slowly. In most cases, abbots leave because they disrobe, though occasionally they will take a position at Wat Pājie, leave the region to study, or die. In most cases, the duties of the *wat* are taken over by a junior monk or a senior novice, who has been acting as the senior apprentice to the abbot. According to monks and older laymen with whom I spoke, this only works when the novice is close to twenty and will soon be in a position to take the higher ordination (and is interested in becoming the abbot, which is not always the case). When there is no one available from the *wat* itself, the temple committee members have a number of strategies that they might draw on to find a new abbot, most of which include drawing on existing networks. Frequently, new abbots are found in the immediate vicinity, coming from one of the *wats* in the district that comprises the *pāṭimokkha* recitation community (another local network). A second route is through kinship networks (lay or monastic) that crisscross Sipsongpannā. I met one abbot living in a *wat* outside of Jing Hong who had grown up in Meng Long (a two-hour bus ride away). He said that one of the villagers had relatives in his hometown, and that when the previous abbot had disrobed, the invitation to become abbot had emerged in this way. A third route for finding new monks is by requesting the help of the monks of Wat Pājie, whose high status for local Buddhist reasons and as the head of the BA intensifies their participation in the local economies of merit, as I have already noted. For example, when a different village outside of Jing Hong was in need of a monk to perform fortnightly services in the village *wat,* they went to Wat Pājie for help. The vice-abbot sent one of the junior monks to fulfill this service, and eventually they invited him to serve as the *dubi long* of the *wat.*

The third local network that I would like to discuss is education. The Buddhist Institute of Sipsongpannā (*foxueyuan*) is a Dhamma school in Jing

Hong that has been housed in two different *wats*. It was begun at Wat Pājie in 1994, and moved to Wat Long Meuang Lue in 2009. This Dhamma school has had monk-teachers and novice-students from around the region. They come to Jing Hong to receive a more advanced Buddhist education than they can normally receive in their local village *wat*. These novice-students then have to travel to Wat Pājie, and live there for roughly three years while they complete a *nak tham* program. Their travel makes visible a network in which education serves as the primary spoke, and the *foxueyuan* in Jing Hong is an important node. While the school is open to novices and junior monks from around Sipsongpannā, as well as to Dai-neua novices from Dehong in western Yunnan, the structure of the network is such that it is fairly uneven. In 2001–2002, the majority of the novices came from two or three different locations: Meng Ce in the northwest of the province, Daluo in the southwest and the Gadong/Gasi region, just to the south of Jing Hong (see figure 3.1). There were relatively few students from Meng La, and none from Jing Hong City. These differences are reflective of several aspects within the local sangha, including the effect of population density and the role played by specific monks in fostering attitudes towards education. For example, Meng Ce and Daluo, both small cities in Meng Hai County in the west, had far more novices study at Wat Pājie than all of Meng La, a county that is roughly a third of Sipsongpannā. At the same time, Jing Hong, the biggest population center in the region, had no students at Wat Pājie. There are probably two reasons for this. First, the schools in Jing Hong tend to be higher quality than those in other parts of Sipsongpannā, which means that students—even novices—have more options to get an education. Second, traditional Dai-lue culture, of which Buddhism is a central part, is simply weaker in Jing Hong, to the extent that Grant Evans referred to it as simply a Chinese city (Evans 2000). Even if this is something of an overstatement (at least when Evans was writing), it is true that "traditional" Lue culture is as much performed in Jing Hong at parks for tourists to consume minority culture as it is lived. One other dynamic of the regional educational network is the difference between Meng Ce and Meng Long, in the southern part of the autonomous prefecture. In 2002, the presence of Khūbā Meuang Jom at Wat Pājie seemed to draw a number of students from Meng Ce to study in the capital of the region. By contrast, there were five Meng Long monks living at Wat Pājie, three of whom were abbots of *wats* in Meng Long, but there were no students at Wat Pājie from the region. When I asked them why none of their students had attended Wat Pājie, all of them replied that their own student-novices were still studying in public school, and so did not need to come to Wat Pājie.

     All three of these networks—economies of merit, personnel suggestions for village *wats,* and the movement of novices to study at the Dhamma school at Wat Pājie or Wat Long Meaung Lue—had, and indeed have, network

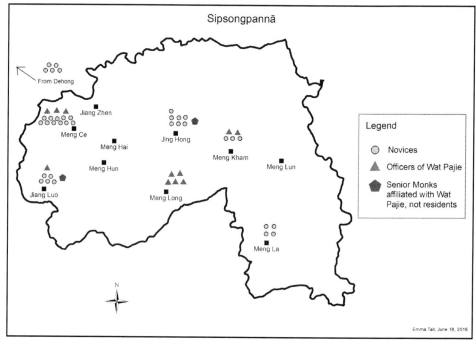

FIGURE 3.1 Map of home regions of monks and novices of Wat Pājie in 2002. Each figure represents one person.

structures that remain within the autonomous region, but a number of other possible local networks had structures that were transnational. For example, throughout the late 1990s and early 2000s, it was possible to find pictures of Khūbā Bunchum in village temples around the region. Khūbā Bunchum is a Tai monk who spent much of the 1990s and early 2000s traveling around Laos, northern Thailand, and the Shan States. He also regularly visited Sipsongpannā. A charismatic monk, his movements have ignored the national borders in the region, moving across them often at will (Cohen 2001). When he visited places, he would leave pictures of himself, and these could be found in village *wats* and individual homes. In other words, they were part of economies of merit or merit networks, as described above. However, unlike those merit networks, which were local, Khūbā Bunchum is not a Chinese citizen, and these pictures have come into Sipsongpannā in the first place through a transnational spoke. There are other networks whose structures may include transnational spokes, but these spokes become localized over time. When villages began reconstructing *wats* in the late 1990s, it became popular to use a less traditional style for the *wihān*. Whereas traditional-style *wihāns* had a thatched, tiered roof,

Dai-lue villages began to build *wihāns* that had Thai-style tile roofs (this is the phenomenon I referred to in chapter 1, when I met a temple committee rebuilding its *wihān* in traditional styles, with the support of a UNESCO project). Because these styles had not been common to Sipsongpannā, there was a need to import artisans and builders to work on them. However, in part through the educational projects at Wat Pājie, and in part through market forces, several former Dai-lue monks (*khanān*) became well known inside the region and they now travel around to either create or guide the creation of the decoration of *wats*.

It is also worth emphasizing that I have been describing local networks for which Wat Pājie has been a central node. Yet while many village monks and lay Buddhists come to Wat Pājie for help, there are economies of merit that do not include the monks of Wat Pājie, and not all village committees come to the senior monks of the sangha for advice when they need a new abbot.

National Networks

While there are many local networks in Sipsongpannā, the national Buddhist networks in which the monks of Sipsongpannā participate are relatively few, and essentially all of these run through the senior monks of the sangha, located at Wat Pājie. That is to say, the Buddhist Association, still located at Wat Pājie even after the Dhamma school moved to Wat Long Meuang Lue, remains the central node that links Dai-lue monks with other Buddhists in China. At the same time, the Sipsongpannā BA is also a node in national Buddhist networks, and while it is probably not a particularly important node on the national level, it is also not inconsequential, either. Or perhaps it might be better to say that despite its marginality, it is surprisingly close to centers of influence. At the dedication of Wannasiri Kuti, there were two different types of monks who were present as a result of national Buddhist networks.[1] The first were those who are visually distinct from the Dai-lue, Theravāda monks, that is, the Tibetan and Mahāyāna monks who performed dedicatory blessings for the building in their respective languages. These monks were obvious and visible by the fact that they wore robes of a different sort from the rest of the monks who attended the ceremony. The second type of monk was less visible: this was a group of monks from Dehong. These monks were Daizu, but not Dai-lue; rather, they were Dai-neua from Dehong, and they could pass as Dai-lue monks unless they identified themselves as Dai-neua.[2] The presence of these monks represents two different national spokes by which the monks of Sipsongpannā are linked to the Chinese Buddhist ethnoscape. The first spoke is membership within the Buddhist Association of China (BAC) and the second are the *minzu* policies of the PRC government that have established the Daizu and generated an ethnic identity since the 1950s. I begin with the BAC.

As detailed in the previous chapter, being a part of the BAC incorporates the Sangha of Sipsongpannā into the governance structures of the PRC. At the same time, membership in the BAC also brings the senior monks of Sipsongpannā into regular contact with other monks in China. This has occurred primarily through three different spokes. The first of these is meetings associated with the governing aspects of the BAC. The officers of the Sipsongpannā BA (who, as previously mentioned, are also the abbot and vice-abbots of Wat Pājie and Wat Long Meuang Lue) regularly travel to Kunming for meetings of the provincial BA; less frequently, they travel to Beijing for national congresses. Fitting for the dual aspects of the BAC's jobs, these meetings had both political and managerial aspects. In 2001, for example, the officers traveled to Kunming on separate occasions for study sessions focused on one of the key policies of the time, Jiang Zemin's policy of the "Three Representatives," a theory that in part was about incorporating the business class into the Communist Party. While not particularly relevant for the monks, they were responsible for communicating it to the rest of the Dai-lue Sangha. They also went to Kunming to discuss invitations from a Shanghai temple and the Sangha of Sri Lanka to send monks to the respective places to study (see chapter 6). The second spoke on the network was a series of meetings associated with the founding and running of the Yunnan Buddhist Institute (discussed in chapter 6), outside of Kunming. The third spoke was a series of travels that might be thought of as study tours, though they also looked like they were simply tourism. It was not uncommon for Han Chinese monks from different parts of China to visit Wat Pājie in an effort to understand conditions there, or simply to see the Daizu, whom they tended to view as exotic. In the other direction, the officers of the BA in Sipsongpannā have traveled as Chinese representatives around Asia, both to major international congresses of East Asian Buddhists, and on smaller study trips. On several different occasions, Khūbā Meuang Jom was happy to tell me of the many different countries he had traveled to with the BA.[3]

The network structure of the BAC has created or intensified the links that Dai-lue monks have with either Han/Mahāyāna or Tibetan monks, which has had two important consequences for the Sangha of Sipsongpannā. The first is that it has opened up resources to the Sangha of Sipsongpannā. Many of these have been educational in nature: Dai-lue monks have traveled around China to further their education, a dynamic I discuss in chapter 6. Invitations to study in Shanghai and Xiamen, among other places, emerged directly from contact at national meetings. Membership in the CBA has also allowed Dai-lue monks to access financial resources. While Wannasiri Kuti was primarily built with local funds, the Sipsongpannā BA received donations from wealthier east coast sanghas to help defray their costs, as well as for the construction of Wat Long Meuang Lue. Moreover, the plans for Wat Long Meuang Lue were first developed in the spring of 2002, soon after a group of novices was delivered to Shanghai for several years' worth of study. All spring, brochures showing the plans of rebuilt temples in Shanghai and Xiamen lay around the BA offices at Wat Pājie, part of the inspiration of Wat Long Meuang Lue.

The second and possibly more important consequence is that participation in the CBA has helped to naturalize the Dai-lue Buddhist place within China. The Dai-lue are Chinese citizens, but they are also ethnically and culturally distinct from the vast majority of Chinese citizens. This difference is not erased by these national monastic networks, but it is softened in some ways. A Dai-lue monk who had gone on a pilgrimage around China on a BAC-sponsored trip celebrating two thousand years of Buddhism in China remarked to me that he had found the trip valuable in part because he had gotten to know other Chinese monks, but also because they had gotten to know him. That is, the Han Mahāyāna monks and the Dai-lue monks had the opportunity to see one another as conationals, as well as coreligionists. This meant that not only were they available to help in dedications for Dai-lue buildings, but they would also be more inclined to invite the minority monks to their own dedications. Similarly, in the early part of the century, there were some exchange efforts that were going both ways. Not only were some Dai-lue monks and novices going to the east coast to receive an education, but at least one temple in Yunnan was sending Han monks to Jing Hong to study Theravāda Buddhism there.[4] The effect of these travels back and forth was to expand the "ethnoscape" of Dai-lue monks so that it included Han monks, and vice versa. That is, these networks made it more likely for the Dai-lue monks of Sipsongpannā to see themselves as Chinese monks, not simply as monks in China.[5]

The second form of national network can be seen through the imbrication of ethnicity and religion that has taken place in the development of Dai-lue identity in contemporary China. Indeed, Theravāda Buddhism and nationality are intimately linked together in China, and there are certain relationships that have emerged and have been strengthened through the state's definitions of the Dai-lue as a certain kind of ethnicity. Most prominently is the development of links between the Sangha of Sipsongpannā and the Sangha of Dehong. I noted in the introduction that the Dai-lue of Sipsongpannā are one group among the Daizu (Hsieh 1995). The Daizu are comprised of four groups of people that were largely independent of one another prior to the 1950s and that had distinct dialects and political relationships, yet as a result of ethnogenesis, they now see each other as being coethnics. We see this perhaps most clearly in the school at Wat Pājie, where five Dai-neua students from Dehong were studying in 2001–2002. They had come from Dehong to study at Wat Pājie because the post-Mao Buddhist revival has not been as successful there as in Sipsongpannā. Thus, while temples have been rebuilt, there are few monks in Dehong. These young men thus were sent to Wat Pājie by the BA in Dehong, presumably to create a cohort of young monks to better propagate Theravāda Buddhism in their home territory.

The Dai-lue monks interact with another group of Chinese minorities (*shaoshu minzu*) through the spoke of "*minzu*-ness": the Bulang and the Wa. While the Daizu are the most prominent Theravāda Buddhists of China, Theravāda is also common among the Bulang, who are primarily located in Sipsongpannā, and the Wa, who spread outside of it, as well as into Myanmar. Historically, the Dai-lue had authority over these other groups, particularly the Bulang, who were often described to me as having been "slaves" of the Dai-lue (and indeed, the Bulang remain an ethnicity that is quite poor, particularly in relation to the Dai-lue). However, for all the damage it caused, the Chinese Revolution also fostered an ideology of equality among the different *minzu* groups in China. Like the novices from Dehong, over the years, a handful of Bulang novices have studied at Wat Pājie, and—according to Dai-lue monks I spoke with—have generally fit in without much trouble. The one Bulang monk that I had the opportunity to interview had largely assimilated to life among the Dai-lue. By the time I interviewed him, he had lived at Wat Pājie about five years, and had studied in Bangkok as well. He told me that his first year had been quite difficult, but that none of the other monks had ever given him a hard time for being a different ethnicity or speaking a different language. (In his first few months, whenever he and the abbot had spoken together, they had to use Chinese because it was the only language that they had in common.) I do not mean to suggest that relations between the Dai-lue and these other nationalities are without problems, rather that the ideology of equality among the nationalities, as well as the shared practice of Theravāda Buddhism, provide a spoke for a network to develop, even if it is a fairly thin one.

These monastic networks, one of which is based on membership in a national Buddhist organization and the other that follows sectarian affiliation along lines of nationality/*minzu,* are structured through the interventions of the Communist Chinese state into what it means to be Dai-lue in the late twentieth and early twenty-first century. They were not created by the Chinese state, but rather by the monks of Sipsongpannā, for a variety of reasons. However, CCP policies that both define what it means to be *minzu* and how religious actors are to be governed (as detailed in the previous chapter) enable the creation of a spoke. These are networks that are "emphatically marked" by the Chinese state, to use Blackburn's (2010) description of British influence on Sinhala Buddhism in the nineteenth century. Without the state's efforts to shape Buddhism (and other religions) to fit within a certain place within the national governance structures and to classify the people along ethnic lines, these networks would not exist. Unlike the local monastic networks discussed above, the structure of the national networks is primarily limited to the monks of Wat Pājie; few monks outside of these encounter Chinese monks on a regular basis, and even fewer lay Dai-lue do. Similarly, while there is a section of southwest Sipsongpannā where the Bulang live, most Dai-lue outside of that immediate region do not regularly interact with the Bulang. Even fewer monks interact regularly with Dai-neua monks of Dehong. Theravāda Buddhism does not provide a perfect tie across Chinese *minzus,* but it is a line of affiliation, and one that is also marked by the effects of state-produced discourse and policies.

While these two networks depend on national ties, there are important differences in the way that the Dai-lue monks treat these networks. First of all, there is a more "natural" relationship between the Dai-lue and the Dai-neua. As I have pointed out, while the Dai-lue in Sipsongpannā did not see the Dai-neua as exactly the same as themselves, they certainly saw them as related. One Dai-lue monk who had traveled to Dehong told me that the reception they had received there was overwhelming. The Dai-neua laypeople cried when they saw the Dai-lue monks who had come to visit them, precisely because of the paucity of monks in the region. This kind of response was because these monks were perceived as coethnics—kin—who had come to help them, not simply because they were conationals. While the shared "*minzu*-ness" seems to be an important factor in this tie, so was the shared religiosity, as the example of the Bulang monk demonstrates. This monk was clearly able to fit into the life of Wat Pājie, and to a much greater degree than the few Han monks who have come to Wat Pājie to study. In other words, the expansion of the Dai-lue Buddhist ethnoscape to include the Dai-neua and the Bulang is relatively straightforward, and requires less work than expanding it to include Han Chinese monks and nuns.

If the Dai-lue treat the Dai-neua as relatively natural colleagues, they treat the Chinese Mahāyāna monks with more distance and also as a resource. The Mahāyāna and Tibetan monks are colleagues with whom they work and interact on a consistent basis, but there remains a distinction between them that is best understood in class, or perhaps "civilizational" terms. The Dai-lue monks are relatively poor, and are seen as relatively backward in Chinese discourse. It is not uncommon for both lay and monastic Dai-lue people to refer to themselves sometimes ironically and other times seriously as *luohou* (backward). They tend to be the recipients of charity from Chinese monks, which shapes how these monks view their (mainly Dai) Theravāda colleagues. For example, in late April 2002, a delegation from the Buddhist Association of Shanghai came to Wat Pājie to give the temple 100,000 yuan so that they might fix the roof on the school building. The delegation consisted of a senior monk and a number of lay female followers. As I discovered after chatting with a few of the guests, the real point was basically a quick sight-seeing trip to exotic Sipsongpannā. The Shanghai monk praised Du Long Jom and Wat Pājie, and the Dai-lue, for their authentic ethnic faith and gave them the much-needed cash, but this also seemed like a performance of Dai-lue ethnicity. The delegation arrived a day early, which required a frenzied importation from a nearby village of dancing women and musicians to welcome the group. The novices, with my clumsy help, put up a bunch of poles with handwoven banners attached to them. While these banners, *dong,* were raised whenever there was a celebration, they were not usually raised when there was simply a VIP (such as Khūbā Siang Lā) coming. Finally, after the arrival of the Shanghai delegation with the attendant dancers, the guests, the dancers, the monks and novices, and myself, trooped into the *wihān* for a welcoming chant. While none of these things were out of the ordinary, they felt very staged, and provided a stereotypical welcome from "exotic" Buddhist cousins, in much the same way that Louisa Schein describes the welcoming of Chinese mayors to a regional conference in the Miao-dominated city of Kaili (Schein 2000, 100–101). This Han Chinese monk was clearly wealthier than his Theravāda colleagues and he was their patron. There was little that the Dai-lue monks could give him. In this, the monks of Sipsongpannā are in a median position, between the wealthier and ethnic majority Mahāyāna, and the poorer (religiously if not monetarily) Theravāda monks of the Dai-neua and Bulang people. It's tempting to use Bourdieu's language and describe them as the "dominant fraction of the dominated class" (1984).[6]

The national networks of the Dai-lue, therefore, have several spokes: membership in the BAC and shared citizenship; shared *minzu;* and Buddhism as a whole, but Theravāda Buddhism in particular. These spokes are not equal in their value and strength. Some provide greater flexibility: membership in the BAC has enabled the Dai-lue to move across more borders (both national and international ones) than shared nationality. Others provide closer affiliation: sharing nationality has created ties between Dai-neua and Dai-lue that are stronger than between either of the Dai and Han monks. The strongest networks combine these.

Transnational Networks

In considering the transnational networks that the monks of Sipsongpannā participate in, rather than using the dedication of Wannasiri Kuti, I would like to begin instead with two other dedication celebrations that took place in the last decade: the dedication of a newly built reliquary in a village outside of Meng Ce in 2007, and the rebuilding and dedication of a reliquary at Wat Mahāthāt outside of Meng Hun in southwest Sipsongpannā in 2002. Like the dedication of Wannasiri Kuti, these dedications included monks from the Shan States in northeast Burma (indeed, some of the same monks), but they were also less official affairs. There was a presence by some members of the local government, particularly the Minority and Religious Affairs Bureau of the Jing Hong government, but there were no higher officials here, such as the governor of Sipsongpannā. These were both, in other words, reflective of networks less mediated by the local government's agenda.

The dedication outside of Meng Ce in 2007 displayed a wider variety of monastic networks. The celebration was taking place in the town of a monk who had been a lay officer at Wat Pājie when I was there in 2001–2002, and for a time had been the Chinese-language teacher there as well, Ai Kham. This was his second stint as a monk: he had been a novice and a monk through his early twenties, and had disrobed in his second year of a three-year technical college in Kunming. After graduation, he had worked at Wat Pājie, and then had reordained in 2003 in order to go to study in Sri Lanka, along with three other monks from Dehong and Sipsongpannā. The building of the reliquary was spearheaded by him, along with his older brother, and attendance at the dedication reflected a number of the networks in which they were embedded. The principal guest was a monk from Sri Lanka who had brought with him a relic (described to me as a "Buddha relic") to be installed in the stupa. This Sinhala monk had been a teacher or sponsor of the Dai-lue monk at his *pirivena* in Sri Lanka. There were also several guests there from Singapore, including some women described to me as part of the Taiwanese transnational Buddhist organization Foguang Shan, but dressed in a uniform that was like a hybrid Buddhist/Catholic nun, and a handful of monks from Thailand, including one, Luang Pho Anan, who ran an orphanage in northern Thailand. The Dai-lue monk had met the Singaporean guests while studying in Sri Lanka, and invited them to join to make merit. His brother knew the Thai guests from his work as a trader between Sipsongpannā and northern Thailand. Each of these guests played an important role in the dedication: the Sinhala monk brought the relic (see figure 3.2); Luang Phuo Anan blessed and energized Buddha images that were placed in the side of the reliquary; and in a telling moment, the brother gave a candle each to one of the Singaporean nuns, to the lay head of the Thai delegation, and to his brother, Dubi Kham, and then asked them to light the candles together before the stupa, saying, "You are a representative of Thailand, you of Singapore, and you of Sipsongpannā, the three countries here."

The other event, the dedication of the rebuilt reliquary, the *mahā-thāt* of Wat Mahāthāt in Meng Hun, was, on the surface at least, a less transnational affair. The reliquary in the town had been damaged thirty years before during the Cultural Revolution and it was finally being rebuilt. When I arrived on the second day of a two-day affair, I found the *wat* grounds filled with

FIGURE 3.2   A Sinhala monk bringing a relic to be enshrined in Sipsongpannā. Behind him are Buddhist nuns from Singapore.

sleeping mats and rolls, since people had been there for several days, both to finish the construction, and also to attend the dedication. On that morning, monks placed the "heart" into the *mahāthāt,* and then we poured concrete into an opening on the top onto a box containing the heart (which I was told contained some small Buddha images and texts, though the men I asked did not know what texts they were). The cost of rebuilding the *mahāthāt* was born entirely by Khūbā Siang Lā, the abbot of Wat Mahāthāt in Tachilek in the Shan States. He had also attended the dedication of Wannasiri Kuti in Jing Hong a few months earlier, and was an important patron of Wat Pājie and its schools—some of their earliest textbooks were donated by Wat Mahāthāt. Most important, however, he had been born in Meng Hun, and had fled to the Shan States in the early 1960s, before the Cultural Revolution. While the presence of this monk was not particularly surprising to me, at the end of the day, after the formal dedication and everyone had returned to go home, it became evident that a large portion of the laypeople who had attended the several-day celebration were actually all from the Shan States: they had simply come across the border for a few days to support Khūbā Siang Lā's efforts. It is interesting to note that what we see in these two cases are translocal monastics on the one side, and translocal villagers on the other.[7]

It should perhaps be no surprise, given what I have said, that at both of these dedications monks from Wat Pājie were significantly involved in running the show.

There is a certain irony in the nature of the transnational networks in which the monks of Sipsongpannā most commonly participate. During the mid-1990s, when scholars began thinking about transnational flows in earnest, it was in the wake of the end of the Cold War and the loosening, if not actual breakdown, of the Bretton-Woods regime that had governed international institutions and the flow of money and people since the end of World War II. Globalization was certainly not a new thing, but there was a tendency to see increased flows as a result of deregulation, the thawing out of the Cold War, and technological improvements as positive and transformative (Appadurai 1996 is exemplary of this). In this sense, there was an emphasis on transnational flows as "new" and national spaces as old and ossified. In Sipsongpannā, however, many of the transnational monastic networks are centuries old (Davis 2003), while the national networks described in the previous section are not more than fifty years old, and probably much less. Despite this irony, I do not mean to suggest that there is a transnational, Tai substratum that permeates the region and supports these transnational networks, though there are some Tais who think this. Rather, and consonant with the general theme of the book, we need to see the ways in which the transnational networks of the monks of Sipsongpannā are both independent of and shaped by both local and national networks and agendas.

From the examples of the reliquary dedications in Meng Ce and Meng Hun, it is clear that the transnational Buddhist networks include both monastic and lay forms. In this, the transnational networks have a greater resemblance to local Dai-lue Buddhist networks than they do to national ones, which are almost solely monastic (there are of course Dai-lue national networks, but they are not specifically Buddhist ones). Moreover, the spokes of these transnational Buddhist networks are also quite similar, primarily entailing educational networks and economies of merit. As the dedication from Meng Ce in 2007 shows, where the monastics from Singapore and Sri Lanka were both linked by the Dai-lue monk's educational travels, these spokes can easily overlap, though only to a certain extent. Dai-lue monks and laity may travel across the border for economies of merit, but only Dai-lue monastics can travel easily outside of China along an educational network spoke. A third spoke along which Dai-lue monastics travel is found among kinship networks. In both Thailand and the Shan States, there are large numbers of Dai-lue who fled Sipsongpannā in the 1950s and 1960s in the wake of the Communist Revolution. While some of these connections were lost, since the "reopening" of China in the 1980s, it has become possible for people to travel back to

Sipsongpannā. Similarly, in the 1980s and 1990s in particular, when Dai-lue monks traveled outside of China to study in monastic schools in Thailand or the Shan States, they were as likely to travel to cities or villages where they had relatives to help sponsor and support them (Lamphun Province near Chiang Mai is a case in point). While kinship was and is not a specifically Buddhist spoke, it has facilitated travel.

A fourth spoke for transnational networks is the pilgrimage/tourism spoke. This is not so much about Dai-lue leaving Sipsongpannā, but rather Thai and Shan coming to Sipsongpannā to see the sights. For example, the Thai and Singaporean groups that attended the 2007 dedication in Meng Ce continued on to Kunming and Wat Pājie to "sight see and make merit." Moreover, as I discussed in chapter 1, especially in the 1990s, Thais came to Sipsongpannā under the assumption that it was a more authentic homeland than Thailand itself (which had become corrupted by modernizing forces).[8] These pilgrim/tourists, who may also be following kinship routes, have often made donations to villages in Sipsongpannā, and it is possible to find Thai donation markers at scattered villages throughout the region. It is also along this spoke that many of the temporary abbots and preceptors who were foreign monks in the 1980s and 1990s traveled to Sipsongpannā. One former monk, a professor at Mahā-Chulālongkorn University in Thailand, told me that he had gone to Sipsongpannā as a monk in the late 1980s because his family had come from there some sixty years previously and he was curious about it. He ended up staying for a year to help a village temple. Another I met was a young monk who was abbot for two years at a *wat* in Gasai, just beyond the Jing Hong airport. He told me that while his own family had not come from Sipsongpannā, he had had a friend in the Dhamma school where he studied who had come from Sipsongpannā, and this had sparked his interest.[9] What these vectors of movement indicate is the ways in which there is an ethnoscape that is constituted by a combination of Tai ethnicity, Theravāda lineages, and family.

The role of the senior monks of the sangha, based at Wat Pājie, in fostering these networks has changed over time. In the 1980s and early 1990s, much of the movement of monks across borders was fairly decentralized. Monks participated in economies of merit and they traveled to Thailand and the Shan States, largely on their own. They often followed kinship networks. In the early 1990s, there was a joint program between the Chinese and Thai governments to sponsor a group of Dai-lue novices to study in the monastic high school of Wat Phra Puttha-bāt Tak Pā outside of Lamphun; around the same time, Wat Pājie was refounded and a school was opened there. Within a few years, Wat Pājie became the central node in monastic education networks in the region, and the senior monks in the BA became increasingly active in sending novices to Dhamma schools in Thailand in particular. Dai-lue monastics could still travel to Thailand to study on their own, but the vitality of individual travel seems to have become less common.[10] Indeed, in part because the senior monks of the BA travel regularly to Thailand to participate in economies of merit, they have many opportunities to develop and foster invitations to study, just as participation in the BAC has opened up opportunities inside China. In other words, once the educational system at Wat Pājie (and latterly at Wat Long Meuang Lue) was established, it quickly became a primary node for Dai-lue monastics for the development and maintenance of transnational networks.

It is intriguing that the Chinese government has been a source both of flexibility and friction in the development of the transnational ties. The most obvious source of friction has been the requirements of crossing borders. Until quite recently, the borders between Sipsongpannā, Myanmar, and Laos have been quite porous. There are many trails through fields and rain forests that enable traders, smugglers, and others to get across, though the roads themselves have clear border crossings—this means that smuggling things across the borders requires a certain amount of labor. In September 2001, I went to Daluo with two junior monks from Wat Pājie and two of the former monks (*khanān*) who worked for the BA. They were on their way to Xiao Mengla, a town across the border in Myanmar, which at that time was filled with markets, casinos, and "dance halls" where Chinese tourists could come and see the exotic life in Myanmar. They were there to buy tiles fabricated in Thailand, which were unavailable in Sipsongpannā, for the roof of the Wannasiri Kuti. I could not go across the border with them because I did not have a visa for Myanmar, so they left me in the care of a senior novice of a *wat* in which one of them had grown up. We drove around on his motor scooter, including along a footpath to the border, where there was a sign marking it, but nothing to prevent us from going from one space to the other. I asked the monk if he ever went over to Myanmar outside of the official crossings. He said, "Sometimes," in a blasé way; it was no big deal.

Despite this, transnational borders remain important even if they are not impenetrable. Over the last fifteen years, the regulations governing monks and novices moving across China's borders have varied. In the late 1990s, it was very difficult to get a passport in China—for monks as well as for ordinary citizens. This meant that for monks to fly to another country, they had to be a part of official delegations. Thus, for example, Khūbā Meuang Jom had a passport, though it was not always in his control Similarly, a junior monk at Wat Pājie who had spent two years in Myanmar on an official educational trip had a passport, though it was only good for the length of his time in Myanmar. He told me that he used the passport in the way it was intended twice: once when he flew from Kunming to Yangon at the start of his time, and once when he returned after the two years. He did return home a few times during the two years, but he did not have the money to pay for a plane ticket, and so he took a bus to the border and walked across without needing to use it. At the time, monks crossing the border merely had to show their identity card (*shenfen zheng*) or their ordination card (*chujia zheng*), or both, to go through the border gates (different monks talked about using different cards). Later (sometime in 2001), I was told, the government required a passport that was limited to the Chinese-Myanmar border. These "China-Myanmar Passports" (*Zhong-Mian huzhao*) were available to Dai-lue living on the border and also to monks, but they were valid for only a few border crossings. Since the early years of the twenty-first century, it has been much easier for monks (and other Chinese citizens) to obtain passports to use at border crossings, but again, so I have been told, they need to have a visa from a Southeast Asian country in order to cross. Even as passports have become easier to obtain, visas have become much harder to obtain. A monk wanting to go to Thailand would need to go from Sipsongpannā to Kunming and apply for a visa at the consulate there. Without a formal invitation from a *wat* in Thailand, this visa is not likely to be forthcoming.[11] These are the frictions that monks encounter as they go from Sipsongpannā to Myanmar or Thailand.

Perhaps more important than constraining the movement of monks back and forth across the border has been the effort to ensure that foreign monks do not stay. When a monk comes to Sipsongpannā from another country, there is often no difficulty in his entering, but foreign monks staying at *wats* in Sipsongpannā for more than a few days are required to register with the local village headman, who is supposed to report it to the government in Jing Hong. This registration is supposed to occur annually, and when I was doing research in 2002, I was told that a few years earlier, there had been an effort to get some of the long-term monastic guests to leave. A similar set of actions was happening in Thailand. In the early 2000s, the Thai government became concerned that there were large numbers of foreign monks staying illegally in the country, and so they began to put pressure on abbots to make sure that the foreign monks all had up-to-date visas (the difficulty of receiving a visa, which was good for a year, depended on one's institutional status). The concern seems to have been not so much to constrict movement, but to restrict long-term immigration.

Yet even as the Chinese government partially restricts the movement of monks back and forth across the border to Southeast Asia, they have also created avenues for the development of networks. I mentioned above the cosponsorship of Dai-lue novices to study in Thailand (see also Hansen 1999). Formal diplomatic relations between China and Thailand in the 1980s and 1990s revolved in some way around Sipsongpannā. A formal trip to China by the late older sister of the late king of Thailand, Princess Galyani Vadhana, included an extensive trip to Sipsongpannā, because she wanted to see the "region of the Thai people" in China (Galyani Vadhana 1986, 1). This trip was initiated by a formal invitation from the Chinese government. The princess' visit in turn helped foster interest in Sipsongpannā as where the Thai people were from, which led in turn to Thai tourists/pilgrims coming to Jing Hong. Finally, the invitation to study in Sri Lanka came not to the abbot of Wat Pājie, but rather to the BAC. In other words, even if the interests of the Sri Lankan monks were specifically to support the Theravāda monks of China, the conduit that they used to foster this was through the institutional structure of the nation-state.

There is one last node of transnational Buddhist networks that needs to be pointed to: international researchers. I, too, have been a node in the development of networks between Southeast Asian Buddhists and the monks of Sipsongpannā. In May 2010, around the time I gave a paper at the Buddhist College of Singapore, which I mentioned in the introduction to this book, I also gave a talk at the Buddhist and Pali College in Singapore about monastic education in Sipsongpannā.[12] There was significant interest on the part of students at the college to contact the BA either in Kunming or in Jing Hong, to foster some sort of donation project. Similarly, as described in chapter 1, the UNESCO project to foster traditional temple arts in Sipsongpannā linked Thai patrons to a *wat* in Sipsongpannā that did not have any previous ties to the village. While these are relatively small linkages, like the networks of the BAC, they open up to the Buddhists of Sipsongpannā resources to which they would not "naturally" have had access.

Conclusion

There is a curious absence in most Chinese scholarship on the Daizu: ongoing connections with Southeast Asian sanghas. Chinese academics whose work touches on the Buddhism of Sipsongpannā, whether in *minzu xue* (nationalities studies), history, or Buddhist studies, are well aware of the fact that Theravāda Buddhism came into Yunnan from Southeast Asia, but discussion of the ongoing interactions described above (i.e., the economies of merit, travels for education, back-and-forth tourism) is absent. The most robust reference that I have been able to locate is in Wang Haitao's *History of Buddhism in Yunnan,* where in a short section on the status of monks after the Cultural Revolution, there is a brief reference to ten monks being sent to Chiang Mai to study at a Buddhist institute there. The role played by visiting monks in the reconstruction of Buddhism is ignored; the emphasis is on the government's role in rebuilding and repairing *wat*s and reliquaries (2001, 509–510). From conversations that I have had with Chinese scholars, whether at Yunnan University, the Yunnan Nationalities University, or the Yunnan Academy of Social Sciences, it is clear that they know about ongoing interactions and movements. And it is also clear that the local government knows about this movement, because at events such as the Wannasiri Kuti dedication, the junior monks and lay officers kept having to go to the Public Security Bureau to report which monks were coming to the celebration from the Shan States. And yet, rendering this knowledge fully legible through scholarly works on the Daizu seems something they are reluctant to do. In part this is because of the degree to which Chinese scholars conceptualize the Dai-lue as part of the Daizu, and so they must talk not just about Sipsongpannā, but Dehong and other parts where these international connections have not been as important. I suspect, though, that it is also due to an ongoing need to conceptualize the Daizu as a *Chinese* ethnic group, whose primary relations are within China. Whether this results from political pressures over what is possible to say institutionally is difficult to say.

Over the course of this chapter, I have sketched the movement of Buddhists around, into, and out of Sipsongpannā. The networks that I have considered have been primarily, but not solely, monastic ones, and they have been primarily focused on Dai-lue monks moving out of Sipsongpannā into China or around Southeast Asia, though we also see monks coming to Sipsongpannā, as at the dedication of the Wannasiri Kuti. The network structures that I have been discussing can be articulated and understood as pertaining to local, national, and transnational frames, but it should also be clear that these frames cannot be fully separated. Images of Khūbā Bunchum come from outside of China and become part of a local economy-of-merit network, and Khūbā Meuang Jom's ability to travel outside of China is a function of his being a member of a national Buddhist organization. The monks of Wat Pājie are central figures in networks at all three levels, but it has to be understood that one of the reasons that Wat Pājie is so central is because of the role that the state's system for governing religion has allotted to the monks who work at and through the Buddhist Association there. Yet, in a sense, this is why the issue of visibility is important to acknowledge. While the state has implemented the structures that condition the movement, and it sponsors or directs some of the movement, there are significant networks that are only partially legible to the state; they are visible to the state from one angle, but not from another. Politics significantly conditions these Buddhist networks, but it is not the only motivator or factor in understanding how Dai-lue monks move, and where and when they do so.

The monks and novices in this chapter have moved in and out of Sipsongpannā along several different spokes: economies of merit, education, and tourism/pilgrimage. However, movement along these spokes has been greased by the building blocks of the ethnoscapes in which the Dai-lue monks of Sipsongpannā are embedded: ethnicity, which follows both national and transnational forms; citizenship and nationality; and Buddhism both as a general form and as Theravāda forms. Each of these provides the monks of

Sipsongpannā with a greater degree of flexibility in their movement, in the way that Ong talks about capital providing overseas Chinese with a "flexible citizenship." The monks of Sipsongpannā do not travel around China or study at Chinese *foxueyuan* without the flexibility that citizenship *and* membership in the Buddhist Association affords them. Yet these flexibilities are not limitless; they are constrained by frictions, in Tsing's terms. Khūbā Meuang Jom's travels around Asia as an agent of the BAC made it more difficult for him to travel outside of China when not under the sponsorship of the BAC, because they controlled his passport, at least through the middle of the decade. And this last point is important, because the network structures that I have described, like the governing structures of chapter 2, are stable, but they change with policy and technology shifts, as well as with the changing concerns of the monks and lay Buddhists of Sipsongpannā as they navigate the changes within Chinese society.

PART 2

**Educating the Monks
of Sipsongpannā**

Learning to Read in Village Temples and Chinese Public Schools

IN SEPTEMBER 1998, I WAS IN MENG HAI County, the western-most part of Sipsongpannā, walking on the road from Meng Ce to Meng Hai, the country seat. Since the 1980s, Meng Ce has been one of the main centers of the return of Buddhism to Sipsongpannā. Many of the monks and novices who studied or worked at Wat Pājie, the central temple in the region, came from this town, including Khūbā Meuang Jom, the abbot of Wat Pājie, and the *sangha-nayok* of Sipsongpannā. Because of this, I had tried to go to Meng Ce to visit some of these temples, but the windy road had caused me to feel queasy and so I decided to get off the bus and walk back to Meng Hai, probably about five miles away at that point. I was in Sipsongpannā doing preliminary research, trying to understand the conditions of Buddhism in the region after the Cultural Revolution. As luck would have it, the road passed through a village and there was a *wat* right along the side of the road. Hoping to find a monk to talk to, I instead encountered ten bald boys running around, throwing a ball. When I walked in, they gathered around, as fascinated by me as I was by them. I asked them whether there were any monks there, and they told me there was one, but he was out. I asked why they weren't in school (it was midday in the middle of the week), and they told me they did not go to school. This surprised me because none of them looked to me to be over the age of eleven, and they were probably younger. I knew that public education was officially compulsory through ninth grade (junior high school; *chuzhongxue*), and was common at least through elementary school. They were a fairly scruffy lot, as nine- and ten-year-olds are wont to be, even if they were bald, and I asked whether I could take their picture. They immediately swept themselves into shape, several of them putting on their outer robes in a somewhat formal way, and arranging themselves without my asking in a highly formal way

FIGURE 4.1 *Pha noy* (junior novice) in village *wat* (monastery/temple), 1998

(see figure 4.1). As I was leaving, their formality left them, and they shouted "hello" and "goodbye" in English after me.

This encounter was fairly unremarkable, but at the same time it was an interesting moment for what lay behind it. Boys like these were and are fairly common around Sipsongpannā, especially outside of the main city of Jing Hong. For example, a group of boys around the same age in a given town decides to ordain. They might have dropped out of elementary school, depending on where they live and the local practices, but often they will still attend school, at least until they finish sixth grade and perhaps beyond. At most temples around the region where novices like this live, it is possible to see a blackboard with Dai-lue letters on it that the boys study, either in the morning or at night. And they learn how to dress themselves, if only to pose for a picture taken by a tourist or ethnographer.

Education at village temples, in Sipsongpannā and beyond, is often understood in fairly stark contrast to state-run public school education. This is sometimes discussed in terms of development and modernization. For example, in "The Proposed World of the School: Thai Villagers' Entry into a Bureaucratic State System" (1991), Charles Keyes discusses these two systems in relation to the emergence of Thailand as a nation-state over the course of the twentieth century. Buddhist monastic education, often an informal process in what Keyes calls *wat* schools, trained young men how to read, thus giving them access to a broader Buddhist culture, and integrating them into local relations, which were in part hierarchically oriented around Buddhist knowledge and attainments. State-sponsored education, on the other hand, incorporated them into the nation-state. It not only directed rural villagers' attention towards Bangkok, but also dampened the enthusiasm of many boys for ordaining as novices and receiving an education within the temples by making public elementary education compulsory (Keyes 1991, 97). While the process that Keyes describes is recognizable as part of the modernization process in Thailand, more than anything else, Keyes suggests, this shift has prepared villagers to accept a subordinate position in the centralized bureaucratic world of the Thai nation-state (1991, 89).

One of the striking points in Keyes' argument is the bifurcation of the two systems of education. State-sponsored education clearly supplants religious education for the majority of Thais. That this is the case is made clear by Keyes' discussion of the transition in Thai education (1898–1930s), when monasteries began to serve as the first public schools. Monks were thus the first public school teachers, not only teaching a variety of secular subjects as well as Dhamma, but also teaching girls as well as boys. Beginning in the 1930s, however, the Thai state began to replace monks with government-trained lay teachers, and built public schools outside of monastery grounds (Keyes 1991, 96). These changes did not take place immediately, and indeed there are still a small number of monasteries that house elementary schools, as well as monastic schools that provide a high school education in Thailand for novices. However, Keyes suggests that the Thai state has found it necessary to try to substitute lay teachers and separate schools in place of monks and *wat*-based ones to "unambiguously orient villagers toward a world shaped by the state" (1991, 101).[1]

Scholars who have examined education in Sipsongpannā have generally taken the same perspective: monastic education and public education are conceptually and institutionally separate, if not indeed in competition with one another (Zhao and Wu 1997; Zheng 1997; Hansen 1999; McCarthy 2000; Shih 2002). The prevailing opinion among scholars who study Sipsongpannā is that most Dai-lue parents and boys are not particularly interested in having their boys educated within the Chinese public schools of Sipsongpannā, and that they would much rather educate their boys within the "traditional" monastic education system.[2] These scholars discuss a variety of reasons for the seeming indifference of Dai-lue parents towards public schools. Mette Hansen reports that parents perceive greater utility in the cultural and religious education that the boys receive in temples (1999, 112). This perception is strengthened, Susan McCarthy suggests, by the deplorable state of the majority of the Chinese schools (2009, 80). Shih Chih-yu points out that many Dai-lue view Chinese education as irrelevant not only to their social life, but to their economic life as well (Shih 2002, 194; see also Zhao and Wu 1997, 319–20).[3] Among these scholars, Shih in particular articulates the distinctions between monastic education in village temples and the Chinese public schools as antagonistic, suggesting that the Commission on Education "sees Buddhism as a threat," and that "schooling is like a fee paid to the state in exchange for undisturbed space for Buddhist practices" (2002, 194).

While the distinction between these systems of education—the Chinese public school and the village temple, are real—in this chapter I want to argue for the necessity of understanding their interactions. I suggested in the introduction that Buddhism needs to be considered from local, national, and transnational perspectives. The education that the boys I encountered in 1998 would have been pursuing was clearly the local form of Buddhism, and there would not seem to be much that is national or transnational about it. However, while those particular novices told me they were not attending public school when I met them, most of them would have attended public school previously. Moreover, I spoke with them not in Dai-lue, but in Chinese, meaning that they had been shaped at least indirectly by Chinese views of the Dai-lue. It is also possible that the abbot of their temple had come from Thailand or the Shan States, bringing a transnational aspect to the Buddhism in the village temple. In both, the national and the transnational do not play an overt role in what happens in the village temple itself, but as will be clear from the material that follows, the education of novices in village *wats* is seldom divorced from these external influences. In other words, I will argue here that to understand how a monk is made in village temples, it is also necessary to be aware of the impact of these external forces, particularly the experience of attending Chinese public schools.

This chapter examines the practices and context of the training of novices in village temples, which should be understood as "apprentice education." Following the discussion of the components of monastic education in the introduction, this chapter will include a discussion of how the different actors (masters/monks, parents, apprentices/novices) understand the point and value of these practices. Apprentice education is in part about content, but it is also about learning how to act in certain ways. Apprentice education produces boys who understand themselves to be members of the community, but do not have a clear sense of themselves as Dai-lue monks. This awareness emerges more clearly in the context of a novice's experience in the public schools. Here they are taught to see themselves as Chinese citizens who possess an inferior civilizational status within the PRC. Because novices are educated in both contexts, these systems need to be considered together, as two systems in tension if not in competition with one another. In particular, the experience of being educated in a public school functions as a "China moment" (Shih 2002) for many novice monks, that is, a realization of themselves both as Chinese citizens, but as minority citizens as well. Even as this demonstrates the impact that national regimes and imaginings have on local forms, it helps foster a subnational identity in which novices understand themselves as Dai-lue, not simply village monks.

Apprentice Education: Learning to Read and Learning to Walk

Apprentice education in Sipsongpannā is the pedagogical action that takes place within village temples. Dai-lue boys learn how to be novice monks, and in so doing also learn how to be Dai-lue men. They are taught by the *dubi long,* the abbot of the temple, the *pha long* (senior novices), and to a lesser extent, the *khanān* and other members of the community, including their parents. The setting is not a formal school, though it is sometimes referred to that way because education happens here in ways that are regular, though not standardized. This type of education is also uncritically referred to as "traditional" (see, e.g., Mendelson 1975, 150–157; Ishii 1986, 25; Zhao and Wu 1997, 319). While this designation might be adequate if we were discussing monastic education in Sipsongpannā prior to the twentieth century, the tradition–modernity binary is less useful when we are talking about pedagogical action in village temples in Sipsongpannā after the Cultural Revolution. The practices themselves may resemble older practices, but the pedagogical context takes place in the contemporary world in reference to projects of modernization. Even rather isolated village temples often have televisions, if not also video compact disc players, donated by the laity (Tan 1995, 185).[4] Thus, rather than concentrating on the condition or state of being of education (i.e., "traditional"), it is more useful to direct our attention to what is the most salient point of this education. Within contemporary Sipsongpannā at least, the relationship between the novice and the monk, which resembles that of an apprentice and a master, is the most important aspect of village monastic education.

In Sipsongpannā, most new novices (*pha noy*) are quite young. They are not yet teenagers, and some are barely old enough to attend elementary school when they "leave home." Consequently, the monk who is the abbot of the temple is often more than simply a teacher. He is largely responsible for their well-being as well as teaching them how to be a monk. Although he does not exactly replace the boys' parents, at the same time, he takes on something like a parental role. As one novice put it to me when describing the difficulties he had when he first began to live in the temple, the monks were there "to take care of me . . . as if they were my own mother and father."

Yet this relationship is not simply about nurturing young boys to manhood. Novices are responsible for learning things, and when they do not do this to the monks' satisfaction, they are punished. Sometimes this entails doing physical labor within the temple, and other times it means corporal punishment, as reported by one eighteen-year-old novice: "When I first became a novice, it was a little difficult. I was very small when I ordained. Every day, the older monks made me do things. If I didn't do them, they would hit me and swear at me. So it was a little hard when I first started."[5] In general, I suspect that parents and relatives approved of this punishment, assuming that they approved of the monk in the first place. Mendelson relates a story of a mother adding to a bruise already inflicted by a monk in Burma (1975, 157). Abuse is certainly a possibility within this context, though all of the monks and novices who commented to me about hardships and punishments noted that they had been punished principally because they had failed to do what the monk or older novice had asked of them. In other words, novices and monks are in a clear hierarchical and pedagogical relationship, in which they both have responsibilities. "A monk's most important responsibilities are to care well for novices and to teach well. A novice's responsibility is to listen to the abbot and study well."[6]

Apprentice education is also about learning how to become a person who knows how to act properly. In January 2002, I observed the novice ordination of ten boys in a small village temple in what is now a suburb of Jing Hong. In most ways that I could see, it was a standard ordination. Taking place over two days, it entailed a festive journey to the temple by the soon-to-be novice and his family, an evening spent in the temple dressed as a little prince and listening to Dai-lue singers sing songs of the Buddha's journey towards enlightenment, and the ordination ceremony itself, during which the boys request ordination, take the ten precepts of a novice, and change into the robes of a monk (see figure 4.2), aided by their preceptors.[7] With the wihān packed with the presiding monks, relatives, and friends of the boys, and Chinese cameramen filming the event, it was an important and festive moment in the lives of these boys.

While watching the ceremony, it was also clear that it was also an early moment in a pedagogical process that would last several years. This became obvious at two different moments on the day of the actual ordination ceremony. The first was before the boys had ordained. I was standing near one of the "money trees" brought by a family member to help support their boy while he was a member of the sangha. The tree was a thick bamboo stick placed in a bucket filled with soap, toothpaste, small towels, and other articles of daily use. Smaller sticks were placed into the central stick and these were decorated with money in small denominations (usually one yuan or less).[8] There was also a card, handwritten in the traditional Dai-lue script, hanging from the tree. Before the ceremony began, I was trying to read what the card said, and one of the lūk kaew walked by. I asked him if he knew what it said. He saw it was written in Dai, and said: "Of course not, I'm not ordained yet. I haven't learned how to read."

The second moment came after the ordination was over. After the newly created pha noy had changed into their robes, the participating monks read out the names and ordination names of each new novice. The paper that this was written on was then tied to the forehead of each boy and they

FIGURE 4.2 *Lūk kaew* beginning to change into *pha noy,* here by taking one arm out of their dress shirts, to make it look like a robe

were presented to the presiding monk. This monk gave a short sermon to the new novices, enjoining them to follow the precepts they had just taken in the process of becoming novices. Among the things that they were not to do was to run around for several days. After the sermon, the monk told the boys to go outside so that a photo might be taken of the group. "But remember to walk carefully," he said to them. By this, the people around me and I had understood the monk to mean that they were to walk in a dignified, quiet fashion, and not to run when they got outside. The boys themselves took the monk very literally, however. As they walked out, they walked very carefully, as if they were on a tightrope, putting one foot immediately in front of the other. Rather than walking slowly and in a dignified manner, they walked out slowly and rather awkwardly, to the great amusement of their assembled relatives and friends.

In reflection, these two moments are similar, indexing the ignorance and newness of these boys. Despite having achieved a new status and position within Dai-lue society, these boys were still unschooled, still raw. They could chant a few *suttas* since they had been practicing them for several months, but they could not read, and they had learned these *suttas* by rote memorization, rather than by reading the words (the meaning is unimportant in this context). Unlike the boys I encountered in 1998, they could not dress themselves as monks (in the ordination ceremony itself, it was the monks who dressed them). And although they may have been inclined to pay attention to the commands of senior monks, they did not really understand what these commands might mean. Not only could they not read, they barely knew how to walk as novices should. Indeed, learning to walk and learning to read are what novices are meant to learn during apprentice education. They are transformed from being "raw" (*dip*) to being "cooked" (*bao dip*). As should be clear, moreover, this process is not simply a cognitive one, but a physical process of learning as well.

What the boys learn during the process and how they learn it relies heavily on the relationship between the monk and the novice, that is, the master and the apprentice. Pedagogically, this relationship is what we would expect of master–apprentice relationships. Apprentice monastic education is a nonsystematized mode of reproduction and entails a pedagogy of modeling. Eugene Cooper commented about wood-carver apprentices in Hong Kong in the late 1970s, "Seldom, if ever, was the apprentice systematically instructed. . . . He learned by observation and imitation, learning to do by doing" (1980, 24). This is how the training of novices in village temples of Sipsongpannā works as well.[9] Like the wood-carvers, novices learn the content of their training by observing the monk and repeating after him. In many temples throughout Sipsongpannā, one can see a blackboard in a *sāla* (pavilion) outside of the *wihān*. There the monk points to a letter and reads it, saying, for example, "*ga*" for one specific vowel/consonant combination. The novices repeat, over and over again, the drilling continuing to the point where the boys had the letters firmly placed in their memories.[10] The same practices are used with writing the forty-four consonants and more than thirty vowels of the Dai-lue alphabet. Novices write letters (and later words) over and over until they have them down to the abbot's satisfaction.[11]

Once the novices get beyond this basic skill in reading and writing the Dai-lue alphabet, what most marks Buddhist knowledge within apprentice education is its lack of standardization. By this I do not mean that there is no coherence to what they learn. It is simply that there are no standards imposed by a central sangha hierarchy, a king, or a national government. Instead, the possibilities for novices' learning are conditioned by their own ambition, the knowledge of their own (and nearby) monks, and regional patterns in both textual and ritual knowledge (Blackburn 2001, 45). For example, in addition to learning the alphabet, novices are supposed to "pay respect to the Buddha" (*naptheu pha-cao*) twice a day. This entails prostrating oneself before a Buddha image and chanting a variety of texts which the novices learn, again, largely through the pedagogy of modeling (this process begins when they are not yet ordained, but trying to learn the appropriate chants for their ordination).[12] There are certain things that almost all renunciants seem to learn, in particular the thirty-eight blessings of the *Mangala Sutta*. Beyond this, however, there is a wide variation in contemporary Sipsongpannā. For example, temples in the Jing Hong region seemed to use a relatively small liturgy, following what is used at Wat Pājie. At Wat Pājie, only two texts are chanted during days that are not part of the full or new moon.[13] On the other hand, novices from both Meng Long (in the southern part of Sipsongpannā near the border with Myanmar) and Meng Ce (in the northwest of the region) both reported having had to learn significantly larger collections of texts than they regularly performed because their abbots told them it was important. There was, in other words, a variety of teaching standards (if not quite distinct lineages) in Sipsongpannā, and a lack standardization in Buddhist knowledge similar to the lack of standard form of the Dai-lue language (Zhao and Wu 1997, 269). Just as there has never been a standard form of the written and spoken language enforced by a central authority, there has never been a standard version of being a Dai-lue novice or monk.

In addition to differences in regional lineages, there are several other factors that determine the type of experiences that a novice might have as an apprentice monk. Among the two most important are the average age of the monks in a collection of villages, and the presence of foreign monks. Age is important pedagogically for the obvious reason that older monks tend to know more, but in Sipsongpannā this is not quite the case as a result of recent history. In 2001–2002, village abbots tended to fall into three different groups: recent monks under the age of twenty-five, monks in their thirties, and monks over the age of sixty. Because status in Theravāda societies is often in part about the time one has spent in robes, it would be reasonable to assume that the last group had the most prestige. However, these older monks have often been men who either disrobed or never ordained as a result of the Cultural Revolution. Many of them ordained after their families were grown up and out of the home. While they are not without prestige, the group of monks presumed to have the most knowledge is actually the group in the middle. These are men who were usually ordained as novices in the early years of the return of Buddhism after the Cultural Revolution. Not only have many of them therefore been novices and monks for between twenty and thirty years, but they have also been more likely to study abroad. Regions such as Meng Long, Meng Kham, and Meng Ce, which have more of these men, have been more likely to have larger numbers of novices.

Foreign monks have also impacted the lack of standardization within apprentice education. During the 1980s and early 1990s, quite a few monks from Thailand and the Shan States came to Sipsongpannā and remained as abbots or preceptors for a year or two, sometimes longer. As discussed in chapter 1, these monks came to Sipsongpannā for a variety of reasons: sometimes they were invited by villages, sometimes they were Dai-lue who had relatives they were visiting, and sometimes they were simply traveling as tourists and decided to remain. The presence of these monks was not the result of a centralized effort to recruit, and many passed under the radar of the local government in Jing Hong. I have been told that cadres knew in theory about the foreign monks but were not aware of how many or where they were. Indeed, these foreign monks were tolerated particularly in the 1980s because of the recognition that human capital was needed to rebuild the sangha. Most I either talked to or heard about stayed for a few years (sometimes "urged" to leave by the local government; see Hansen 1999, 111n3), and then returned to their native countries, though a few disrobed and remained in the village in which they had lived as a monk. The effect of these foreign monks has been varied. Those who were from Thailand brought with them the standardized knowledge of the Thai *nak-tham* course (i.e., the three-year training in Buddhist knowledge), while those from the Shan States often brought with them knowledge that was not very different from what was present already. At the same time, they also brought with them living proof of a wider Buddhist world. While foreign monks have been important in the reconstruction of post-Mao Buddhism in Sipsongpannā, because their numbers were not tracked in any public way, it is difficult to fully gauge their impact on the Buddhism in the region.

The second major component of apprentice education is less about Buddhist knowledge and more about the embodied practice of learning how to walk and act in a way that is deemed proper comportment for a monk. Learning how to walk focuses on how a monk or novice is supposed to act and relate to people, whether monastic or lay, stranger or kin, in public or private. For example, the new novices walking out of the *wihān* were trying to act as the presiding monk told them monks should act. This learning extends far beyond that first day as a novice, however. Indeed, for many years—perhaps for as long as a man is in robes—he must consider what it means to walk like a monk. This extends to the most mundane of activities: is it appropriate for a novice to ride a bicycle? Is it appropriate for a monk? Perhaps the first instinct that scholars have had in trying to answer that question is to go to the Vinaya, the disciplinary codes of Buddhism. This is certainly reasonable, since one of the main things the Vinaya codes do is to try to regulate the bodies of monastics. Since novices only take ten precepts (and not the full 227 that Theravāda monks are supposed to follow), however, the Vinaya is not always directly relevant, and even with those who have undergone the *upasampadā,* the higher ordination, the Vinaya is only a part of the dynamic in which appropriate monastic behavior is determined.[14]

For example, we can examine a straightforward rule about shaving the head. According to one modern commentary on the Vinaya by the early twentieth-century Thai *sangha-rāja,* Prince Wachirayān, "The hair of the head should not be allowed to grow for longer than two months, or more than two inches in length" (Wachirayān 1973, 2:4; Thanissaro 2001, 10). Clearly, two months and two inches provides for a great deal of variety. In

Sipsongpannā, and in Thailand, the general practice seems to be for renunciants to shave their heads once a month (usually the day before the full moon),
though there are some traditions in the Shan States and the rest of Myanmar
in which monks are to shave their heads every two weeks. While it may seem
to be a minor matter whether monks and novices shave their heads every
other week or once a month, the appearance of a monk matters. Thanissaro
Bhikkhu notes that a monk who does not follow the custom of when to shave
his head "tends to stand out from his fellows" (2001, 6). How he interacts in
public is in part a consequence of how he looks and how this appearance is
perceived by the laity that supports him. For example, Seneviratne reports
that a number of ordained university students in Sri Lanka were mocked by
some laity for keeping their hair a little bit longer and well groomed, calling
this a "*samenera* cut" ("novice cut"; see Seneviratne 1999, 204). The criticism
arose not so much because of the length of the hair itself, but because the
way they kept their hair was indicative of the way these novices seemed (in
Seneviratne's reading) to be too attached to the goods of modern society.
Rather than being tied to a village temple and working for the good of the
people, these young men sporting snazzy haircuts were seen as selfish, modern
monks. The point here is not so much that there is any meaning intrinsic to
when shaving takes place, but that there are local traditions, which are extra-
textual, that are important in determining when acts should take place.

Monks smoking, another noncanonical issue, reveals that standards
of comportment are variable, even when "timeless" materials such as the
Vinaya act as an anchor for these standards. In Thailand for the last fifteen
years, members of the sangha have been encouraged to give up smoking ciga-
rettes, though as much as one-third of Thai monks smoke, and smoking-related
illnesses are the leading cause of death among monks. There have been some
efforts to enlist monks into the antismoking ranks, ostensibly on the grounds
that since smoking is addictive it is therefore "against core Buddhist values."
Discouraging monks from smoking and enlisting them in antismoking efforts
is reasonable in Thailand from the perspective of the financial burden that
smoking-related illnesses produce and also the efficiency of effecting a policy
change. However, neither of these are the reasons that people I have talked to
support a ban on monks smoking. When I have asked people in northern
Thailand (some monks, some lay) what they thought of monks smoking, the
most common response was that they felt it was "not attractive." People did
not seem to be interested in the health issues per se; rather it was the aesthetics
of a monk, that is, his appearance in public and his demeanor, which was
important. With both the length of hair and smoking, the point is that the
public appearance of a monk is very important.

That the public appearance of monks is important has consequences
for the way that we think of discipline. Monks are supposed to act and appear

in certain ways in public. They are generally not supposed to run, for example, because it is deemed unseemly.[15] Much of what is deemed seemly, or not, is determined not so much outside of the Vinaya, but in conversation with it. Rupert Gethin has suggested that the Vinaya is deeply aware of the importance of how monks are perceived by the wider community (1998, 92–94). Monks are supposed to be dignified, but what makes a monk seem dignified varies across time and space. Relatively recently it has been determined by a number of people in Thailand that the smoking monk does not look attractive in public, which means in part that he does not look dignified. It is significant, however, that not all people believe this is the case.[16] Indeed, in Sipsongpannā, I have never heard laypeople criticize monks for smoking. In a sense, the issue of monks smoking is particularly interesting because we can begin to see the progress of change with regard to the aesthetics of being a monk. This also means that the disciplining process is actually a pedagogical one. Monks and novices need to be taught what is appropriate behavior.

Monks teach novices how to be proper novices through what Jeffrey Samuels has called "action-oriented pedagogy" (2004). Samuels argues that novices and young monks in Sri Lanka learn how to be proper renunciants not through the memorization of texts, but rather by doing things. Content (such as the Dai-lue letters) is important in the long run, but acquiring a monastic identity requires the regular performance of a variety of tasks, such as worshipping the Buddha or cleaning the temple. Significantly, it is not simply the doing of these actions but the attitude that is encouraged by the community during their performance. As one novice told him, "It was not what we studied. It was the way we were supposed to act in the temples, such as standing up when the teacher came in, cleaning the temple, and talking properly to our teacher" (Samuels 2004, 964). Samuels also quite rightly stresses the communal nature of action-oriented pedagogy. More than the instructions of a teacher, it is the atmosphere created by both the teacher and the other student-novices that fosters a particular monastic ethos within new novices.[17]

This form of action-oriented pedagogy in apprentice education does not always produce universally respected monks and novices. We can see this when we think of the labor done in the temples throughout Sipsongpannā. In the village temples of Sipsongpannā, there is a lot of work to be done. They need to be continually swept, buildings need to be repaired, weeding needs to be done, food needs to be cooked, and sometimes animals need to be cared for. Villagers who come to give their help at the temple to gain merit (bun) do some of this work. Much of it—indeed most of it—is done by the novices of the temple, however. Most of the novices do not talk about this labor as a pedagogical act, as Samuels' informants explicitly do. Instead, it is something they do because the abbot told them to do it. However, I would argue that this labor becomes a pedagogical act in two ways. Negatively, labor is often the

punishment for not adequately completing tasks aimed at acquiring information, such as learning the Dai-lue alphabet. Positively, labor is an important
part of the pedagogy of modeling taking place at temples. Novices learn standards for what temples look like from the abbot, and also how monks act.
When an abbot is lazy, novices are more likely to be lazy; conversely, if his
notion of discipline is strong and he is strict in the maintenance of the temple
and in his personal habits, then his standards will be reflected in the behavior
of the novices as well.[18]

While the abbot is the most important educator, the surrounding
laity also have an important role to play. The wider community determines
and maintains local monastic aesthetics. They reinforce what is deemed to be
appropriate behavior, often by talking about a particular behavior as "unattractive."[19] In a sense, the laity are the final arbiters of what kinds of behavior
are appropriate for monks. This is especially the case in apprentice education
where the laity and monks live in close proximity. Parents and other relatives
(in particular, grandmothers) do not hesitate to criticize their sons and grand-
sons if they are acting out of line, regardless of whether they are novices. But
they also enforce their standards in other ways. Whereas a layperson, even the
pu cān or other khanān, will rarely directly criticize abbots of temples, indirect criticism and gossip are not uncommon if an abbot is not supported for
some reason. The laity also assert indirect control over the support they give
the temple. If the abbot would like to build a new wihān, or even just repair
the roof, he has to marshal support for these relatively expensive and labor-
intensive building projects. Although families of a village will rarely withhold
the alms of food from a temple, there are many more ways that they support a
temple that give them opportunities to express their pleasure, or displeasure,
with the way an abbot acts.

The performative aspects of being a novice mean that there is significant variety within the temples of Sipsongpannā in terms of disciplinary standards, educational goals, and aesthetic presentation.[20] For example, there was
one temple I visited regularly where the abbot had significant control over the
behavior of the novices in the wat. The temple grounds were always properly
weeded by both the monk and the novices, and the temple itself owned a large
tract of land with a grove of rubber trees. The novices harvested the sap to help
defray the costs of maintaining the temple. The villagers only had good things
to say about their abbot (who had had an extensive education by Dai-lue standards), and when it came time to rebuild the roof of the ordination hall (bosot),
they all happily contributed (see figure 1.1). On the other hand, another temple
I visited regularly did not have the same kind of support from its villagers. It
was rather run down, and the bosot in particular seemed on the verge of col-
lapse. The villagers never directly criticized the abbot to me, but they also did
not do a lot to support the temple. In fact, unlike the first temple, this second

temple did not seem to be a center of the community. The point is not that there is a direct correlation between temple maintenance and lay support; rather, it is that villages maintain the temples that they want, and if the monk acts in ways they find most important, they are happy. The village temple outside of Jing Hong, which had the ordination I discussed at the beginning of this section, is a good example of this. The abbot of this temple was a pleasant man, but seemed lazy to me. He slept late and drank a little bit more than a monk should.[21] However, he was doing a decent job teaching the novices the Dai-lue alphabet, which was what the parents I talked to wanted for their sons. Their approval of his outcomes (if not his general attitude) was reflected in their support (in cash and labor) of several building projects at the temple (i.e., they paved the grounds of the temple and rebuilt the roof on the *wihān*).

Educating monks and novices through action-oriented pedagogical practices has certain consequences for our understanding of what kind of student is produced within apprentice education. In general, the novices produced in village temples are members of the community. The novices remain in regular (if not constant) contact with their family and the broader village community, and this community has a hand in policing how the boys are to act. The village community generally does not have direct control over how these novices are trained, or the way that they learn to walk, but it does have indirect input. Yet novices produced in apprentice education in Sipsongpannā do not seem to have a broader Dai-lue or Buddhist identity. They do not see themselves as Dai-lue so much as members of their village (e.g., they are not Dai-lue monks but monks of Wat Bān Yāy), and their roles and responsibilities are not so much to the Dai-lue people as they are to their fellow villagers. This is not to say that apprentice education is in contradiction with a broader Buddhist or Dai-lue identity. The importance of the Dai-lue letters could be the impetus for producing a regional identity within pedagogical practices; the presence of foreign monks could help produce a pan-Theravāda identity (Keyes 1992, 26), but they are not sufficient by themselves to produce this regional identity. The lack of standardization within the Dai-lue letters (i.e., regional differences among vowel uses) undermines its power as a unifying symbol, and foreign monks are simply not widespread enough to significantly foster a transnational identity. Thus, when we look at apprentice education alone, before considering the influence of the Chinese public schools, we see the production of local monks, in whom a broader Dai-lue identity remains a potential rather than a reality.

Producing the Daizu: Novices in Temples and in Chinese Public Schools

It is necessary that we not examine apprentice education in isolation. I argued in the introduction for the necessity of examining Buddhism at multiple levels. I noted above (as well as in previous chapters) how "transnational monks" have served a central, though only partially visible, role in the reconstitution of the Sangha in Sipsongpannā. In a sense, this connection is an obvious one, because the monks from Thailand and the Shan States were often from Lue communities in their respective countries, and so despite being "transnational," they were also in some sense "local." National dynamics in China have a more direct impact on apprentice education because of links to public schools. And yet it makes sense to discuss these systems separately: they are ideologically distinct, and viewed from the angle of the Chinese government, they are (implicitly at least) in competition with one another. Indeed, scholars have widely reported that cadres and Chinese scholars are likely to see apprentice education as an impediment to Dai-lue boys' participation in the public schools in Sipsongpannā (Hansen 1999, 108; Shih 2002, 194; McCarthy 2009, 78). However, while there does seem to be some evidence pointing to monastic education reducing participation in public schools of Dai-lue boys (McCarthy 2009, 78), government officials are more likely than Dai-lue stakeholders in the educational system to see these systems as being in conflict with one another.

Novices have been attending public schools in Sipsongpannā since the mid-1980s. Their numbers fluctuate, but they are far more common in the lower grades than they are in middle school (i.e., secondary education). The first Dai-lue novice graduated from the Nationality Middle School (Minzu Zhongxue or MinZhong) in 1993, the second best high school in the autonomous prefecture. He told me that he had ordained when he was in elementary school; after graduation, he attended the Nationalities Institute in Kunming (Minzu Xueyuan), along with another monk. They both disrobed after graduating from college. Since then, a handful of novices and monks have attended either three- or four-year colleges in Kunming, usually having graduated from one of the higher-ranking high schools such as MinZhong. Although there were nine novices at MinZhong during my 2001–2002 fieldwork, even more novices have attended some of the vocational middle schools in Sipsongpannā.

For the most part, novices who attend the public schools of Sipsongpannā are like other Dai-lue students, with a few important exceptions. In elementary school, novices live at the temples (which are usually quite close to their homes), and walk or ride their bicycles to school every day. Most boys who attend junior high school continue to live in their home temple, though some board, depending on how far away the school is. Most of those who attend high school, board at school. In what would seem to be an acknowledgment of their status as novices, they generally do not share dorm rooms with lay students. For example, the nine novices studying at MinZhong in 2002 shared two dorm rooms. Lay students generally had at least eight students per room, but the novices got to have more space. Despite this separate space, however, the students did not make this a particularly Buddhist place.

They told me that they did not have any particular Buddhist items in their room. There were no Buddha images or Thai pictures of either Jātaka stories (previous lives of the Buddha) or the Buddha's life, which are common in temples throughout Sipsongpannā. This lack of Buddhist paraphernalia indicates that many of the students who board (particularly at the level of upper middle school) lead a rather minimal religious life. These novices are often too busy with schoolwork to return to their home village temples regularly, and they do not seem to seek out a local temple to serve as a replacement. This extends to the other things they learn in the temples. One novice I met from MinZhong had to think for a few moments before he could remember how to write his name using Dai-lue script. He somewhat sheepishly told me that he had not had much chance to practice writing in Dai-lue. Of course, there are exceptions to this situation. In May 2002, a novice who was a senior at MinZhong underwent the *upasampadā,* which requires far more knowledge of Dai-lue than barely being able to write one's name.

Students at all levels told me that they did not feel that being novices had particularly affected their experiences in the Chinese public school. Despite continuing to shave their heads and wearing robes instead of school uniforms, they take all the same classes, including physical education, and they felt as though the teachers treated them the same as they treated nonordained students. That does not mean that they all got along with their teachers; rather, it is that they did not perceive the problems they had with their teachers as a function of their being novices. For the most part, they did not receive special dispensations because they were novices (with the possible exception of the dormitory space), and were expected to do all their homework. That these boys essentially study two different courses at the same time (the Chinese public school course as well as the apprentice education course) makes it much harder for them to achieve academically in both, though some do. Indeed, the novice who took the *upasampadā* at Wat Pājie went to Kunming to study at a technical college after graduation from MinZhong, but he was already over the age of twenty when he graduated from high school (or else he would not have been able to take the higher ordination). Both his ordination and his postsecondary education were supported by the abbot of Wat Pājie.

This support suggests that at an official level, the monks of the region have been supportive of Dai-lue novices remaining in the public schools. Since at least the late 1990s, the Buddhist Association has actively encouraged novices to study in the public schools, as well as in temples. The number of novices in public schools remains somewhat elusive, though in 2007 the BA office reported to me that two-thirds of the Dai-lue novices around the region were also attending public schools. In 2001–2002, many of the monks who worked and taught at Wat Pājie were also the abbots of temples around the region. They told me that the novices at their temples (who were not studying at Wat Pājie) were all still studying in public school (this was particularly the case with those still in elementary school). On one level, this support might be read as a need for the monks to pay public lip service to the demands of the local government. The local government wants novices in school, and so the monks pay attention to that to avoid trouble. Indeed, McCarthy has reported that some school districts have sought to make abbots responsible for the continued attendance of their novices (2009, 79). Although this is certainly possible, many of the abbots were generally also in support of novices studying in the public schools. While some were principally concerned with the "moral and spiritual development" of the boys (2009, 79), I found that most abbots were also concerned with mundane success as well. When they did have students who had done well enough to test into the upper middle school, they were happy to inform me of it.

This does not mean their support was without qualification. Abbots tended to complain that the public school schedule precluded boys from giving enough time or energy to their studies of Buddhism or Dai-lue culture (e.g., they had to study the Dai-lue script at night). This means that the novices face significant burdens in their studies. It takes them longer to learn how to read Dai-lue, thereby limiting what can be passed on, but it also makes it more likely that they will not be successful in completing either of their studies. Almost half of the novices studying at the Dhamma school at Wat Pājie told me that they dropped out of public school because their scores on entrance exams were not sufficient for them to matriculate to either lower or upper middle school. They might have scored too low to continue anyway, but working on two different curricula surely did not help. Nonetheless, most of the abbots that I interviewed also seemed resigned to the fact that the novices would be attending public school, and so they could only concentrate on the religious life of the boys in the early morning and late afternoons or evenings.[22]

This ambivalence seems to be shared by the Chinese teachers and administrators. On the one hand, as noted above, Chinese officials are widely reported as viewing the education of novices in village temples as an impediment to Dai-lue boys receiving what they perceive as a proper education. On the other hand, many actually working in the school systems have at times made an effort to accommodate novices, though this was often about accommodating Dai-lue culture at least as much as it was about novices themselves. A vice-principal at a technical high school outside of Jing Hong told me that novices were often allowed to miss school to participate in specific cultural events in their villages (McCarthy 2009, 78–79), but she also said that other students were allowed to attend as well. There have also been some efforts in Sipsongpannā to teach a bilingual curriculum, particularly at the elementary school level, though these have been sporadic and focused on the new Dai script, which is universally reviled by monks and most Dai-lue in Sipsong-panná. In other words, schools have occasionally accommodated the needs of novices, but usually in terms that make sense to the state and not geared towards the needs or desires of the students. Teachers, however, seemed to be more supportive of the novices in their classrooms. Those whom I interviewed told me that they felt as though they did not treat the novices any differently from lay Dai-lue students. They might have been embarrassed to say that they were much harsher towards novices than other students, but I never heard teachers criticize the religious life of their students—in fact, quite the opposite. Public school teachers (Han, Dai, and other nationalities) told me that they generally liked having novices in their classes because they were well behaved and worked much harder than their lay counterparts. Like the abbots, they viewed the double curriculum that the novices studied as an unfortunate situation, but these teachers were positive about the novices themselves.

The last major stakeholders in the life of novices in public schools are the families of the novices, and like the abbots and school administrators, parents also seem ambivalent about their sons' educational experiences and opportunities. As noted at the start of the chapter, Hansen, McCarthy, and Shih all mention the disinterest exhibited by Dai-lue parents towards Chinese public education. In particular, this is because the parents do not see public education as relevant for the economic or social lives of their children. While I have certainly met parents who seemed to be very happy about their son's ordination, I also met quite a number who expressed anxiety over how the ordination would affect their child's performance in the public schools. Part of this is probably an urban/rural divide: parents of novices near Jing Hong, where the public schools are of a higher quality than most of the schools throughout the region, are more likely to support their ordained sons continuing in the public schools. Moreover, while many boys living near Jing Hong in particular will become farmers like their parents, they also have many more opportunities to find jobs beyond agricultural than do their coethnics who live in more isolated regions. The question of a boy's ordination is thus rather complicated for these parents, because the possibility that ordination will hinder their future opportunities has greater consequences than it does for their rural peers. The families of the novices near Jing Hong thus hope that apprentice education and the public schools are not in competition with one another. As one father of a new *pha noy* put it to me: "We were very happy when [our son] ordained. If he also goes to junior high school and high school, we will be very happy with that as well."[23]

I see this ambivalence in terms of a desire to see their sons succeed, and there are in fact significant structural obstacles to this. In addition to low test scores, exacerbated by the need to study two curricula, the other major reason novices quit schools was that attendance in the public schools can be a major financial burden to the families of novices. While public education is required in Sipsongpannā, it is not free, and after elementary school, it can become quite expensive. In addition to tuition, students (and their families) were often responsible for a myriad of fees (books, water, electricity, etc.), which could push the costs of going to school up to as much as 1,000 yuan per semester (about $120) for junior high, and even higher for high schools. I was told by a Dai teacher that there is some public assistance, but it goes to the most impoverished villages and most Dai-lue villages are comparatively well off. Both financial and testing reasons refute the common impression among educational cadres that the reason novices quit school is because they are lazy and their parents do not make them work hard.[24] In fact, we might say that these boys did not quit school so much as they were kicked out by the schools. For some monks, then, the financial and testing burdens that cause novices to leave the public schools are potential "China moments." That is, they are moments when a minority subject must comply with a demand of the Chinese state (in this case, in the guise of the school), and in so doing, is confronted with being a minority (Shih 2002).

There is another type of "China moment" that occurs within the public schools for Dai-lue students—novices and lay alike. While being a novice may not have affected the way that the boys experienced being public school students, I would argue that the reverse is not the case. In fact, remaining in schools seems to affect significantly how novices view being Dai-lue and being a novice. Part of this has to do with the ideology that these students regularly receive at school, or what Mette Hansen nicely calls their "lessons in being Chinese" (1999). The principal lesson that all Dai-lue learn in the public schools is that they are backward (*luohou*). It is true that the Daizu are not portrayed as being as backward as other Sipsongpannā minority groups, such as the Hani or the Jinuo, both because the Dai-lue have a traditional script, which is an important marker of civilizational status, and because they practice a religion that receives official recognition and is not something classified as superstition, such as spirit worship. Nonetheless, in comparison with Han Chinese, for example, both textbooks and teachers reinforce the notion that the Dai-lue are still somewhat primitive. While it can be hard to quantify the effects that these "lessons" have on students, Hansen has argued that there is a clear difference between the attitudes of first-year junior high school students and senior high school girls. She found that the younger girls had far more positive views of Dai-lue boys, and that they generally felt it was important that a future husband will have lived for some time as a novice or monk. Many of the older girls, on the other hand, were quite dismissive of boys who had been novices as potential mates. This was because they felt that most of these boys would not be good students. It was not that they felt that ordination was a bad thing, but they also did not want a boyfriend or future husband who had no future prospects. They had largely been incorporated into the unequal ideology of the Chinese state (Hansen 1999, 147–149). I found a similar shift in attitude with regard to novices who were in high school. They do not denigrate their experience as novices, but they tend to downgrade its importance with regard to other educational experiences.

It is also possible to discern some of the longer-term challenges these attitudes pose to the Sangha of Sipsongpannā. I mentioned above that parents with whom I spoke in the Jing Hong area expressed some ambivalence about their sons' ordinations. This concern was largely over whether apprentice education would hinder a boy's public school education. It is interesting to note that this was a concern shared by both some *khanān* and novices who were in senior high school. The *khanān* were men who were affiliated with Wat Pājie, but now had jobs in Jing Hong (one was an editor for the local newspaper and the other worked for an official cultural organization). Neither of them had gone beyond elementary school. I asked these men and *pha long* about what they hoped for their own children (one of the *khanān* I asked had a son; the other *khanān* and the novices obviously did not), and whether they wanted them to ordain. The *khanān* and the students all said that they wanted their (real or hypothetical) sons to ordain, but only for a short time. They thought it important that they learn the Dai-lue language, but that it was more important for them to concentrate on Chinese and English. In other words, they did not want their offspring to repeat their own experience.

There is another consequence to these lessons in being Chinese, however, beyond the question of inequality. What students have learned is not just the fact that they have a lower civilizational status than the Han; they have also learned that they are Daizu. Prior to these lessons, they would obviously know that they are Dai-lue, but it is only when they are confronted with Chinese (a language they may only partially know) and lessons about how the Daizu are a minority group within China that they start to learn what it means to be Dai, and not simply members of their own community. We see this, for example, in the matter of Daizu history. Very few Dai-lue students know much of their history. Most of the novices I talked to said that they wanted to know more about Dai-lue history, but that it was something that was really only known by elderly people. Even so, there were several who did know something of Dai-lue history. When I asked one where he learned this history, he pulled out a Chinese-language textbook about the peoples of China and showed me the five-page section he had studied on Dai-lue history (or rather Daizu history). What he knew of being Dai came from his knowledge of also being Chinese. Indeed, what we might suggest is that the lesson in being Chinese that Dai-lue students learn is simply that they are Daizu.

Conclusion

In the early 1990s, monks around the region told me that when novices first started attending the Chinese public schools in more significant numbers, older Dai-lue villagers were resistant to them attending for two different reasons. The first was that they felt as though the novices did not really need to know the information they would learn in the public schools. The novices came from farming families, and what they learned in the temples—about how to read and be a proper Dai-lue man—was deemed sufficient. The second was more of a culture and gender issue. These older villagers were especially concerned about Dai-lue novices attending secondary schools, which primarily have two-story buildings. The problem is that it would be possible that girls would be seated over the heads of novices (i.e., girls in a second-story classroom would be literally over the heads of novices in a first-story classroom). While the Dai-lue are not as height/status conscious as some other Tai societies, such as Thailand, there is still a clear hierarchy that links height and status, and higher parts of the body as more valuable than lower parts. To have a laywoman "standing" over the head of a novice was troubling for many Dai-lue villagers. A *khanān* told me that over time, even these older villagers came to see that this was not a significant problem, and that it was important to have Dai-lue boys gain an education that was valuable outside of the village context. This vignette speaks to the implicit clash of the systems of education that Dai-lue boys face, but it also highlights the degree to which Dai-lue society has accommodated its changed circumstances, and the willingness of people to experience and support new forms of education.

In this chapter, I have situated the basic education of novices in the formation of the Dai-lue community. Pedagogical practices in village temples, that is, apprentice education, creates boys who are embedded in their local communities, with skills and knowledge that are salient for their local communities, though not the sangha as a whole. Their knowledge is not oriented to their *cheua kheua,* their ethnic group, or to the *meuang,* the imagination of the polity. Rather, they are oriented towards the needs of one in belonging to the village. At the same time, most of these boys also spend time in the public schools, which are generally run in the Chinese language. The lessons learned in these schools are directed at teaching the students about the place of the *minzu* (the nationalities of China) in the civilizational hierarchy of the nation. Dai-lue children learn where they are situated within the Chinese imagination as a civilized but not very modern group. Novices who study in middle schools generally study with other children from around the autonomous region, and this fosters the development of a sense of themselves as Dai, not just as residents of Meng Hai, Meng Long, or Meng Ce. The overall experience of studying in the public schools, then, is a "China moment." The public schools are places where boys who have learned in village temples that they are members of village communities become faced with a discourse of China. This interaction with "China" forces them to understand themselves not just as Chinese, but also as Daizu.

Apprentice education is very much the way of passing down local forms of Buddhism, a Buddhism that has no systematic standards, but is relatively consistent across the region. Most of the boys who experience this education, like those I described at the beginning of the chapter, will ordain for a while and then become farmers like their parents. Yet this is no timeless village life; just as older Dai-lue came to accept the value of middle school, despite the danger of boys sitting below girls, this local Buddhism has been affected by national and transnational forces. Transnational monks have helped preserve this local form, and national visions of China have created a wider vision of what novices should be. In this context, it is important to understand how Chinese power works in this context. The Dai-lue are Chinese citizens, and Chinese forms of governance are widespread throughout the region. Dai-lue culture is "emphatically marked" by this state power, but that power does not always operate actively on Dai-lue Buddhism.

The Fragility of Autonomy

Curricular Education at Dhamma Schools

ONE DAY EARLY IN AUGUST 2001, I WAS working in the computer room of the Dhamma school (*hongheyn pha-pariyatti-tham*) at Wat Pājie with Ai Kham. We were working on getting the temple's Macintosh computers to print on the Lexmark printer that they had bought in China. At the time, pre-iPod and iPhone, Apple products were extremely uncommon in China, and Wat Pājie was in fact using them only because there was a font that had been developed in the Shan States that was close to "classical" Dai-lue script, but it was only for Macintosh computers. The senior monks and *khanān* of the sangha were working on the Dai-Chinese dictionary that used the old Dai script, and not the new Dai script that had been devised at the Yunnan Nationalities Institute in the decade before the Cultural Revolution (as described in chapter 2). And so we were trying to harmonize the printer and the computers so that they could print out the draft of the dictionary. At the time, Ai Kham was the Chinese-language teacher at the Dhamma school. He was (and is) Dai-lue, and had been a novice for several years during and after middle school. He had attended a three-year technical institute in Kunming, and during part of this time, he was still in robes. It was on the strength of this education that he was teaching Chinese to the monastic students at the Dhamma school at Wat Pājie. In the mid-2000s, he would again ordain, this time as a monk to travel to Sri Lanka to study (I discussed his reliquary dedication in chapter 3), but at the time of our walk, the invitation to study in Sri Lanka had not been extended; Kham was a lay Buddhist with a girlfriend and was happily ensconced as both teacher and computer guy at Wat Pājie.

On this particular day, though, he was not happy, and not just because of our inability to get the computer to print. He was upset about the local government, which he said was going to enforce some of the rules regarding students. Apparently, boys were not supposed to ordain until after they had finished elementary school, and they were not supposed to attend the Dhamma school without first having finished junior high school (*chuzhongxue*). Of the forty or so novices who were studying at Wat Pājie in 2002, at the time only a handful would have been able to fulfill both of these requirements. I asked Ai Kham why this change was coming, and he told me that it was because the government did not particularly like the school, or the sangha more broadly. He told me it did not actively oppress the monks, but it did try to hinder the projects at the school. When I asked when they would start to enforce the rules, his answers became vague, both as to where the decision was coming from and when it would happen.

Ai Kham's annoyance and anxiety was in sharp contrast to the actual presence of the local government at Wat Pājie. While the monks were regularly in conversation with certain members of the local government and security bureau, only on a handful of occasions did anyone from the government come to the temple or school. One of these occasions was the end of term exams in October 2001, when the students of Wat Pājie had to take the exams for the first year of their Dhamma course (*nak-tham tī*). They were joined by the third-year students (*nak-tham ek*) of the only other Dhamma school active in Sipsongpannā at the time, based at Wat Manchuanman in Meng Kham, a half hour down the Mekong (and near the *salāt soy* of chapter 1). Three of the four members of the Minority and Religious Affairs Bureau (Minzu Zongjiao Bu) came to Wat Pājie, watched the novices taking their tests, chatted for a few minutes with the monks, and then left. These men were in fact Dai-lue, and one had been a teacher at Wat Pājie before Ai Kham, though he had never ordained. While there was no doubt that conversations took place behind the scenes about what could and could not be done at Wat Pājie, the local state was not an ominous, or even regular presence, at Wat Pājie. In fact, while it did become common for students at the school to have finished junior middle school by the middle of the decade, I was told this was a choice the monks themselves had made (though whether they made this decision for pedagogical reasons or in anticipation of governmental decisions is unknown to me). The disjuncture between Ai Kham's view of the local government and my own observations of its absence at the temple, and in particular at the Dhamma school, points to the uneven power of the Chinese state, and its consequences for the educational project of the monks of Sipsongpannā.

The Dhamma school at Wat Pājie opened in the spring of 1994, after several years of applications. It was the second Dhamma school opened in Sipsongpannā, and in terms of numbers of students and continuous activity, it has been by far the most important. Up until 2009 when the school was relocated to new space adjacent to Wat Long Meuang Lue, the school was housed in a large three-story building built in 1995 in the center of Wat Pājie.[1] This building also served as the dormitory for the students, all but a handful of whom boarded at the school, and until the construction of the Wannasiri Kuti in 2002, it also housed most of the monks and the temples offices as well. The Dhamma school's overt purpose has been to provide Dai-lue novices with a different kind of Buddhist education, and more of it than they receive within the context of apprentice education; that is, its goal is to create a cohort of Dai-lue Buddhist intellectuals. For this, the monks of Wat Pājie have relied on a curriculum that they borrowed from the monastic schools of Thailand and the Shan States. This does not mean that this school was only to be focused on Buddhism. Mette Hansen (1999, 115) reports that permission to open the school was predicated on also teaching Putonghua (Mandarin Chinese) to the students, who are either novices or young monks. While it extends the mission of the school beyond simply teaching about the Buddhist tradition, this require- ment is largely consistent with other Buddhist institutes of Southeast Asia and China. Buddhist institutes in these other places all teach the classical languages in which Buddhist texts are written, such as Pāli or Sanskrit, and many also teach other subjects as part of their formal curriculum. However, it also means that the teaching of Chinese is at the heart of the school's curricu- lum and learning how to be a Dai-lue Buddhist intellectual includes learning (to be) Chinese.

In the previous chapter, I discussed how "lessons in being Chinese" in the Chinese public schools shapes the Buddhist education of novices in village temples in important, if sometimes passive, ways. In village temples, boys learn to be Dai-lue men, a status that has Buddhist knowledge at its base. Being Chinese has an indirect impact on what the boys learn because they often train in a village *wat* and attend a public school at the same time. In the cur- ricular education at Wat Pājie, there is a different kind of problem. While the government is normally not actively involved in the regulation of the school, the educational project at the school is shaped much more clearly by its rela- tionship to China, or its imagination of what it needs to be in relation to "China"—in essence, what I have been calling "China moments." The argument in this chapter has two parts. The first is a modified form of the question of how monks are made, to think about what kind of monk is made. By examin- ing the curricula of the Dhamma school in Jing Hong at Wat Pājie, and looking at this in relation to other projects at Wat Pājie, I will argue that the Dhamma school seeks to create a cohort of Dai-lue monks who understand the close relationship between "Dai-ness" and Buddhism, and who see themselves as responsible for upholding both. The second argument has to do with the con- sequences of these "China moments" and the limits of autonomy for the Sangha of Sipsongpannā. While the sangha has had a significant amount of freedom in pursuing its pedagogical agenda at the Dhamma school, at the same time, in direct and indirect ways, "China" presses in on the school, making the creation of Dai-lue leaders a difficult, even fragile, project. To begin to make sense of this, I turn first to Wat Pājie and the Dhamma school.

A School in a *wat* in a Tourist Park

Wat Pājie has been an important location, even an actor, in this book so far, and will obviously be one in this chapter. Up to this point, however, most of the discussion about the temple has been about the roles that its monks play, whether in governing the sangha or participating in economies of merit. To understand the school that was there between 1994 and 2009, it is important to include an understanding of the space of the *wat* as well. With the exception of Wat Long Meuang Lue, with which it is closely tied, Wat Pājie is the largest *wat* in Sipsongpannā. During the time of my primary research, it was comprised of four main buildings: the *wihān* in the center, with a large three-story building perpendicular to it that housed the school and dormitory of the novices. Catty-corner to these two was the Thai-style ordination hall (*bosot*) dedicated in the late-1990s with the support of the Thai royal family. Wanna-siri Kuti, the abbot's house dedicated in 2001, is situated in the corner between the school building and the *bosot*. There have been small pavilions and sheds that have been constructed or torn down over the years, and the space of the *wat* has changed significantly since the dedication of Wat Long Meuang Lue in 2007. Since the Dhamma school moved to Wat Long in 2009, the school building and the *wihān* have both been torn down, and a large new *wihān* was dedicated on December 12, 2012 (12/12/12, an auspicious time for a place named "the twelve regions").

The *wat* is located at what has been the edge of Jing Hong proper. When opened in the early 1990s, it was essentially surrounded by rice fields and villages. Since then, however, the city has developed up to and around it. Indeed, over the course of visits to Wat Pājie between 2001 and 2011, I have seen more and more large buildings go up around the *wat*, and the villages adjacent to it have largely disappeared to become part of the city. The most important development, though, has been the construction of Manting Park, one of several that opened up throughout the 1990s to cater to large numbers of domestic tourists who came through Sipsongpannā after the airport opened. While distinct from the park, which includes a small zoo, ersatz Dai houses, a performance stage, and a lake with a zip line and paddleboats, Wat Pājie is at the same time incorporated into it, and tourism is a constant presence on the temple grounds. Although the number of tourists coming to Wat Pājie is not consistent and varies greatly with the time of the year, even at its slowest periods, Chinese domestic tourists come to the temple every day. At times, as during the spring holiday period in early May and around the time of the

Water-Splashing Festival in mid-April, thousands of tourists come through the temple.[2] The temple had to post signs in Chinese and English that people should take off their shoes when entering the *wihān,* and monks have been required to tend to tourists in a variety of ways (Borchert 2005b). In 2001–2002, tourists would occasionally make their way up to the third floor of the school building, and would start taking pictures of me teaching the novices English. While most of these tourists were well behaved and unobtrusive, their presence also diverted resources from the school and brought relatively few benefits. Both monks and novices did their best to avoid being the subjects of cameras.[3]

The majority of the temple's finances come from donations of various sorts. Although a certain amount is offered by tourists visiting the temple, the monk in charge of the accounts on several different occasions told me that the money brought in by tourists hardly covers the costs associated with their presence. The temple has received help from a variety of government offices and Buddhist foundations in and outside of China, particularly for the construction and repair of buildings, and for the purchase of land. Labor for construction and much of the food consumed by the monks and novices (in particular rice) has been donated by Dai-lue villagers throughout Sipsongpannā. Another source of money is tuition for the school, though this is relatively minor. During 2001–2002, families gave the temple 600 yuan for the three-year course. The treasurer also told me that this did not cover the costs the boys incurred. For the 600 yuan, the boys received room and board as well as textbooks. This fee was in sharp contrast to the public schools, which could be as much as 1,000 yuan per term. Nonetheless, the temple's finances have seemed to be relatively healthy. Although life for its residents has never seemed particularly ostentatious, and the employees are not paid much, nor has the temple particularly struggled to get things when it needs or wants them. Its members have also consistently purchased land and engaged in building projects since the *wihān* was built in 1990.

The population at Wat Pājie has been diverse, and has also fluctuated over the years. Until the time when the Dhamma school moved to Wat Long, the primary population included the novices and young monks who were studying, the monks who served as their teachers, and the monks who worked for the temple (such as the treasurer) or for the Buddhist Association. Regarding the monks who ran the place, as described in chapter 2, those running the BA offices and those running the school have tended to be the same monks; indeed, a single monk might be a teacher, a vice-abbot at Wat Pājie, and the head of one of the regional offices of the BA. In other words, while each of these entities (school, BA, temple) has a distinct space in an organizational chart of the sangha, they also overlap, and there was often a sense that when something needed to be done, it would be done by whichever monk was available and had sufficient seniority. Beneath Khūbā Meuang Jom, there were two vice-abbots (*hong cao aowat*) and a head teacher (*khū yāy*). These monks normally did not teach, but they were also the monks who accomplished most of the tasks in the temple. They were also the ones sent to Kunming to take part in official study sessions. Two other monks, both from Meng Long, were the principal teachers of the Dhamma course, and the head teacher of the Dhamma school at Wat Manchuanman in Meng Kham was often in residence. An eighth monk served as the treasurer. All eight of these would qualify as senior monks (and all but one of these was already in his thirties). Since 2002, the tasks of teaching in the school have expanded somewhat, with some of the senior monks going to Kunming to teach at the Yunnan Buddhist Institute (described in chapter 6), and younger monks returning from Thailand in particular taking on the jobs of teaching at the Dhamma school in Jing Hong (whether at Wat Pājie or Wat Long).

During my fieldwork in 2001–2002, there were between thirty and forty students and ten monks. In other years, there have been as many as eighty student-novices in residence. As I noted in the discussion of local monastic networks in chapter 3, the students come from all over the region, though there are regions of Sipsongpannā, such as Meng Ce, that seem to attract more students. The vast majority of the students at the Dhamma school over the years have been Dai-lue, but since 2000 there has consistently been a group of Dai-neua from Dehong, as well as a handful of Bulang monks and novices studying there. In the class that I spent ten months teaching, these regional differences did not affect the interactions between the novices very much. With the exception of the novices from Dehong, who were much younger than the Dai-lue novices (and who also spoke a different dialect when they arrived), close friendships among the student-novices at Wat Pājie tended to be linked to educational background and age more than by region (i.e., the seventeen-year-olds who had graduated from junior high school tended not to spend as much time with the fourteen-year-olds who had dropped out of elementary school). The same was not true in a vertical sense. Senior monks were more likely to patronize those novices who were from the same region as themselves, though it should also be noted that this patronage was often more about making the novices do work on their behalf than about providing favors. That is to say, when a senior monk needed some low-level job done, he was more likely to order a novice or junior monk from his region to do it.

The educational levels of the students also varied a great deal in 2001–2002, although this came to change several years later. In 2001–2002, the students ranged in age from thirteen to twenty-two years old, with most being sixteen to eighteen. Eleven had attended middle school, nine of these having graduated. Of the remaining twenty-four students, all of the rest had been to elementary school, and fourteen of these had graduated. Most had dropped out for either financial reasons or because they were not good enough students, but they did not seem to generally view the Dhamma school as a poor substitute for the public schools. They appreciated the opportunities of Wat Pājie, and most of them expressed a clear desire to study at Wat Pājie (i.e., it was a good substitute for the public schools). As one of them said when I asked whether he came because he was not able to study in the public schools: "No, it's not that. If I wanted, I could go to a Chinese school to study, but then with regard to *sutta* and Dai literature (*jing wen, daiwen*), they would be lost. It would be the same (for me) as those who did not ordain. Therefore, I came to study at Wat Pājie."[4] While this attitude remained common when I interviewed students in 2007, in 2006 the policy of the school changed, and they began to accept primarily only novices who had finished junior high school. As we will see below, however, this was not because it was imposed by the local government as Ai Kham had feared—or at least not completely.

While the Dhamma school was the primary project at Wat Pājie, it was not the only one, and it was not always the privileged one. There were a variety of religious and construction projects that occurred during the 2001–2002 school year that I taught at the Dhamma school. Some of these, such as the preparations for the Tai new year of Song kān were open to tourists, and indeed hundreds, if not thousands, of (primarily) Chinese tourists made their way to Wat Pājie to watch the washing of the Buddha image discussed in chapter 2 and to wash it themselves in the day before water play began. Others were official holidays that were not tourism related, such as Auk wasā, the ceremonies marking the end of the rainy season retreat. These were well attended events, but the only non-Dai-lue people there were my family and me. Similarly, there were a variety of celebrations at the *wat,* such as an impromptu visit by Khūbā Siang Lā from Tachilek in October, and the more formal visit by Khūbā Bunchum, which took place in January 2002 and entailed two days of celebration, ceremony, and merit making. Like the preparations for the dedication of Wannasiri Kuti discussed in chapters 2 and 3, these more formally religious events resulted in the cancelling of classes for a period of time, ranging from a day to several weeks, both because the labor of novices was required to prepare for the events, and because the monks who taught the classes were needed for other work.

There was an additional project that took up much of the energy of the monks of Wat Pājie: publishing, and it has continued to do so. Wat Pājie, or perhaps it might be better here to say the BA of Sipsongpannā, has had a substantial, ongoing publishing project that has been multifaceted in its projects and agendas. Since the late 1990s, Wat Pājie has published a series of books and pamphlets either in Dai-lue or in both Chinese and Dai-lue, for use in the *wat,* in Dai-lue villages more broadly, and in Jing Hong as well. Among the most important have been the series of textbooks used in the Dhamma school that were adapted from textbooks from Tachilek or transliterated/translated from Thai. The latter books, which were not brought into use until 2004, are the textbooks used by the formal *nak-tham* program run by the Thai Sangha (within which the vice-abbots and head teacher of Wat Pājie in 2002 had all studied in the early 1990s). In addition, they have published several different handbooks and language books that the BA distributed throughout the region in the late 1990s and early 2000s. These include a Dai-lue alphabet book, *Akkhara,* and liturgical texts used throughout the region (including the one with *Mangala Sutta* used at the *salāt soy* discussed in chapter 1). The monks also published guidebooks for both new abbots and *pū cān,* the lay leaders of village *wats.* These included instructions about the responsibilities of these offices as well as abbreviated forms of the texts that they were responsible for on a regular basis. The logic behind these was that such handbooks were necessary in a context where the chain of knowledge had been broken as a result of the Cultural Revolution. While most common at *wats* in the immediate region of Jing Hong, I have encountered these texts at village *wats* throughout Sipsongpannā. The third project along with textbooks and handbooks is more public and less religious: advertisements and signs. Wat Pājie has been the place where one could get things translated into Dai-lue easily and accurately, and they have been used by restaurants, hospitals, and tourism parks to translate and publish (or provide proofs for publication) menus, medical information, and signs in the classical Dai-lue language.[5]

Perhaps the single most important publishing project that the monks were involved in starting in the late 1990s was the development of the Dai-Han dictionary (Dao, Cao, and Dao 2002) discussed in chapter 2. While there are a few small dictionaries that had been developed by Daizu scholars in Kunming, these all used the new Dai script developed at MinDa in the 1950s. As has been already noted, while the ostensible purpose of the script was to facilitate literacy, it has generally been ignored and is little used among most Dai-lue (and never by the monks, most of whom told me that they could not read the script). Nonetheless, while the government normally uses Chinese characters in its written communications, when it uses Dai-lue, it uses the new script, and as reported in chapter two, individual cadres have sometimes grumbled about the efforts to foster the use of the traditional script by the monks of Wat Pājie. Ironically, even while these cadres complained about the dictionary, its development and publication were supported by the local government, at least financially.

Governmental pressures and support were not the only things that make this dictionary worth our attention: it was impacted by both transnational aspects and local pressures. In 2001, the only font available for use on Windows-based machines (which were the most common computing platform in China at the time) was in *xin daiwen*. There was an "old Dai" font available for use, but it had been developed in the Shan States and it used a Macintosh platform. As a result, while Wat Pājie had a few Windows-based computers, they primarily used iMacs they had purchased in Bangkok. Because no one in China used Apple products at the time, and because the manuals were all in English, whenever a problem arose (which was frequently), they either needed someone like me to read the manuals or they had to take the computers to Bangkok. Alongside these transnational computer flows (and woes), there was an additional irony to the dictionary. Even as the monks faced criticism from some in the local government about their use of "old Dai," they also faced criticism from some villagers over the use of the Shan font because it was not traditional enough! In other words, the monks faced pressure from both above and below, as they were utilizing transnational resources to produce this dictionary. In a sense, the dictionary encapsulates the dynamic that I have been emphasizing throughout this book about the interplay of local, national, and transnational influences on the way that people experience and understand Buddhism as a whole. These dynamics are also evident in the educational programs of the Dhamma School of Sipsonpannā more broadly.

FIGURE 5.1 Novices studying at desks at the Dhamma school at Wat Pājie

Sitting at Desks: The Characteristics of Curricular Education

Before examining these programs, it is worth considering the form of pedagogy taking place at Wat Pājie, which I referred to in the introduction as curricular education. Modern curricular education takes place within institutional contexts that we can easily recognize as schools. I mentioned in the beginning of the previous chapter that Charles Keyes (1992, 27) refers to apprentice education as taking place in *wat* schools, but also that it is perhaps misleading to think of the pedagogical context of village temples as taking place in schools. This is because these are not formal institutions of learning, but instead institutions where pedagogy is folded into other practices and types of relationships. In the twentieth century, however, it has become increasingly common for Theravāda monks and novices of Southeast Asia to be educated in institutions that resemble public schools in important ways. In part, this is because the education of monks has been seen as one aspect of shaping the population, and in part because monks trained in schools run by the state, even indirectly, can be used in nation-building efforts. I focus on three aspects of curricular education as essential, especially in contrast with apprentice education: the organization of time and space, standardization of knowledge, and the pedagogical relationship.

In contrast to village temples, time and space in monastic schools is clearly demarcated for pedagogical activities. As detailed in chapter 4, educational space in village temples is not dedicated primarily to education, but is part of a common space used for a number of different activities. A blackboard might be set up in the *wihān,* the *kuti,* or in a *sāla* off to the side. There is never a separate room, let alone a separate building, in which the monk trains his novices. On the other hand, Dhamma schools in Sipsongpannā and Thailand all have spaces dedicated to pedagogy. When students are not in class, these spaces are generally not used for other tasks, though students might use them for independent study.

The use of time is similarly organized and differentiated. Curricular education clearly demarcates times in which students are to be in classrooms. At the schools I have observed, this is generally punctuated by the use of an alarm bell to tell students that class is beginning and ending. Again, in apprentice education, while there may be times that are generally reserved for the teaching of novices, these are informal designations. For example, there were two villages I visited outside of Jing Hong and in Gasai District near the airport that both had schedules posted announcing the study times for novices. However, in my visits to these *wats* (timed to coincide with these schedules), the novices never actually studied at those times. By contrast, the Dhamma school at Wat Pājie had two or three formal class periods each day (9 a.m., 3 p.m., and sometimes 8 p.m.), and outside of special events, this schedule was followed regularly.

The effect of this organization of time and space is both to set aside and to privilege pedagogical action. Novices in these places are not simply there to learn how to become novices who can perform rituals, but to become well-educated novices who might be considered intellectuals. Setting aside time and space for regular classes indicates that pedagogy is a temple priority.

Along with the organization of time and space, knowledge practices are the most important aspect of curricular education. Unlike in apprentice education, which is marked by the relative unevenness of the presentation of knowledge, curricular education has a standard collection of materials (the curriculum) that is delivered in regular, and even standardized, ways. The presentation of knowledge depends on textbooks, often produced specifically for use by a school, that present the knowledge in a standardized way. Wat Pājie, for example, has used textbooks produced by temples in the Shan States and the Thai government for their own *nak-tham* courses and textbooks approved by the Chinese state for its Chinese-language course. In addition to standardizing knowledge, these textbooks clarify and delimit knowledge, especially with regard to Buddhism. At the same time, however, the knowledge they present is far broader than in apprentice education, during which novices learn very specific things that will be useful to them as ritual leaders and community members. The knowledge within curricular education, while not unlimited, is much broader and includes far more of the translocal Buddhist tradition. The process of transmitting this knowledge often is aided by exercises included in the texts, and enforced through the use of exams, which are themselves generally standardized. In other words, the students are formally tested on materials in the textbooks, and the successful completion of these exams ultimately provides them with proof of their knowledge acquisition, or in some cases, acts as a credential.[6]

The standardization of knowledge extends to bodily practices. Part of this takes place in the classroom: novices sit at desks, not on the floor. The desks are in neat rows and students are often assigned to a specific desk. Students stand and greet the teacher at the beginning of class and thank her or him at the end. Moreover, comportment is often an explicit concern within curricular education, in both knowledge and performance. In places such as Thailand where the development of a monastic school system has been driven in large part by the agendas of the Thai state, a *vinaya*-centered scripturalism has been a central focus (Schober 1995, 313). At the same time, these schools are also distanced from specific lay communities. As a result, unlike the dynamics of discipline discussed in the last chapter, comportment in curricular education has to be enforced by monks. Presumably, this leads to stricter enforcement (since monks know better than laypeople about how monks should act), but it also puts a much higher burden on the monks themselves to maintain standards. This can be a challenge if the number of senior monks is limited.

In apprentice education, the primary pedagogical relationship is between a master monk and an apprentice-novice. In the school setting, the fundamental nature of this relationship is changed; instead of apprentice and master, the novices become students and the monk is a teacher. This is, I would suggest, a more distant relationship, predicated on the exchange of knowledge more than the formation of a person (though these are obviously related concerns). There are more students, and while a teacher might take some of them under his wing (thus establishing something of an apprentice–master relationship), he (or she)[7] is not directly responsible for the well-being of the students. Instead, it is the institution as a whole that is responsible for the students. In the same way, the teacher is not beholden to the village, but to the institution. What this means is that the teacher fills a position within an institution, in contrast to the village monk, who functions within a network of relationships. This is perhaps a fine distinction, since institutions function via relationships and village monks have positions. The relationships in curricular and apprentice education are not the same, however. If we were to map them, the teacher-monk's position in the institution would be best displayed with an organizational chart, but this would not be feasible for village temples, at least not in Sipsongpannā. Instead a web of lines denoting types of relationships to other villagers would be a more useful way of conveying information.

The three differences that I have outlined above suggest that we view curricular education as a more efficient mode than apprentice education in that it provides broader knowledge that is standardized to more people. It is not surprising to note that it has been seen as a key place where a patron can build support within the sangha. In general, there are two types of actors who have both the interest and resources necessary for creating systems of curricular education: the state and large monastic institutions. For both, their interests should be thought of in terms of reproduction and legitimation. Curricular education has been seen as an efficient means for fostering the moral support for the state, by trying to produce students who view the political order and the moral order as closely aligned (Swearer 1976, 66–68). It can also be an effective means to gain some measure of control over regional sanghas. In Thailand, this has been done in part by linking advancement in the sangha to educational achievements. Ishii has argued that this has meant that monastic examinations become a catalyst for the homogenization of monastic knowledge (1986, 77). This homogenization is perhaps a by-product of the effort to create a cohort of capable administrators loyal to the duopoly of the Bangkok-based sangha and the royal family, a central goal of the monastic education reforms that began at the end of the nineteenth century (Reynolds 1972). This is not to suggest that setting up a school will automatically produce support within the sangha for a state's rule. The Pāli schools set up by the French in colonial Laos have been seen as unsuccessful in their efforts at producing a Lao form of Buddhism

(*Bulletin École française d'Extrême-Orient* 1909, 823–827, and 1931, 834–835; Edwards 2007). While the military rulers in Burma certainly provided the requisites for the sangha during their decades of direct rule, support within the sangha was by no means absolute (McCargo 1999). Indeed, as I argue in the introduction, while educational and other types of support for the sangha are important avenues for legitimacy, legitimacy can be difficult to produce (Blackburn 2001, 90).[8]

The situation at the Dhamma school at Wat Pājie is different from these Southeast Asian examples in several ways. It is not run by a state, though the local state has a certain degree of oversight, and has also contributed to its construction and upkeep. Rather, it was largely founded by monks and former monks, and it is run by monks. Instead of being a mechanism for the production of legitimacy, its founding seems to be an act, by turns desperate and strategic, meant to foster a vision of being Dai-lue, partially inscribed within being Daizu and Chinese. Before examining some of the ways that the curriculum of the Dhamma school demonstrates this, it is necessary to consider what "autonomy" means in the context of Sipsongpannā and the minorities of China.

Autonomy and Minorities

Sipsongpannā is an "autonomous prefecture" (*zizhi zhou*). It is, moreover, the *zizhi zhou* of the Daizu. In official terms, this means that the Daizu are designated as having a certain degree of control over their own development. What this autonomy means in practical terms is not always clear. Tan Leshan (1999–2000), for example, has argued that the Dai-lue have had relatively little actual self-rule during their sixty years of being a part of the People's Republic. While the governor (*zhouzhang*) of "Xishuangbanna" is Daizu, few other influential members of the local government have been. While political and economic policies are implemented at the local level, they are normally determined either at the provincial or national level, and the local government is generally more beholden to Kunming (and, ultimately, to Beijing) than to local concerns. As a result, most scholars have not taken the category very seriously. Emerging from the compromises that the CCP had made to gain the support of ethnic groups during the civil war with the Nationalists, "autonomy" was a substitute for the possibility of independence from the PRC. Even though in the last thirty years there has been a promotion of minority culture and the subsidizing of minority status at a variety of levels of both government and popular culture (Gladney 1994), "autonomy" has meant little to most minorities. In this reading, the concrete benefits that accrue from being a minority—the ability to have two children, quotas for minorities in educational settings, an autonomous government (which means representation in the central government), and sometimes the ability to retain more taxes (Schein 2000, 96–97)—are essentially bribes to tie minorities to the nation, the efficacy of which is debatable. At its core, this analysis highlights the irony of autonomy for China's *shaoshu minzu:* the ability of the group to decide its own fate is necessarily subsumed to the authority of the party and state. It is autonomy in name and appearance only (Heberer 1989; Tan 1999–2000). On the other hand, Susan McCarthy has argued for a more positive reading of the conditions of "autonomy." Without ignoring the asymmetrical power dynamics between the (largely) Han state and China's minorities, McCarthy suggests that the laws about the rights of minorities on the books have in fact provided minorities with a certain social space in which to foster their own vision of their culture and identity (2009). In other words, while autonomy is not true independence, nor is it completely meaningless.

What is at stake in this discussion is the extent to which minorities can shape their worlds. The agency of China's minorities is certainly constrained, but there is some ability to act. There are costs associated with being a minority (such as being seen as more "primitive" by the wider culture), but at the same time, groups have generally sought to attain minority status for the benefits that it provides (Schein 2000, 97). Erik Mueggler has noted:

> Present-day "minority nationalities" are neither outside a cohesive entity called "Chinese culture" nor in any simple process of being assimilated by it. Instead these peoples seed a diverse cultural field with fresh influences; they selectively appropriate its elements, reworking or embellishing them; they imagine coherent versions of it against which to pose self-consciously, inventing themselves as different. (2001, 19)

This is a point echoed by Dru Gladney, who has argued that it is necessary to understand ethnic identity in China as not simply the result of state definition, but a "dialogical interaction of shared traditions of descent with sociopolitical contexts, constantly negotiated in each political-economic setting" (1998, 109). These negotiations, however, take place in the context of powerful images produced by both state and nonstate actors of what it means to be a minority in China. Sara Davis (2005) has spoken of this as a "simplification project," which emphasizes certain aspects of minority cultures, such as dress forms, religion, language, and in particular, song and dance. These might be understood as a part of the state's efforts to render minorities legible—to use James Scott's (1998) formulation—and therefore subject to policies for development and control. These forms are reproduced in public schools, in the propaganda organs of the state, and in policies that have encouraged the development of a tourism industry in Sipsongpannā that fosters images of the region's minorities, which can be commodified. This is the context in which the "autonomy" of the Dai-lue monks needs to be understood.

This can perhaps be best understood with reference to the development of Wat Long Meuang Lue, and the experiences of the monks there. The temple was opened with great fanfare in 2007, and as I have already discussed, it was the product of a partnership between the local government, a real estate developer, and the BA of Sipsongpannā. Aspects of the partnership have been very fruitful for the Sangha of Sipsongpannā. In particular, they have a large new temple complex with a new school that they could not afford to build themselves, which they have wanted for a number of years. Throughout the construction, however, they argued with the real estate developer about the aesthetics of the *wat* and whether there would be any Dai-lue construction workers. In the years since its construction, they have had conflicts with the developer (who manages the *wat* in exchange for tourism revenue) over entrance rights as well as the presence of monks. At one point, in 2009, the real estate developer dressed workers up as monks to give Han Chinese tourists a taste of "real" Daizu Buddhism—an effort that the BA strongly and publicly resisted.[9] That they were able to do so is a testament to the avenues of action available to them; that they felt compelled to do so was a consequence of how "Dai-ness" is manipulable by both state and economic actors. Indeed, the experience with managing their own temple complex can be seen as a "China moment" when the Dai-lue monks are faced with their subaltern status vis-à-vis the local government and wealthy Han real estate developers.

It may be useful to think of minority status and autonomy as similar to their religious status. Just as being Buddhists (and in particular, Theravāda Buddhists) opens certain resources for the BA in Sipsongpannā, being a minority constrains the Dai-lue at other moments because of the political economies around them. The same forces constrain and enable them in the context of the Dhamma school.

The Pedagogy of Wat Pājie

When I have asked the younger monks of Wat Pājie about the mission of the school, I have generally received two different answers. One answer subsumes the school's mission into the temple's mission as a whole: if there is no Wat Pājie, then in a few years, there are no Dai people, Dubi Gaew Law told me. On the other hand, there is a sense that the school's mission is separate, natural, and obvious. Dubi Sam Bian told me that the student-novices study what they do because they are Buddhist monks, and they should know about Buddhism.[10] These two separate understandings suggest multiple agendas at the temple, even when the residents themselves do not see them as distinct.

There are two different formal curricula at the Dhamma school: Buddhist (*nak-tham*) and secular. The former is taught every day for roughly six months out of the year, and culminates in a set of exams sometime around the end of October. The secular curriculum, which is generally taught throughout the year, has been more diverse, featuring a variety of non-Buddhist subjects that have varied over time. For the first decade of the Dhamma school's existence, this program was largely informal and unaccredited, but since around 2005, the Dhamma school has had a formal relationship with the technical college in Jing Hong, providing a more formal curriculum and process of instruction. In conjunction with these two formal curricula, however, there is an informal curriculum spread throughout the pedagogical activities at the Dhamma school focused on Dai-lue culture. I suggest here that an analysis of these three curricula reveals the dynamics described above, and that these point to the challenges and dynamics of being a minority religious actor in contemporary China.

The Buddhist Curriculum

The Buddhist curriculum is divided into training that occurs in the classroom, and training that occurs in the *wihān,* usually during and after the evening's chanting and meditation. In the classroom, the novices study five different topics: the Dai-lue script (*akkhara*), the life of the Buddha, Buddhist discipline, Buddha Dhamma, and the exegesis of Pāli aphorisms for the purpose of sermons (*suphāsit*). In the *wihān,* the novices memorize texts for chanting, practice the performance of *suphāsit,* and also practice the chanting of Pāli, principally through a redaction of the Vessantara Jātaka in Dai-lue script that the monks at Wat Pājie produced in the late 1990s. Instruction in the *wihān* has also included practice at sitting in meditation for fifteen to thirty minutes each night after chanting the evening service. While there has often been talk about the desire to implement the study of reading and translating Pāli, there had been little progress at implementing such a program, at least as of the time of my last visit to the Dhamma school in 2011. The Buddhist curriculum is a modified version of the *nak-tham* curriculum of the Thai monastic school system, which was experienced directly by the senior monks of the sangha in the 1990s.

In contrast to apprentice education in village *wats* in which texts are normally not standardized, curricular education at the Dhamma school at Wat Pājie and Wat Long has been based on a series of textbooks. For the first decade or so of the school's existence, the Dhamma school received their books from Wat Pha Thātu Sāy Meuang, the temple in Tachilek that has been the home temple of Khūbā Siang Lā (see chapter 3). These books were often handwritten, and then photocopied and bound. With some of these, the monks at Wat Pājie typed them up in the "classical" Dai-lue font, and published them through Wat Pājie. In the beginning of the millennium, senior monks began to translate/transliterate[11] the textbooks from the Thai *nak-tham* curriculum. These textbooks, initially developed by the Supreme Patriarch of Thailand from the early twentieth century, Prince Wachirayān, were part of the effort by the central government to standardize and domesticate the regional sanghas of Thailand (Zack 1977; Ishii 1986; Kamala 1997), and are the ones that are currently in use at the Dhamma school. It is interesting to note that these Thai origins are not acknowledged in the publication information of these books, which describes them as coming from Wat Pājie.

Despite their initial use in Thailand, the majority of the information contained in these textbooks should be seen as decontextualized and religious, not political. There are neither implicit nor explicit claims about politics, Sipsongpannā, or the Dai-lue people. With the exception of an alphabet book (discussed below), these textbooks are filled with information about the life of the historical Buddha and the *puttha sāsanā*, the teachings of the Buddha. They contain no references to times and places remotely connected with the contemporary world. In other words, they are not chronicles about Sipsongpannā, or relics there, but are solely about a translocal (delocalized) Buddhism. Indeed, the preface to the book on the life of the Buddha states quite clearly that the book was put together specifically for Buddhists who do not know much about the Buddha, but would still like to study and know, and that this book will allow them to "understand the conditions of the true teachings of the Buddha" (*Wichā Puttha-bawatti* 2004, foreword). The most explicit statement these texts make about the agenda for their reception is in the foreword to *Handbook to the Vinaya*, where it states, "Those who study will know and understand the regulations revealed by the Buddha; this will help them be leaders who implement these rules in daily life."[12] While this statement invokes the relevance of Buddhism to daily life and the value of learned monks as leaders, there is not an obvious or overt political agenda articulated by the text. A decontextualized, universal tone is common throughout these textbooks.

This "classical," decontextualized Buddhist knowledge can be seen in a brief examination of *Puttha* (The Life of the Buddha) and *Wichā* (The Teachings of the Buddha), two of the textbooks used at the Dhamma school. Both of these books provide knowledge that would not be out of place in a textbook on Buddhism anywhere. Divided into fifty-six chapters organized into ten sections, *Puttha* describes the world into which the Buddha was born, his last life, and the production of the *sāsanā*. The first three sections provide background for the Buddha's life, including descriptions of Jambudvipa; the four *varnas* (castes) of India; the Sakya clan; the lineage of the Buddha; and the supernatural powers (*aphinihān*) of a *mahā-purusha*, the "great man," of which the Buddha is an exemplar. Section 4 describes the young prince's experiences between leaving home and his enlightenment, while section 5 discusses some basic central doctrines of the *sāsanā*, such as the four noble truths and *anatta*, the Buddhist concept of not-self. Later sections focus on the construction of the early Buddhist community, including talking about important disciples of the Buddha, key places that the Buddha traveled during his preaching lifetime, and the various events surrounding his lifetime. Ending with the first council, the book contains no focus on the *jātaka* narratives, reflecting, perhaps, the modernizing influence of the Rama V on Thai Buddhist curricula (Jory 2002). Nor is there any mention of the journeys that the Buddha was said to have taken to Southeast Asia during his lifetime in local chronicles such as the *Jinakālamālipakaraṇam*. Instead, stereotyped and universal knowledge of the life of the Buddha, available in almost any textbook on Buddhism, is preferred to that which might be seen as "local" knowledge.

Wichā focuses on the basic philosophical content of Theravāda Buddhism—though it does not identify it as such. It is simply *puttha-sāsanā*, the teachings of the Buddha. To do this, it has two different strategies. The first strategy is to explain words or phrases. Thus, it sets out two to three words around a given theme, such as "the Three Jewels" (*ratana sām yang*) or the three roots or conditions of goodness (*kusala-mūla*). If the word is not well known or is a Pāli word (as in the three *kusala mūla*), it will give a short gloss, such as "*alopha bao khāy dāy khowng khao*" (*a-lopha* [nongreed] means to not desire to attain his things). Then it provides a longer explanation of what each of these terms might be. The second strategy of the text is to have questions and answers at the end of each larger section (there are fifteen) to reinforce what was said in the explanation. For example, one of the questions asks about the Three Jewels: "The Lord Buddha, the Dhamma, the Sangha are called *ratana*, which means 'jewels.' Please explain what this means." The answer explains that there are people who do what is good and this elicits respect in others, and in doing what is necessary, they bring about joy and comfort. The Buddha who knew the truth in everything and taught it to others did this, and the sangha did likewise. "In doing so, they are like splendid gems" (*Wichā Dhamma-wiphāk*, 38–39). Information like this is conventional Buddhist knowledge, though more extensive than novices generally receive within apprentice education.

Transmitting the knowledge contained in these textbooks is in important ways the formal, official rationale for the existence of the Dhamma school in Jing Hong, and the monastic students are required to take a series of exams based on the textbooks. The examination questions themselves are quite straightforward. For the exam about the life of the Buddha, the students were asked about the Buddha's grandparents, the Buddha's first discipline, and the donor of a *wihān* at Veluvana. The exam based on the teachings of the Buddha was somewhat more extensive. Like the textbook described above, the students were asked to both gloss the meanings of specific words and recapitulate Buddhist explanations for how the world works. Exam questions from 2001 included being asked to describe the types of anger and indolence, as well as different types of fear as described in the teachings of the Buddha. They were also asked to describe the characteristics of a good or bad person.

In 2001, these exams took place at the end of October, about eight months after the academic year began (and right before the dedication of the Wannasiri Kuti). They required several weeks of intensive preparation by the teachers (all monks) who were focused on the Buddhist subjects. Indeed, during the last week or so before the exams, the other subjects the students were studying (in particular my English class, and a Chinese-language class) were suspended for the purpose of exam preparation, which mainly consisted of taking practice exams. While they found them to be quite stressful, most of the novices passed the exams. The exams were observed by the officers of the MRAB; despite this official show of surveillance, the entire process for the exams was internal. The exams were written by the monks at Wat Pājie and graded by them as well. There was no external accreditation in this process.

The Non-Buddhist Curriculum

The non-Buddhist curriculum is largely focused on helping the novices develop skills that the senior monks feel are necessary for the novices as adults in the PRC and for the sangha to survive in twenty-first-century China. While one of the stipulations for permission to open up the Dhamma school in 1994 was that the novices learn Mandarin Chinese, there were no other requirements, nor, according to former monks who were involved with its opening, were there clear discussions for how this requirement should be fulfilled. The education of novices and young monks in Sipsongpannā has never been the province of the local government, and the monks engaged in this educational project have had to develop a program for training novices on their own. Moreover, in contrast to debates that took place in Burma around the appropriateness of novices acquiring non-Buddhist knowledge (Dhammasami 2007), the post–Cultural Revolution Sangha in Sipsongpannā has not had this kind of debate. There has been no resistance to the development of a robust secular curriculum at the Dhamma school, from either the local government or the local Dai-lue community; nor has there been much help either.

While the monks of the BA have been able to construct a Buddhist curriculum based on materials that were either donated to them or they took from monastic education in Southeast Asia, the development of a non-Buddhist curriculum has been ad hoc. For the first decade of its existence, the

Dhamma school sought to train its students in math, English, Thai, and word processing/computer work in Chinese and Dai-lue, in addition to Putonghua. These courses were often focused on specific skills that they might need as monks, or that might be needed by the sangha. For example, the study of Thai was primarily for those novices who were going to be traveling to Thailand to study at a monastic school there, while the word processing and computer work helped develop students who could assist in Wat Pājie's publishing projects. In both cases, however, there was no consistent time set aside for this training; rather, it was squeezed into other classes, or at the end of a session to prepare the novices who were about to travel to Thailand to study.

The ad hoc nature of the non-Buddhist education was more widespread than these classes, however. The monks regularly struggled to find someone who could teach the classes that they felt were needed to train the students adequately. I taught English at the Dhamma school for ten months, two hours a day during the week. In many ways, my class resembled other English as a second language (ESL) instruction I had done in Japan in public high schools, but there I had gone through a rigorous application process, and in Sipsongpannā, I showed up one day and volunteered to teach in exchange for some Dai-lue-language lessons. If I had not arrived, it is not clear that the monastic students would have had the opportunity to study English. Similarly, Chinese was often taught, not by a trained teacher but by someone who was available who had some postsecondary education. For example, among the Chinese teachers at the Dhamma school in its first decade were Ai Kham, mentioned earlier, a Dai-lue man who moved from Wat Pājie to work in the MRAB, and a Chinese woman who had studied Thai at MinDa in Kunming. None of these people were trained as Chinese teachers, any more than I was trained in ESL. It is not that they did a poor job, but, like me, their best qualification was that they were available.

Curricular materials were generally dealt with on a similar ad hoc basis, with the school using what was donated and available. In 2001, the textbook that was used for Chinese language was one that had been developed for adult language learners, published by Yunnan Educational Publishers (Alexander and He 1997). The text claimed to have a "practical" focus to its lessons and contents, but it was largely about the importance of returning to school and attaining skills through education. Ironically, it also contained lessons on Chinese minorities that discursively incorporated minorities into the Chinese body politic. For example, two lessons are concerned with the Daizu: chapter 19, which presents a famous song said to be about Sipsongpannā (though of course it refers to the place as Xishuangbanna, the Chinese transliteration of the region), "There Is a Beautiful Place," and chapter 26, "A Memorable Water-Splashing Festival."[13] The lyrics of the first talk about the beauty of Xishuangbanna but then slip in a few lines about the "kind" and "liberating" CCP. It does not quite attribute Xishuangbanna's bucolic nature to the CCP, but it does have the "Daizu following you forever." The second chapter does not really say much about the Water-Splashing Festival, but it does talk about the 1961 celebration when Premier Zhou Enlai famously joined in the celebration. In other words, to the extent that the Dai-lue people are present in the textbook, they are incorporated into the nation. While the monks complained about this book to me, they did use it for several years, potentially reinforcing the messages of the text regardless of whether they wanted to or not. They used it, I was told, because it had been donated to them.

Since the middle of the last decade, the Dhamma school made a significant shift in the way that it handled the non-Buddhist curriculum. Instead of the ad hoc procedures described above, they made an arrangement with the technical college in Jing Hong. The college provides the instruction in non-Buddhist subjects, and in exchange, the students would be eligible to take the entrance exam to go to the technical college. This has had several different consequences. First, it has regularized and standardized a curriculum that had not been either. Second, it has brought about the conditions that Ai Kham was concerned about: rather than students having a wide variety of educational backgrounds, from elementary school dropout to middle-school graduate, all of the students at Wat Pājie are required to have at least graduated from junior middle school. The difference, however, is that this was a decision made by the monks of Wat Pājie rather than imposed from the top as Ai Kham feared. The third consequence is that this provides what is really an alternative middle school, but using the same kind of curriculum provided at the public schools. Thus, instead of learning Chinese, a bit of math, and perhaps English, the student-novices learn Chinese, English, mathematics, social studies, legal studies, and music. This means that in social studies and legal studies, they learn about the PRC, serving to further incorporate them into the body politic.

I have heard two different rationales for this shift. One came from a lay administrator working at Wat Pājie in 2007. She said that this had come about because of the difficulty of teaching the novice-students under the previous situation. The difficulty was about how to teach students in a single class who had such radically different skill bases (personal communication, Jing Hong, June 2007). The second came from Khūbā Meuang Jom when I met him at Midway Airport in Chicago in 2003. He was concerned about the lack of accreditation—or indeed, really recognition of legitimacy by the wider community—because it limited the opportunities available to the graduates of the Dhamma school, and he wanted the students to be able to participate in the economic potential of China (personal communication, Chicago, February 2003). By this logic, then, while the change to formal affiliation with the local technical college limited the autonomy of the monks in controlling the

Dhamma school, the hope was that it would open up opportunities to participate in modernizing Jing Hong.

Dai-lue Cultural Curriculum

Neither the Buddhist nor the non-Buddhist curricula described above are particularly focused on the Dai-lue, or Sipsongpannā. Indeed, both rely on materials from outside of the region, in ways that could be read as either universal
and translocal (the Buddhist curriculum) or national (the non-Buddhist curriculum). This is particularly the case with the agreement between the Dhamma
school and Jing Hong's technical college. Yet there has also been a very clear
ethos within the school regarding the need to foster and maintain an awareness of Dai-lue identity, and in particular one that links being Dai-lue to
Buddhism. In this, the Dhamma school fosters an identity that is distinct
from that of apprentice education. This identity is fostered through what we
might call an informal Dai-lue cultural curriculum.

The cultural curriculum is manifested both explicitly and implicitly.
Explicitly, there have been a variety of efforts to introduce Dai-lue culture
inside extracurricular classes. These have been classes outside of the formal
structure that is devoted to specific aspects of Dai-lue culture. For example,
for several years, after the afternoon class, the students were given the opportunity to study what was described to me as *Daizu gongfu,* martial arts of the
Dai-lue. Each day, half of the classes would do the labor required to keep up
the appearance of the *wat,* and half of the class would do martial arts forms
with a Dai-lue man. While novices getting exercise is not always seen as a positive (since they get sweaty and are not good models for laypeople), Khūbā
Meuang Jom told me on several occasions that it was important for novices to
get exercise, to stay out of trouble. Prior to coming to Wat Pājie in the mid-
1990s, he had novices in Meng Ce participate in an intramural soccer program. Having the novices work on *gongfu* was simply attending to a concern
that they know about Dai-lue culture while also getting sufficient exercise.
Another Dai-lue culture class was an art class that was sponsored by UNESCO.
Novices studied with a monk who had studied Tai arts as a novice in Thailand,
and part of the idea was that they would be able to find work either as monks
or, after they disrobed, doing the decorations for rebuilt village *wats.* In both
cases, these courses were met with enthusiasm that waned after a few years.
They were also largely dependent on the energy of a specific person who organized them, and when that person moved on, the effort died. We see a similar
kind of difficulty with the effort to develop a Dai-lue history class within the
curriculum. Many of the students told me that they would like to study Dai-
lue history, but there have been no textbooks, and no one really in a position to write one. Moreover, since the alignment was made with the technical

school, the history taught at the Dhamma school has been nationalist Chinese history.

At the same time, there has been an implicit focus within the formal curriculum to make the novice-students understand who they are as Dai-lue. One small but telling fact was that the Buddhism curriculum was, at least in 2001–2002, referred to as "Dai language class" (*daiyu ke*) rather than in terms of Buddhism. Neither the students nor the monks thought much of this; when I asked them why, they said because it was in Dai-lue, but it seems to be also something that incorporates Buddhism within the broader framework of Dai-lue culture.[14] A more explicit example of a focus on being Dai-lue was in the alphabet language textbook that the Dhamma school used at the beginning of its *nak-tham* course. Unlike the other textbooks used subsequently in the course, the alphabet book, *Bap heyn akkhara* (Letter Study Book), displays a clear political perspective and an awareness of the political situation that the other textbooks of the Buddhism curriculum do not. The messages embedded in the text's lessons emphasize the importance of Dai harmony and the fact that it is threatened. Language is an essential ingredient for maintaining the harmony and the community. In lesson 51 (of 88), for example, the text states: "Not having feet is better than not having the words of the ethnic group; not having life is better than not having one's nationality; not having flesh and blood is better than not having one's own lineage." Language is not the only factor, however. In the vision of this text, Buddhism is just as essential for the well-being of the Dai community; indeed, it is deemed the glue that will make the future possible. This idea, and the anxiety that it might not come to pass, is expressed clearly in lesson 50:

> Worry for the Dai nation . . .
> Future *meuang* will be civilized[15] because we have a desire for unity
> Future *meuang* will be civilized because we always have the Vinaya
> Future *meuang* will be civilized because we have the Buddha's
>   Dhamma.

The material of *Bap heyn akkhara* is not explained, but rather is recited over and over again to standardize pronunciation. Although the students do not understand all the words,[16] they understand most of them enough to understand the messages I have just described. The words of the book draw their attention towards being Dai-lue, and what is important about being Dai-lue. Thus, they are taught at the Dhamma school not just what is important within Dai-lue culture, but also that their job is to protect this culture.

It is clear that many of the student-novices have learned the messages of this Dai-lue curriculum. In village *wats* of Sipsongpannā that I visited, novices usually gave rather imprecise reasons for why they wanted to ordain. Often they told me either it was because they felt like it, or because their friends were also ordaining. The student-novices at Wat Pājie were rarely as vague, however. Most of them told me that they ordained because it was a tradition of the Dai-lue people. Clearly, a link had been made in the minds of these boys between ordination, being Buddhist, and Dai-lue culture. It was not that novices in village temples were unable to make this connection, but they did not clearly express it. In contrast to the student-novices of the Dhamma school, the village novices also did not tell me that they ordained because it is a Dai-lue practice. These boys who have only been educated within an apprentice system also do not describe their responsibilities in ethnic-wide terms. They say that they are supposed to study and learn, follow the abbot's orders, and perhaps teach the younger novices. While some of the novices at Wat Pājie say the same thing, there are more who frame their answers in broader terms in response to questions about their responsibilities. They are to "protect Buddhism" and "teach the people." One student-novice put it this way: "I feel like the greatest responsibility of monks and novices is to develop and spread greatly the culture of the Dai people, protect Dai culture and traditional practices, and do not let others destroy it" (personal communication, Jing Hong, May 2001). It is these connections, between Dai-lue culture and Buddhism, and the monastic responsibility to protect them both, that the school at Wat Pājie seeks to teach its students.

Conclusion: The Challenge of Development and the Fragility of Autonomy

This last point would seem to be part of a triumphal narrative, or at least a successful one. The senior monks of the sangha, who are also the officers of the BA, and who founded and continue to run the Dhamma school, have succeeded in fostering students who closely link being Dai-lue and being Buddhist, and who feel responsible for this. They have been able to do this by utilizing resources from Thailand such as the Buddhist curriculum, as well as their own experiences in the *nak-tham* program to serve as a model. They have also done this in part by working the system in China: by being good minorities who work with the local government and develop relationships within the local government. This has also allowed them to foster a relationship with the local technical college, which has meant that the students at the Dhamma school are also receiving an education that might possibly be recognized outside of the Dai-lue community if and when the novices disrobe. I also suspect that the continuing support for the Dhamma school in Jing Hong, or at least tolerance for it, is linked to the way in which the Chinese state has come to see Buddhism as a "good" religion—because it is not Christianity—and because it can be appropriated to development plans.

The Dhamma school is now at Wat Long Meuang Lue, has signs in English and Chinese that tell tourists about it, thus demonstrating the ways that the monks of Sipsongpannā have been able to work the system, to use international resources and models, to hide openly in the cracks of an atheist system, to foster Dai-ness, and to act autonomously. And yet this is a fragile project, and it is important to remember that autonomy in the official conception is an autonomy within the official Chinese system.

There are many pressures on the Dhamma school that make the development of an independent educational system difficult, and many of these challenges are less about an oppressive state than an overwhelming one. When I visited the Dhamma school in 2007 (for the first time in five years), I noticed that one of the students was reading a book entitled *Xishuangbanna Daizu Shenghuo Xisu yu Chuantong Wenhua* (Traditional Culture and Life Practices of the Dai People of Xishuangbanna) (Yi 2006). Written by a Dai-lue scholar who has taught at the Nationalities University in Kunming, the book contains many short essays about Dai-lue culture on matters both religious and not (how to protect a person's spirit [*khwan*], worship of the spirits, rules about funerals, roles of Buddhist monks, etc.). Looking at this, I was excited to see that it looked like a distinct resource had been made available to the school, and indeed the Dai-lue people, that would help them preserve and maintain their culture. Yet this new resource of the Dai-lue in the form of this book is also a bilingual text that is published in both Chinese and Dai-lue. However, the Dai-lue is the "new" Dai-lue script, the one that very few people read. When I asked the novice who had the book, he confirmed that they read the Chinese portions because none of them can read the new Dai-lue script. Was this a "China moment" in the midst of the Dai-lue curriculum?

The monks of Sipsongpannā have autonomy at the Dhamma school to pursue their vision of Dai-lue culture and of Buddhism. It is not independence, however; it is autonomy, framed and hemmed in by the politics of religion in China, and by the lack of resources to pursue things as they might in a perfect world. The fear that Ai Kham expressed in our conversation in the beginning of this chapter came true, though not for the reasons that he expected. The monks running the Dhamma school made the choice to require the novices to finish junior high school, in order to fulfill the agreement with the technical school in Jing Hong. They made this choice because they want their student-novices to have greater opportunities; it was a rational choice based on the development of the Chinese economy, and not compelled by the Chinese government. While the Dhamma school has autonomy, creating and maintaining a clarity of mission within contemporary China is a fragile project.

6

Transnational Buddhist Education and the Limits of the Buddhist Ethnoscape

ONE AFTERNOON IN JANUARY 2008, I JOURNEYED TO Wat
Paknām, a temple in the Thonburi section of Bangkok, to talk with some Dai-
lue novices. Wat Paknām is an interesting temple, not least because the late
abbot there was Luang Pho Sot, the discoverer or creator of the Dhammakāya
meditation technique, which is at the heart of the Dhammakāya movement.
Wat Paknām has long formally disassociated itself from Wat Dhammakāya,
which has (in)famously had problems regarding embezzlement of funds. Wat
Paknām is nonetheless important, if not as famous as Wat Dhammakāya. Its
abbot has long been a member of the Supreme Sangha Council, and since the
death of the Supreme Patriarch (*sangharāt*) of Thailand in 2013, most Thais
assume that the abbot of Wat Paknām will become the next Supreme Patriarch.
I was able to find the Dai-lue monastics at Wat Paknām largely through the
aid of an English monk who had been at Wat Paknām for several decades, and
who has served as an advisor for novices and monks who come to Thonburi to
study. I had been put in touch with him by a Dai-lue officer of the Yunnan BA,
who sometimes helped arrange for Dai-lue monastics to travel abroad for an
education. They had, of course, come to Bangkok to study Pāli within the *nak-
tham* course. I chatted with these monks, some of whom I had taught at Wat
Pājie in 2001–2002, for about an hour, inquiring about their studies, the conditions of their life in the Thai capital, and their plans for the future. For the
first bit, the English monk sat and listened to us, but as most of our conversation was in Chinese with the occasional Dai-lue thrown in, after a while, he fell
asleep.

This moment is not interesting because of the fact that it was an
extraordinarily international moment, though it was that. Of course monks
have been international travelers and exchange students for centuries. The
Chinese monk Xuanzang, whose experiences were reimagined in the *Journey*

to the West, traveled to South Asia in the early seventh century and studied at the Buddhist university Nālandā; Japanese monks traveled to China for hundreds of years for both study and diplomatic missions; and Theravāda monks have traveled around both the Indian Ocean and mainland Southeast Asia for several hundred years, as part of official missions, recreating lineages, delivering images, and, of course, getting an education (McDaniel 2008). And as chapter 3 showed, Dai-lue monks, too, travel and are embedded in a number of local, national, and transnational networks. In the case of the Dai-lue at Wat Paknām, the English monk told me that there was a long relationship with Sipsongpannā. He said that the abbot of Wat Paknām had been a major donor for building the school building at Wat Pājie, and that a few years before my visit, the abbot had gone to China to see the tooth relic there.[1] Khūbā Meaung Jom had also been there, and it was during this visit that they had arranged for some Dai-lue novices and junior monks to study at Wat Paknām. Here we were, then, at a Thai temple outside of Bangkok, citizens of China, England, and the United States, speaking about Buddhist education in Thailand, mainly in Mandarin Chinese. This was perhaps remarkable only because during the conversation, none of us remarked on the remarkableness of these movements; this was a clear example of the Buddhist ethnoscape.

And yet to my mind, perhaps what is more interesting is not the contours of the Buddhist ethnoscape revealed here, but the limits to the flexibility embedded in it. Of the monks and novices there, only one, the Englishman, would be at Wat Paknām within a few years (I would be gone within about three days of that visit). The Dai-lue monastics were studying Pāli, in the *naktham* course at Wat Paknām, similar to what they had studied in the Dhamma school (still at Wat Pājie at that particular time). While they were studying, their visas were straightforward, and relatively easily maintained. Foreign monks have to renew their visas every year, traveling to an office in Bangkok with letters confirming their continued study. Even the English monk, who had been living in Thailand for three decades, had to re-register every year, confirming that he was still occupied at Wat Paknām. I have been told that for most monks studying in Thailand, this is a straightforward process. Once the Dai-lue finished their studies, they were supposed to leave and return home, unless they were given an official position or job within the *wat* (like the English monk). The burden of reporting the presence of foreign monks is on the abbot of the *wat,* and while this has normally not been a particularly big issue, during the last decade, there has been pressure put on abbots to make sure that there are no illegal monks at the *wat* (or rather, no legal monks in Thailand illegally). However, as the English monk noted, he (as the officer of the *wat*) is shown the identification papers of a monk (ordination cards, or national identification card). If it is a forgery, how is he to know? While it is unclear how many non-Thai monks are living in Thailand illegally, or whether there is any real effort to contain them, there has been a certain threat in the air over illegals. In other words, while an understanding of Buddhism as a unified and universal object enables movement and connections, as we shall see in this chapter, state policies or national discourses sometimes work with and sometimes work against the flexibility provided by Buddhism.

Much of the discussion about monastic education in this book has been about identity, at least implicitly. The questions I have asked about how monks are trained and what they learn are directed at thinking about what kind of monks or *khanān* they will become. In chapter 4, the identity created within village temples is that of a "cooked" (*bao dip*) Dai-lue villager, for whom Buddhism is a central resource of local connection. In the last chapter, the discussion focused on the curricula at the Dhamma school in Jing Hong, as one of the projects that the BA is engaged in to create groups of novices and monks that understand themselves as guardians of Dai-lue identity and Buddhism in Sipsongpannā. In both cases, the Dai-lue aspects of this identity were mitigated and shaped by the governance regimes of both the local and national Chinese governments. Thus, I argued that because of experiences within the Chinese public school system, the Dai-lue village monk comes to understand his place as a member of the Daizu. The Buddhist intellectual trained at Wat Pājie (ideally) gains an understanding of his responsibilities through the crisis that incorporation into the Chinese political economy brings to the very existence of a Dai-lue community and identity.

Transnational monastic education (TME), the subject of this chapter, is a different kind of phenomenon than what I have discussed so far. It is not a specific institution or mode of instruction; rather, it is the experience of a monk or nun who travels across a "national" border to study in a monastic education system where he or she is an outsider. TME is not a new phenomenon, but in important ways, crossing contemporary borders in the early twenty-first century for an education is distinct from what it would have been a century ago, or even more recently in some cases. When Lue monks traveled to study in Chiang Mai in the era before Thailand existed (i.e., prior to 1939), they probably traveled without papers of any kind, except perhaps a letter of introduction, and they certainly traveled without understanding themselves as citizens of a particular nation-state. They undoubtedly saw themselves as members of a polity, but those notions of belonging have been transformed in crucial ways by the formation of modern nation-states, and the efforts by modern states to foster national modes of belonging. It is perhaps comparable to the idea of "China moments," except that it is not necessarily the awareness of "China" that the student-monastics experience, but an experience of otherness that travels along a track of "Buddhism." It is, in other words, an experience of monastic education that exists only because of universalist notions of Buddhism, but these universal forms are constantly and consistently shot through with the experience of difference that comes from this border crossing.

TME is a diverse phenomenon. It is not a single phenomenon run by a centralized institution, but rather a series of institutions of different Buddhist sects, located in different nation-states that have more or less awareness of one another. In some ways, what unifies these locations in this chapter is simply the experience of the Dai-lue as they travel across boundaries and borders of sect and nationality to further their education. Yet as we saw at the start of the book where I encountered the Dai-lue novice at the Buddhist College of Singapore, TME is not limited to the Dai-lue, but is rather a broader experience for Asian Buddhists. Chinese monks travel to Singapore; Taiwanese and Chinese monks to Sri Lanka; Thai monks to India for tertiary education; and Nepali and Bhutanese monks to both Burma and Thailand. These are simply some well-worn tracks within intra-Asian educational networks.[2] While this kind of travel has become an important aspect of Dai-lue Buddhism, it should also be understood as a source of prestige among and between national monastic systems. In other words—and as we shall see in this chapter and consonant with the argument throughout the book—TME is as much about national prestige between monastic systems as it is about translocal forms of Buddhism, or "Buddhism" enabling local movement. In other words, what is interesting about TME is not that monks and nuns travel for an education, but rather what it reveals about the ways that education and economies of prestige shape how "Buddhism" is used by monastics in the early twenty-first century. In this chapter, I will examine the Dai-lue experiences of TME, primarily in Thailand and China, as well as their efforts to create their own TME institution, the Yunnan Buddhist Institute outside of Kunming. What we will see in this examination is how universal notions of Buddhism and ethnic and national identity enable and constrict the movement of monastics within Asia and across China.

Journey Out of Sipsongpannā to TME Institutions

While Dai-lue monastics have probably left Sipsongpannā for centuries in order to attain a monastic education, their participation in TME should be understood as being a post-Mao phenomenon, and its transformations as a part of the development of the current forms of post–Cold War globalization. During the first decade and a half after the return of Buddhism to Sipsongpannā, Dai-lue monks traveled to the Shan States and Thailand to further their education, undirected by any single institution. Exemplary of this was a monk who was once the abbot of Wat Bān Gong. In his midthirties when I met him in 2002, he told me that after he had attended the first two years of junior middle school, he had traveled to northern Thailand and studied at a monastic school outside of Lamphun. His own education, monastic and otherwise, had taken place before the development of Wat Pājie, and so his travel was not directed by the BA in Sipsongpannā. He was not traveling into the complete unknown, however. He told me that he had cousins in Lamphun, and they helped him get established there, and supported him during his years studying in Thailand. How many monks took part in this educational travel remains unknown, and to a certain extent unknowable, as most of these men have either disrobed or remained in Thailand or the Shan States. The local government of Sipsongpannā and Yunnan began to participate in this travel in the early 1990s, when, along with the Thai government, they cosponsored ten Dai-lue novices to study at Wat Phra-Putthabāt-takphā, a different temple outside of Lamphun (Hansen 1999, 147). This sponsorship was a part of PRC efforts to foster ties with Southeast Asian nation-states as a part of their post-Mao development (much like the trip that the sister of the Thai king took to Sipsongpannā in the early 1980s [Princess Galyani 1986]), and while it initially appeared that the government would sponsor more Dai-lue students to study in Thailand, this was not the case.

Instead, in 1994, the Dhamma school opened at Wat Pājie, and as the leadership of the Buddhist Association of Sipsongpannā stabilized in the late 1990s, the movement of novices out of Sipsongpannā for study became the purview of the BA, more by the concentration of resources that has taken place than by a specific design. For many of the same reasons that were discussed in the last chapter, such as a desire to foster both knowledge and skills in novices that could be used to preserve and protect the Buddhism of Sipsongpannā has led the senior monks of the region to send novices out of Sipsongpannā. The primary location that Dai-lue novices have gone for "study abroad" trips has been Thailand, and in particular, northern Thailand, but they have also sent student-monastics to Buddhist institutes (foxueyuan) on the east coast of China (Shanghai, Xiamen, and Guangzhou), to Yangon, and to Sri Lanka.[3] The opportunity to study in these places has emerged in a variety of ways: some have been pursued by the BA, others have emerged when Khūbā Meuang Jom or one of the vice abbots meets senior monks, such as Somdet Wat Paknām discussed above or Chinese monks from Shanghai; still others have fallen into their lap, as when an invitation came to study at Vidyodaya and Vidyalankara pirivenas in Sri Lanka came to the Yunnan BA in 2001. While the last invitation went through governmental channels, the majority of these invitations and opportunities come through high-level monastic connections. These connections may be enabled by the state or quasi-state institutions such as the BA, but they are not really state-level interactions. In other words, since the mid-1990s, what had been a "transnationalism from below" (Guarnizo and Smith 1998) during the first fifteen years of the post-Mao sangha has become a "meso-level transnationalism," directed by nongovernmental or quasi-governmental institutions.

In this, the experience of the Dai-lue seems to be fairly reflective of the educational peregrinations of Buddhist monks and nuns more broadly. Monastics sometimes travel on their own, sometimes through state channels, and sometimes along routes established by prior monastics in the lineage to which they belong. In July 2013, I met a group Arakanese monks who were studying at the Chiang Mai campus of Mahā-Chulālongkorn University (Mahā-Chulā) in the English-language program there. They were not a group, in that they had traveled to Mahā-Chulā separately. One of them told me that he had studied first at the International Buddhist College (IBC) for several years (first in Hat Yai in southern Thailand, and then outside of Bangkok). He had gone to both places (IBC and Mahā-Chulā) because they were places where he could study Buddhism in English, as his ambition was to propagate Buddhism to the wider world, and English was a necessity for this (I had met him in a program called "Monk Chat," which gives monks the opportunity to chat with tourists in English). He also said, however, that it was somewhat happenstance that he had ended up at IBC; he had found it online. After he arrived in Thailand, he had met a group of Arakkanese monks studying in Thailand, who networked with one another online. It was these monks who informed him of the program at Mahā-Chulā where he was studying when I met him. This experience was very different from that of the monastics who were studying at the Buddhist College of Singapore (BCS) (where I met the monk at the start of the book). The monks at BCS were primarily Mahāyāna monks from the PRC, and their process of attending the BCS came through advertisements that had gone through BAC channels (such as the invitation to study in Sri Lanka). This Arakanese monk's experience traveling on his own was also somewhat different from the path of Chinese and Taiwanese monks that has become increasingly common: going from China to university in Sri Lanka, and from there to universities in the United Kingdom. This educational spoke has not necessarily been directed by the institution, but it has become a common path traveled by certain communities of monastics, such as those who have ended up teaching at the BCS in Singapore.

TME institutions around Asia are quite diverse, ranging from nonaccredited religious programs to PhD-granting institutions, such as Mahā-Chulā, whose main campus is outside of Ayutthaya, or some of the Indian Buddhist universities, such as Ambedkar University.[4] Given this, their relationship to their respective national governments and the process for both funding and accreditation is also quite diverse. Universities such as the Buddhist universities in Thailand and Sri Lanka receive state funding and accreditation, and are, in fact, part of larger tertiary educational systems. Other TME institutions have a more distant relationship to public education systems. The BCS, for example, is a private institution, supported primarily by the monastery that houses it, Kong Meng San Phor Kark See Monastery, and that monastery's patrons. It is not a part of the larger educational system in Singapore. This caused difficulties for the BCS, in that it had difficulties in its initial establishment with proper accreditation. Because it is distinct from the public education system, and the Singaporean government is officially neutral with regard to religion,[5] the BCS could not rely on public educational resources in its efforts to develop its two programs, one in English and one in Chinese. Ultimately, they went to Buddhist universities outside of Singapore for the development and accreditation of their programs.[6] Perhaps related to this, different TME institutions also conceptualize their "transnationality" in different ways. Places such as Mahā-Chulā and Mahā-Makut in Thailand[7] have many foreign monastics among their students, but these foreign monastics are part of a larger program dedicated to teaching Thai monks as well. They may also have programs that are for lay students as well as monastics. At the same time, an institution such as the BCS is primarily focused on non-Singaporean students coming to study in Singapore. In other words, some TME institutions conceive of themselves primarily as TME, while others have TME programs within them.

Given the diversity of TME institutions, it is important to be careful about making global claims about them. Nevertheless, there are several consistent aspects. First, these schools, institutes, colleges, and universities are filled with monks who cross boundaries. These boundaries are racial and ethnic, national, linguistic, and perhaps hardest to conceptualize, sectarian. We saw this at the beginning of the book with the presence of the Dai-lue monk at the BCS, but there are many more Theravāda monks who have come to study at the BCS from Thailand, Cambodia, and Myanmar. At the BCS, moreover, cross-sectarian dynamics are embedded in the curriculum, exemplified by the fact that their English-language program is accredited by the University of Kelaniya in Sri Lanka. Although it does not have a Theravāda program per se, the students in this program learn primarily about Pāli forms of Buddhism when they study in English. However, when I asked one of the BCS students who was a (Han) Chinese monk about this (while we were both eating the Singaporean food court delicacy *laksa* at a Vesak event outside a mall in Singapore), he said to me: "I came [to the BCS] because I am very interested in English. But here, I learn Buddhism in English. How marvelous!" (personal communication, Singapore, May 4, 2010). In other words, the border crossing, between Mahāyāna and Theravāda, did not bother him. One of the reasons why this might have been so was articulated to me a few days later by an administrator at Mahā-Chula outside of Ayutthaya. When I asked him about the incongruity of a program focused on Chinese Buddhism being accredited by a Thai Buddhist university, he explained, "In terms of study, [there is] no

Mahāyāna, no Theravāda, no Vajrayāna . . . it is all the Buddha's teachings." Indeed, while he acknowledged the differences between different types of Buddhism, he told me that these were only "culture" (personal communication, Mahā-Chulā, May 10, 2010).

The second point is an aspect, or perhaps consequence, of the first point. One important aspect of monastic education in more located places such as the apprentice forms discussed in chapter 4 is that it reproduces lineages. It does so in terms of the personal relationships between students and teachers, and also within the context of (re)constituting "fraternities" within the broader Buddhist world that share institutional structures such as ordination practices. While the permeability of lineages varies according to the time, place, and form of Buddhism, monastic communities generally function through logics of lineage. However, TME institutions do not. They are focused instead on transmitting Buddhist knowledge (and sometimes secular knowledge), which is partially conceived in sectarian terms, and partially conceived as transhistorical *religious* knowledge. Part of what makes this possible is very much the ideas articulated by the monk at Mahā-Chulā, which assumes the possibility of a Buddhist ethnoscape, linking all the Buddhists of the world.

Passing in the Dhamma Schools of Thailand

As noted above, the Dai-lue novices crossing borders to study have tended to go to two different institutions: the Dhamma schools (*rongrian phra-pariyattitham*) of Thailand, and the Buddhist institutes (*foxueyuan*) of the PRC. These are diverse institutions that span nationalities,[8] and Buddhist sects. They include formal religious schools, which have secular and religious components and tertiary education. Dai-lue have tended not to be able to matriculate into postsecondary institutions, in part because of the limits of their educational backgrounds, and in part because of the limits of what these institutes are willing to accept. While far more have attended Dhamma schools in Thailand than have attended Mahāyāna Buddhist institutes in China, it is worth thinking about them together because they represent similar possibilities for the novices.

The Dhamma schools of Thailand are part of a large network of schools that has developed over the course of the twentieth century. Like the Dhamma school in Jing Hong, these schools train novices in both secular and Buddhist subjects, though unlike the school for the Dai-lue, the Buddhist component also includes the study of Pāli. In my experience teaching English at a Dhamma school in Chiang Mai (1994) and Bangkok (2014), the students spend most of their time working on the secular curriculum and Pāli (which they study most days). The *nak-tham* course such as the one described in the last chapter tends to be studied primarily on Wan Phra, the Buddhist "Sabbath" in Thailand that follows the phases of the moon.

Over the last half century, these schools have tended to cater to boys from rural communities, and to serve as an alternative secondary school system to the public education system. Up until recently, secondary education in Thailand was not compulsory, and public high schools required both high test scores and high fees. For teenage boys who were either unable to test in or to pay, the Dhamma schools provided an opportunity to continue their education. It is for this reason that scholars have tended to focus on monastic education in Thailand as a matter of social mobility (Tambiah 1976, chap. 14; Palanee 1982; Wyatt 1994). While this has undoubtedly been an important aspect of ordination and monastic education in Thailand, we should not presume that the Dhamma schools are therefore solely about crass materialistic goals. For example, when I taught English in northern Thailand in 1994, students told me that they had ordained in order to get an education and because they "loved the Buddha," seemingly without noting any tension between these two things. On the sociopolitical side, these novices also receive regular messages that being a good Buddhist and a good Thai national are virtually the same thing. Swearer notes in his discussion of a monastic high school in northern Thailand that religious instruction and the ethics component of social studies in the secular course "serve to reinforce the moral-ethical basis of the socio-political order and . . . Pāli studies sanctify and perpetuate the religious order in particular" (1976, 63).

While the Dhamma schools are very Thai places, they are also at the same time surprisingly transnational, and often have monastics from other Theravāda countries studying in them. In schools in northern Thailand, it is common to encounter students from the Shan States or Sipsongpannā, and depending on the Dhamma schools, one might encounter novices that belong to a hill tribe such as the Karen who are probably from Thailand, but just might be from across the border. Abbots or head teachers are technically required to get copies of ordination cards, national ID cards, or both, when they allow a novice or young monk to live in their *wat* and study at the Dhamma school there or that of a nearby *wat,* but not all monks are equally zealous in these matters. At different points in time, the Thai government has put pressure on abbots to confirm that no novices or monks are living in their *wats* under false pretenses, but the ability of the Thai government to enforce this is limited. The English monk from Wat Paknām said to me in this regard that if a novice comes to Thailand from the Shan States to study in the *nak-tham* course, he speaks Shan, which is quite close to northern Thai, and after a few months, he speaks central Thai with an accent. If he then takes his higher ordination, sponsored by a Thai family, he has been brought into the institutional structure. When he comes to study in Bangkok, there is no simple way to tell if he is not actually a Thai citizen (personal communication, Bangkok, January 2008). In other words, it is easy to pass as Thai for certain kinds of novices and monks, and Dhamma schools in Thailand often end up having a far more transnational population than is obvious at first glance.

This is an important facet of the experience of Dai-lue monastics who have come from Sipsongpannā to Thailand to study. As noted above, there has been a shift in the way that these novices have traveled south for foreign study. Where once they traveled on their own to study, since the late 1990s, they have increasingly followed network spokes that have been established by the officers of the BA in Jing Hong. The Dai-lue monastics that I met at Wat Paknām had been brought there by monks from Jing Hong. Similarly, when I interviewed Dai-lue novices in the Chiang Mai region in 2002 (primarily at Wat Phra Puttha-bāt Takpha outside Lamphun and Wat Sri Sodā on the outskirts of Doi Suthep in Chiang Mai), they had been brought south. However, once Dai-lue novices have attended school for a year or two, a number of them decide to go to Dhamma schools in other places (primarily Bangkok). When they do this, it is easy for them to effectively disappear into the larger Thai Sangha. A number of them do this because they have heard of a place where they can get a better education than the Dhamma school where they have been placed. Or they do it because they find life in Thailand congenial; a number of Dai-lue novices told me that they appreciated life in Thailand because Thai people tended to treat monks with more respect than the Chinese tourists that novices regularly encounter in Jing Hong. While most of the novices that I interviewed wanted to eventually return to Jing Hong and work at the Dhamma school there, many of them were pleased to be able to spend time in Thailand, studying and passing as Thai.

Life in Thailand has also had challenges for Dai-lue novices. While most encountered the routine difficulties that life in a foreign country presents (almost all of them told me that the single hardest thing to adapt to was the food, which tends not to be as spicy as food in Sipsongpannā), a number also encountered problems with the educational opportunities available to them. Prior to the late 1990s, Dai-lue novices who came to Thailand found it easy to enroll in all of the curricula of the Dhamma schools, studying not just the *nak-tham* course and Pāli, but secular subjects as well. Sometime around the turn of the century, however, the policies regarding foreign students began to fluctuate, and the Dai-lue novices were prevented from enrolling in the secular curriculum. Between 1999 and 2008, novices told me different stories about what would allow them to study the secular subjects. Some told me that foreign students were only allowed to study in the *nak-tham* course; others said that if they had finished junior high school, they could study in the secular program; others told me that they had to bring a document from their schools saying that they had finished junior middle school. This shift came as something of a shock to the students from Sipsongpannā, in part because monks who had traveled earlier on their own had been allowed to study secular subjects, as had the students who had studied at Wat Phra Puttha-bāt in the early 1990s, cosponsored by the Chinese and Thai government. Indeed, one monk at Wat Pājie told me that before 1999, the Thai government had freely handed out "student cards" to Dai-lue students so that they could easily enroll in Thai Dhamma schools.

This shift in educational opportunities reflected a difference in attitude between the Thai Sangha, and the Thai government. The monks of Thailand seemed rather uniformly to desire to aid the development of Buddhism in Sipsongpannā. Several different monks with whom I spoke asked me what they could do for the Sangha in Sipsongpannā. Did they need computers? Did they need teachers? Did they need money? This same desire seemed to be the inspiration for taking Dai-lue students into the monastic high schools. The administrators with whom I spoke who had visited Sipsongpannā spoke disparagingly of the "low level" of Buddhism there. While they laid most of the responsibility for this at the feet of the Chinese government, it was also clear to me that they felt the Dai-lue and the monks (both Thai and Dai-lue) would themselves have to address the problems caused by the Chinese. Consequently, teaching students Dhamma and Pāli was the least they could do for Sipsongpannā Buddhism. Over the course of the 2000s, on the other hand, the Thai government was increasingly concerned about the possibility that Shan or Burmese would enter Thailand illegally, using their status as ordained monks as a cover for mass migration (personal communication, Ministry of Religion, February 2002). It was for this reason that pressure was put on abbots to confirm the legitimate status of foreign monks. Although the policy was not focused on monastics from Sipsongpannā, they were caught up in it, and several monks told me that they felt a need to carry their ordination cards with them regularly. It is also here that we see that it was not just possible for monastics of Sipsongpannā to pass as Thai, but that some of them felt it a necessity to use Thai names and generally keep it under wraps that they were not Thai citizens.

To a certain extent, the challenges that Dai-lue monastics have encountered in Thailand have been about expectations. The monks I interviewed at Wat Paknām in 2008 had not expected to be able to study secular subjects when they came to Bangkok, and as a result, they were not disappointed in the ways that monastics were at the beginning of the decade. The shifting policies of the Thai state towards foreign monks, it is worth noting, was also a surprise to the Sipsongpannā BA. In the spring of 2002, I asked the head teacher of the Dhamma school at Wat Pājie about the students going to Thailand to study, particularly about whether it was a good opportunity for them. It also came as a surprise to the Sipsongpannā BA, which for a time in the early part of the decade reduced the number of graduates that it sent to study in Thailand precisely because its members felt as though studying in Thailand was not as good an opportunity for the novices. "It's a good opportunity," the head teacher said, "and we need to send our students there, because the sangha needs the skills that they learn there . . . but [it is] not as good as it used to be."[9]

Buddhist Charity for Theravāda Monks in Chinese Buddhist Institutes

In the fall of 2001, eleven graduates of the Dhamma school at Wat Pājie left Sipsongpannā by bus to go to Kunming. From Kunming, they boarded a train to Shanghai, where they were placed at Yuan Ming Jiang Tang, a temple in the western part of the city that is a sibling temple of Long Hua Si, one of the three major temples of Shanghai. Here they were to live and study at the Hua Lin Buddhist Institute (BI). They were sponsored by the Shanghai BA, and were overseen by the monks of the Yuan Ming Jiang Tang. Although these students were the first group from Sipsongpannā to go to Shanghai, they were not the first group to leave Jing Hong to travel to an eastern seaboard city, but rather the third. In 1998, and then again in 1999, graduates from Wat Pājie traveled to Xiamen and also to Guangzhou to study, as guests of the respective BAs. In both these cases, it was smaller groups that went to study with four to each city. While the group that went to Shanghai was originally scheduled to remain for only a year and a half, it ended up staying for three, and a second group of students from the Dhamma school in Jing Hong was also able to study in Shanghai.

Unlike the Dhamma schools of Thailand, the Mahāyāna BIs in China are not part of the public education system. Most of the BIs in China are akin to the public colleges and universities of the rest of the country, though rather than being under the auspices of the Ministry of Education, they are run by specific temples in conjunction with BAs. They are usually three- or four-year courses that require an entrance exam, and usually require their students to have finished their secondary education in the public school system.[10] As a consequence, BIs function more as professional training for Chinese monks, who are adults, and less as an alternative form of public education, which is primarily for teenagers, like the Dhamma schools of Thailand. While the Dhamma schools of Thailand are split between secular and Buddhist subjects, Chinese BIs tend to have a greater share of their instructional time (approximately two-thirds) dedicated to Buddhist subjects (Long 2002).

Despite this overt Buddhist orientation, BIs in China are imbued with nationalist discourses. In examining several BIs in Sichuan for both monks and nuns, Darui Long has pointed out how the charters of these schools explicitly claim to be aimed at "train[ing] Buddhist nuns who love the country, and support the Party leadership and the socialist cause" (2002, 192). Another school's charter said that its purpose was "to train Buddhists who are patriots and faithful to Buddhism so that they become knowledgeable and able persons for the development of Buddhism." It goes on to say that:

> Students should support the leadership of the Communist Party of China. They should be patriotic and faithful, with good virtues and abilities. They should observe state laws. They are trained to be managers of the monasteries and researchers for Buddhism. (Long 2002, 199)

This was language that was similar to what Dai-lue novices would have encountered when they studied in Shanghai at the Yuan Ming Jiang Tang. The rules of the BI there began with a statement that students should "Fervently love the socialist motherland, support the leadership of the Communist Party, defend the unity of the Nationalities, and support the motherland." This set of rules, which has language consonant with the demands of Document 19, was given to the Dai-lue students before they traveled to Shanghai. It may be the case that we should read this language as prophylaxis, put in to assure local governments that religion is embedded within and tied to national projects. Nevertheless, it is language that new students at BIs are forced to encounter, if only in preparation for attending, and while on a daily basis monk-students may not be forced to confront or acknowledge their citizenship as Chinese, it is not far from the surface. Moreover, occasionally, BIs may force these monks to acknowledge the way in which Buddhism is linked to the nation.[11]

In 2008, there was a "Seminar on Buddhist Studies in Foreign Languages," based at the Jade Buddha Temple (Yu Fo Si) in Shanghai, in which young monastics from China, Taiwan, and Hong Kong gave speeches in English, Korean, French, Thai, and Spanish about Chinese Buddhism facing the world (Gu 2009). The seminar was a warm-up event for the second World Buddhist Forum, which took place in 2009 in Wuxi, and many of the essays published in the volume were by young monastics studying at BIs throughout China (the Jade Buddha Temple has a BI as well). One of the primary themes of the conference was "Chinese Buddhism Facing the World." Many of the essays straightforwardly talk about the challenges for Chinese Buddhism in the face of both massive economic development and internationalization. For example, some essays suggested the need to "throw off the 'Temple model'" (Gu 2009, 122), or to develop good websites to foster proper interaction with the world (154). Others sought to provide a balance by focusing on how the transmission of Buddhism to China from India 2000 years ago indicated that what we see now is simply a new version of old challenges (68). Part of what is fascinating about these essays by students in BIs is that they naturalize the relationship of Buddhism and China. The monastics are focused on the development of "Chinese Buddhism," not Buddhism in China. One monk, for example, ends his essay with a clear rearticulation of the language of the rules cited above: "To meet the expectations of the people around the world, Chinese Buddhism should stick to the principal of loving both our nation and Buddhism, unite closely around the [Communist Party of China], cooperate sincerely with other fraternal religious groups and people of different ethnic religions, and make unremitting efforts to build a harmonious socialist China. . . . I am proud, I am a Chinese. I am proud, I am a Chinese monk" (178). There is a certain overdetermined quality of a comment like this; of course, when "facing the world," a monk is going to respond in a patriotic fashion. The point is instead that BIs will place their students into such situations, even as they are training them in Buddhism.

This can be seen clearly in the courses that the Dai-lue novices studied at the Yuan Ming Jiang Tang. When I visited the Dai-lue students in May 2002, they told me that they were studying English, "computers," geography, and Mahāyāna Dhamma (a Taiwanese monk who had grown up in Hawai'i informed me that it was a "Pure Land Lineage"). They also studied tai chi, Chinese language, and Chinese history. The vice-abbot of the temple, who was their advisor, told me that he taught them Chinese law (secular, not Buddhist). The curriculum, in fact, resembled much of what the Dhamma school in Jing Hong came to resemble after it made its pact with the technical college. They were also encouraged, but not required, to take part in the meditation practice and chanting that occur at the temple. The Dai-lue students told me that they did this, but they found that chanting sutras was particularly challenging. This was partly about being unfamiliar with a style of chanting that uses rest marks and bells. It was also, however, due to their unfamiliarity with classical Chinese. In the Chinese class, they were using a ninth-grade textbook that barely got them to the level they needed to follow the texts they were chanting.

Even as these students were being integrated into the Chinese curriculum, they were regularly marked as outsiders. The Dai-lue wore monks' robes, but they continued to wear the orange/saffron of the Theravāda world rather than the gray (and occasional mustard) that the Han Chinese monks of this temple wore. At mealtimes, they seemed to eat apart from the Han monks, and they tended to find the food far too bland, if adequate.[12] While the Dai-lue told me they attended the chanting, they were not required to go to it. Moreover, unlike the Dai-lue students, the Han monks did not practice tai chi. Many of these Han monks were also students, but unlike the Dai-lue students, they all studied at the main school connected with the Long Hua Temple, and they all studied above the level of high school. The Dai-lue students alone studied at the Yuan Ming Jiang Tang, taught largely by teachers who were brought especially to teach them a modified high school curriculum.

This attitude of distinction from the Dai-lue monastics seemed to be shared by both the monks of the temple and the teachers who were brought in from the outside. The monks I talked with spoke of the Dai-lue students with obvious fondness, and seemed to enjoy their presence. They appreciated the students' hard work, and one of the monks mentioned to me how two of the students in particular were quite smart. Yet they also spoke of them from above, as if they were children. One of them told me that these two novices are quite *taopi* (naughty). He also told me that he scolded them for not knowing my name (they had simply referred to me as *laoshi* [teacher]). I should note that this was a tone that the Chinese teacher and I tended to use when talking together about the students at Wat Pājie, though it was not the tone the monks themselves tended to use when talking about their students. In my own case, I would say that age was the principal factor causing me to talk of the students as I did (being the same age as some of their fathers), though it is possible that in the case of the Han monks, ethnicity was also playing some sort of factor.

Their teachers also seemed to emphasize their outside status. When I observed a Chinese-language and a Chinese history class, both teachers emphasized the length of their stay and also their ethnicity. The *yuwen* teacher, who was a retired Chinese professor of Fudan University, referred to "when you leave" throughout his class; as in, "this is a *cheng-yu* [aphorism] you should remember when you leave." During the history class, the teacher emphasized both Buddhism and ethnicity. For example, the lesson for that day focused on the Five Dynasties period between the Tang and Song dynasties (907–960 CE). When he sketched out each dynasty's key points, they included dates, ruler, seat of power, famous Buddhist temples, and what their attitude was to Buddhism and whether they were "minorities" or not. He also asked the students, after noting specific changes in Buddhism during one of the dynasties, "What about your Theravāda Buddhism?" I do not want to make too much of these remarks; in their 1989 textbook on China, Fairbank and Reischauer make largely the same point about the Five Dynasties, and the students are indeed Theravāda Buddhist. Nonetheless, the regular references to their returning to Sipsongpannā, as well as references to minorities and their own brand of Buddhism, served to distance the students from their place of study (a point born out in conversations with the Dai-lue students). Indeed, while not meant pejoratively, this attitude functions as a "China moment" for the Dai-lue monastics at the Yuan Ming Jiang Tang.

A TME of the Yunnan Buddhist Institute

The experiences of Dai-lue monastics in transnational monastic education are, at best, uneven. On the one hand, traveling outside of Sipsongpannā to continue their education, whether in Theravāda contexts in Southeast Asia or in Mahāyāna BIs in China, is pursued as a viable and positive option by both senior and junior monks of Sipsongpannā. While fewer Dhamma school graduates traveled from Jing Hong to Thailand to study in the middle of the decade, when invitations arose from the abbot of Wat Paknām, they were accepted. Similarly, the senior monks actively pursued exchanges with Mahāyāna monks, sending Dai-lue novices to the east coast, but also accepting a small number of Han monks to come and study at the Dhamma school in Jing Hong. Moreover, since the late 1990s, young Dai-lue monks and older novices have told me that they wanted to go study Buddhism outside of Sipsongpannā. On the other hand, however, when they have traveled outside of Sipsongpannā, they have not always been met with a robust welcome. Dai-lue monastics in Shanghai are constructed as outsiders, the recipients of charitable gifts; those in Thailand, hide in plain sight in part because of intermittent pressure from the Thai government.

This highlights one of the intense ironies of the conditions of the Dai-lue monastics: their liminal status, on the edge of China and of Southeast Asia enables them to cross borders or nation and sect, but it does not necessarily allow them as a group to belong. In other words, their citizenship and their religious identity provide them with the flexibility to move across boundaries, but crossing these borders, they do not leave their subaltern status. Without being both Theravāda and Tai, these young monastics would not be able to go to Thailand, or once there, to pass as Tai. They would certainly not have the opportunity to go to Sri Lanka. Without being Chinese citizens, these Theravāda monks would not be able to go to Shanghai or other east coast cities to study (or probably even to Kunming). Yet just as these subject positions make them more flexible, the frictions of regimes of governance limit the effectiveness of the Buddhist ethnoscape. They cannot stay in Thailand indefinitely without breaking the law, just as they could not easily remain in Shanghai over the long term without a residency permit. While the Mahāyāna monks were willing to interact with and even support their conationals, they did not seem to be interested in permanent associations unless the Dai-lue were willing to "convert" to Mahāyāna Buddhism. Indeed, the irony of this transnational education is that precisely what provides the monks with flexibility, creates the friction that limits their opportunities.

It is perhaps for this reason that the Buddhist Association of Sipsongpannā strongly supported the creation of the Yunnan Buddhist Institute (Yunnan Foxueyuan; YF) in the middle of the decade. The YF is about an hour outside Kunming, very near Anning, a hot spring resort town. It was built on a hillside, essentially in a forest, on land that was donated to the Yunnan BA. The YF was the idea of Dao Shuren, a Dai-lue bureaucrat who was a vice-president of the BAC up until the early part of the first decade of the twenty-first century and who became the head of the Yunnan BA afterwards.[13] The initial vision seems to have been to capitalize on the relatively unique nature of Buddhism in Yunnan, which is its diversity. While it is certainly an accident of history and geographers, Yunnan is a place that has had native, local sanghas of the three major streams of Buddhism for half a millennium. Indeed, the monks and BA officers that I talked to claimed that Yunnan was the only place in the world where this is the case. All other places where diverse Sanghas coexist is the result of recent migration, but in Yunnan, Theravāda, Mahāyāna, and Tibetan forms of Buddhism have existed for significant periods of time. The YF was meant to capitalize on this, and become a Buddhist institute where monastics of all sorts could study together.

This is also where it makes sense to think about the YF as a TME institution. Like the BIs of the east coast of China, the students are all Chinese citizens; however, here the crossing of boundaries of nationality—of "*minzu*-ness"—is built into the very idea of the school. Moreover, while it is in some ways a small thing, the YF has in the past been a member of the International Association of Buddhist Universities (IABU), and Dao Shuren spoke at a conference in Bangkok in 2008 at the founding of the IABU, in which he linked the project of the Buddhist Association of China to the project of the IABU in fostering Buddhist education, as an international project. "I believe that under the joint efforts of the participating countries of Buddhist education, senior monks are bound to promote friendly exchanges and the development of Buddhist education in various countries and regions, and make new contributions to the world."[14] While to a certain extent this should simply be seen as boilerplate bureaucratic language, it nevertheless does explicitly link the BAC and the YF in particular into an international Buddhist project.

In broad outline, the YF program as described by the monks who worked there and the lay teachers might be seen as something of an amalgam of the programs at Wat Pājie and the Yuan Ming Jing Tang. There were eight subjects that were being taught at the school: English, modern Chinese literature, classical Chinese literature, *mishu xue* (what they described as "secretarial matters"), Chinese legal studies, accounting, computer usage, and Buddhist materials. Students from the different streams of Buddhism do not study a Buddhist curriculum in common; rather, they study the Buddhism of each of their traditions separately (though they do study the other courses together). The Buddhist curriculum was (and is) taught by monks of the various traditions, and in the Theravāda case, the YF has largely been staffed by the monks of Wat Pājie (of which more will be discussed below), and the Theravāda curriculum largely matches the *nak-tham* course at Wat Pājie. The rest of the curriculum is taught by faculty from the Yunnan Nationalities University (MinDa). Like the changes to the Dhamma school in Jing Hong, which made it something like a prep school, the YF was designed to make it possible for monks to attend colleges in China. Monks who successfully made it through the several-year program were entitled to take the entrance exam to MinDa, something that they would only be able eligible to do if they were enrolled in high school programs, and indeed, several of the (lay) teachers with whom I spoke suggested that at least some of the Dai-lue students would be capable of passing the exam (when I visited the school, no one had yet taken the entrance exam).

Like the Mahāyāna BIs discussed above, the transnationality of the YF is implicit rather than explicit. Its logic—or perhaps better the marketing behind it—is trans-sectarian, and relies on an idea not all that different from what was expressed by the monk from Mahā-Chulā that Buddhism is one.

Nonetheless, the conditions at the school are complicated. Students are supposed to enter the program through an entrance exam, and they are also supposed to have finished junior high school. A number of the Dai-lue students came to the YF after studying at Wat Pājie. Some of them had been to Thailand or Shanghai, and for these students, the program was largely a repetition of what they had learned already. Others came to the YF after studying in the public schools, and had never attended the Dhamma school in Jing Hong. Despite this, the monks at the YF told me that they did not see the YF program as being in competition with the Jing Hong Dhamma School, but rather part of the same project. There were some difficulties in matching students, however. According to the MinDa teachers I spoke to, the Dai-lue students tended to be pretty good, and to have a reasonable knowledge of Putonghua. On the other hand, they said the Tibetan students were quite low-level. This made the classes very difficult to teach. These teachers did not know whether the Tibetan students had been to middle school or not, but they felt as though the Tibetan students were for the most part not prepared to enter a Mandarin-based program.

There are problems of integration. While the interactions that I saw between Tibetan and Theravāda monks seemed perfectly pleasant, they were neither particularly intimate nor frequent. Part of this may have been a language problem; if the Tibetans' Chinese skills were as poor as the Han teachers suggested, then the various monks would not have shared a language in common. Part of it was also cultural differences. While it seems minor, the food served at the school was described by the Dai-lue monks as Chinese: the Dai-lue did not like Tibetan food, and most Han and Tibetans found the Dai food to be too spicy. Hence, their sustenance became the lowest common denominator. Ironically, during my two visits to the school, it was clear that there were almost no Mahāyāna/Han monks studying there. This makes sense given the discussion in chapter 4 about the age of ordination, and the fact that Tibetan and Dai novices can ordain at a much younger age than Han can. While there are, of course, exceptions, as a general rule, Han men need to wait until they have graduated from middle school before ordaining. For these monks, then, there is less benefit to attending the YF, even if it is the only

Buddhist institute in Yunnan. Regardless of the reason, this meant that the YF has become de facto a minority Buddhist institute.

Perhaps related to this, the YF seems to have become not just a minority Buddhist institute, but much more a Dai-lue Buddhist institute. Most of the administration is done by Dai-lue monks and laymen. The head teacher of the YF has been one of the vice-abbots of Wat Pājie. Moreover, the two men most responsible for the administration are the head and vice-head of the Yunnan BA, and both of these men are Dai-lue (one of them is in fact a *khanān*). They do not seem to have created the YF for Dai-lue monks, but they are also not acting against the interest of the Dai-lue Sangha in their administration. Finally, while there are certainly some Tibetan monks involved, the office at the YF is largely staffed by Dai-lue. What is also interesting about this is that this administration seems really to be Dai-*lue* and not Dai-*zu*. The trilingual gate to the YF, for example, uses Dai-lue characters and not Dai-neua ones. The textbooks used in the Theravāda training similarly use Dai-lue, and the teachers are Dai-lue, not Dai-neua. There are undoubtedly practical reasons for this, such as the fact that the Dai-lue Sangha is more developed than the Dai-neua. Even if it makes sense, however, it can make non-Dai-lue Theravāda Buddhists feel as though they are inferior to the Dai-lue. Indeed, when I asked some of the Dai-lue monks about this (and these were monks I had known for six years and we were speaking in private), they acknowledged the prominence of Dai-lue, and even looked a little sheepish, but they did not say they thought it should be changed.

In a sense, then, the YF repeats some of the same experiences that the Dai-lue have had in Thailand or in Shanghai, except in this case Dai-lue monks are shaping the experience, and Tibetans are the ones for whom the school is somewhat uncomfortable.

Conclusion: the Limits of the Buddhist Ethnoscape

Throughout this chapter, I have regularly referred to food, and often in a negative way. When I have met Dai-lue monastics in schools outside of Sipsongpannā, the subject of food has always come up. This is because I have asked them about what they feel about living where they are, and adjusting to new types of food looms large in their experience. This is admittedly a prosaic fact, but it also points to a simple but important fact that bodies traveling across distance need to be fed, that it is not always easy for young men to acclimate, and that many of them end up feeling lonely, and wanting to return to Sipsongpannā, even when they are grateful for the opportunities to study, and appreciative of their teachers. Disliking the food creates friction that disinclines one to stay in a place.

Transnational monastic education is marked by frictions such as these, but also flexibilities. When young Dai-lue monastics leave Sipsongpannā, they do so because they are ambitious—to learn, to develop themselves, and to help protect their sangha. They travel along spokes that have generally been laid down by the teachers at the Dhamma school in Jing Hong, spokes that were developed in their own experiences in Thailand, or in the experience of working within the Buddhist Association of China. These are spokes that rely on affiliations of ethnicity, of nationality, and of Buddhism. All of these enable travel across borders and boundaries, for the Dai-lue monks, but also for monks and nuns of other countries as well. TME is a much wider phenomenon than scholars have sufficiently acknowledged.

Yet even as we acknowledge the border-crossing capacity of Dai-lue and other monks, this chapter has highlighted the difficulties with it as well. When Dai-lue monks cross a border, they do not go from a location of regulation and webs of power and authority structures to one of freedom; rather, they enter into a different set of authority structures and class conditions, where they may or may not have a location that enables them to stay. That is, to return to Talal Asad's (1993) point, we are all of us located; it is just that when we travel, we enter into a different set of equally located relations. Buddhism enables the monks of Sipsongpannā to escape for a time how they relate to their state authorities, but it does not enable them to escape state authorities and regulation.

Afterword

DURING MY SECOND VISIT TO THE YF in the summer of 2009, the monks and laymen who were working in the office were developing a proposal for a "Theravāda Buddhist Pāli College." This would be a tertiary program that would give the Theravāda Buddhists of China—that is, the Daizu and Bulang people—the opportunity to study Theravāda Buddhism and Pāli at levels that they had not yet been able to do in China. It would finally move them beyond the knowledge embedded in the *nak-tham* curriculum taught in Jing Hong and at the YF. It would also, so they said, put Theravāda Buddhism at the same level as Mahāyāna and Tibetan Buddhism, which, they told me, already had their own colleges in China. I was struck by the fact that they had only gotten the YF up and running for a few years, and they were already looking at opening up yet another institution, one that would not be transnational in the way that the YF is. They were not given permission by the Yunnan government, and I have not heard of continued efforts to develop such a college. Yet this was the experience that these monks had with developing Wat Pājie in the early 1990s, and it was also the experience with Wat Long Meuang Lue in the first years of the twenty-first century. It would be no surprise, in other words, if there were a dedicatory celebration of the Theravāda Buddhist Pāli College in 2022, but nor would it be a big surprise if this project never saw the light of day. Not all business ventures are successful, and these Buddhists have shown themselves to be highly entrepreneurial over the years.

Indeed, they have had to be. As has been clear throughout this book, while the monks of Sipsongpannā have been fairly successful in recreating their sangha, in developing programs for maintaining language and culture, and in sending their student-novices to a number of different places to study, they have not always had great opportunities for doing this. Dai-lue monks have tended to have good relations with the Han majority and the local government, for reasons that have been touched upon at various points in this book, which has meant that they have been participants (sometime active, sometimes reluctant) in the transformation of the local economy towards domestic tourism. This has flooded the region with cash; although it has not always benefited Dai-lue villagers in significant long-term ways, it has provided a clear space for the maintenance of Dai-lue cultural forms, including Buddhism. But the development of these forms into commoditized and consumable bits can distort what is practice and ossify living culture. To the degree that the monks of Sipsongpannā want to develop their culture, it is always in the face of this development, and an overwhelmingly large government system that is at best suspicious of the agency of minority groups, including religious ones. This does not mean it is impossible to achieve their aims, but they must always be pushing, even as this pushing cannot be perceived as stepping out of the limits imposed by the government. As a group, the monks of Sipsongpannā are too few to fight the system, but it is also not in their interest to do so in overt ways. The sangha as a whole has benefited from being able to build and rebuild *wats,* and their continued ability to foster development relies on continued good relations with the local government. They do not want to be seen as "troublesome" like some other minorities. Rather, they seem to be adept at finding places in the system where they can exist so that they can develop a community that interests them. It is an ongoing process that requires constant management.

This book began with a series of questions about what makes a monk. The answers to these questions reflect the idea that the development and redevelopment of a religious community is always an ongoing product of competing agendas, political structures and economic development, local concerns and national politics, and the particular way that ideas about "Buddhism" have become naturalized in the early twenty-first century. Moreover, while there is an assumption that "Buddhism" is a stable object, what gets naturalized and privileged as "Buddhism" varies depending on the context of the interaction (local, national, or transnational) and the actors involved (lay villagers, Dai-lue monks, state actors, Chinese Mahāyāna, or international Theravāda Buddhists). Part of what this means is that while there are Buddhist discourses and practices that have remained consistent in some ways over the centuries, Buddhism itself does not have any kind of essential nature. Instead, it is a location around which and through which some communities such as the Dai-lue have debated what it means to be Dai-lue. This does not mean that it is absolutely flexible (there are, after all, cleavages between different kinds of Buddhists), nor that it is the only location around which such negotiation takes place. But as I have shown throughout the book, Buddhism is a resource for Dai-lue development, where Dai-lue people can engage with the state on terms over which they have partial control. Part of this is the way that the Chinese state has chosen to define religion as a legitimate form of culture (within certain parameters) and sees Dai-lue Buddhism as both useful (for development) and legitimate. It is relevant that the monks and *khanān* were trying to open a Theravāda Buddhist college, and not one focused on history or culture. This minority form of Buddhism has come to be seen as something that is socially useful, in part because the senior monks and *khanān* play by the government's rules, even as they exploit resources from outside the borders of the country. In a sense, it is notions of what Buddhism is that enable both of these actions.

In saying this, I am suggesting that we need to understand new models for thinking about how religions work in the contemporary world. Thomas Tweed has recently argued that religion should be seen as a social phenomenon that both orients communities and enables their movement in space, that is, it is about both crossing and dwelling (2006, 55). Much of this is resonant with the conditions I have been describing in Sipsongpannā, and it is clear that Buddhism does multiple kinds of work for the Dai-lue. It performs this "locative function," conditioning what it means to be Dai-lue, but it also provides a strategy and a resource for movement across political and cultural borders that are not otherwise easily crossed. Yet at the same time, there is a curious limitation to the way Tweed describes the crossing function of religion. The examples he utilizes are focused on aspects that are redolent of religious discourses or institutions, such as pilgrimage. While Tweed clearly understands that people go on pilgrimage for multiple reasons, his examples highlight religious actors moving in religious ways to follow religious agendas and projects, ignoring the ways that religious motivations can be partial or tied up with other types of motivations. The boys who become novices (see chapter 4) and travel outside of their home village to further their education (see chapters 5 and 6) do so for both religious and nonreligious reasons. Some do so because they love the Buddha, others because their friends are ordaining. These nonreligious reasons are not trivial; indeed, they are essential to understanding the role(s) of Buddhism within a society. In understanding Buddhism, it is therefore necessary to emphasize a "both/and" perspective. The second dynamic that Tweed's analysis misses is the role played by the imagined essence of a religion. Scholars have argued for the last several decades that Buddhism is an unstable referent. According to this viewpoint, it has no essence, it varies across time and space, it is multiple phenomena, and so forth. While this is true in some ways, I have also aimed to show here that "Buddhism" has a social life and a social impact to which we must pay attention. States govern religions—Buddhism, for example—as if they have stable referents, and Buddhist actors and states assume a tie with other Buddhists because they are Buddhist. The strength of that tie varies, but it is there nonetheless.

The Chinese state has loomed large throughout this book. It conditions the possibilities of choices that the Dai-lue have, and it is difficult to completely escape the state, even in "Zomia." At the same time, I have also tried to show that there are limits to state control in the practice of Buddhism in the region. Or perhaps it would be more accurate to say that there are limits to the state's efforts to control the practice of Buddhism. Hence, the monks of Wat Pājie and the Buddhist Association and of village temples do not always think about the state or about politics. There are local concerns, such as the need to pay back an invitation to a ritual or the need to make sure that the text-books are available for the next class of novices to use. There are also transnational relationships that shape people's lives and enable their capacities. In highlighting this, I do not wish to suggest that these local concerns or trans-national connections are part of a pure religious sphere that is outside of the political sphere. The rules that enable and constrain religious practice were established as a part of the playing field, affecting religious practice in explicit and implicit ways. Yet even as monks have to pay attention to local politicians and their concerns, they also have to pay attention to other relationships, in Jing Hong, among Dai-lue elsewhere in China, and among the Dai-lue and other Buddhists in mainland Southeast Asia. In the process of rebuilding the sangha, the monks of Sipsongpannā constantly face the world in multiple frames of conceptualization. If the state is never far away, neither are monks and nuns who live under different state systems. Dipesh Chakrabarty (2000) has talked about the need to "provincialize Europe" in understanding modern Indian history. His point is to acknowledge how European models of social development are central to understanding what has taken place in South Asia and India over the last two centuries, while also acknowledging the ways in which these models are completely irrelevant. In a sense, what I have tried to do here is to "provincialize the state": to describe its foundational role in the practice of Buddhism in Sipsongpannā, but not reduce everything to a conflict between the state and religion.

Much of the discussion throughout the book has functioned at the level of the sangha, or decisions that monks and novices as a class might make. Yet it is important that we remember that the sangha is made up of boys and men who are making life decisions, and that their status as a novice or a monk is shaped by a variety of factors that are normally beyond our vision. In 2011, I spent a day in Jing Hong, and while chatting with some former students at the Dhamma school, I again met the Dai-lue monk who had attended my lecture at the Buddhist College of Singapore the previous year (whom I described at the start of the book). He had left the BCS and returned to Sipsongpannā because he needed a break from studying. Being at the BCS was a good opportunity, he acknowledged, but it was difficult as well, and he was not really sure it was what he wanted. I have been told that he has since disrobed, and is working for a cross-border trading company. Decisions like this have not been moments of regret within the sangha: he did not become a transnational Buddhist intellectual, but some opportunities end up not being the right fit for a given individual. A monk's parent might die, for example, and someone needs to take over the land that they have been working. Or perhaps the young monk falls in love. Most Dai-lue men with whom I speak recognize that everyone has a very specific set of factors that lead them to ordain, but also to disrobe.

The idea of specificity leads me to my final point: Sipsongpannā is a very specific place. The Buddhists there are minorities who practice Theravāda Buddhism in a country where Mahāyāna is the majority form of Buddhism. The politics of religion in Yunnan and Sipsongpannā is a specific product of the recent history of China and the way in which the Chinese state has defined and managed both religions and minorities. The ability of Dai-lue Buddhists to develop and move across a variety of Buddhist networks is a specific product of their location in China, as a part of the Tai world with coethnics throughout Southeast Asia and as Theravāda Buddhists. Yet rather than seeing the Dai-lue as unique and incomparable, I would suggest that their experiences highlight certain practices and forms that are common throughout the Buddhist world. Buddhists everywhere are also citizens, and they practice their Buddhism within legal frameworks that define religion either explicitly or implicitly. Some of these are repressive and others are not, but all of them are productive in the sense that they lead religious actors to privilege some acts over others. Not all Buddhists have had to develop and rely on transnational networks as much as the monks of Sipsongpannā, but Buddhists of all sorts travel, assuming and creating ethnoscapes that have local, national, and transnational aspects. In other words, I wish to suggest that what the monks of Sipsongpannā show us are some of the ways that Buddhists exist in the political landscape of the early twenty-first century.

I began this book by asking what makes a monk. The answer—which is overdetermined in some ways—is that monks are the products of communities, of state systems of governance and control, of capitalist development, of local and national forms of Buddhism, and of the imagination of what Buddhism is universally. The answer also lies in the individual life choices of the men who have become monks.

Notes

INTRODUCTION

1 "World religions" is a category that has become normalized over the last century through usage, publication categories, and course titles. However, following the implications of Masuzawa (2005), when I refer to Buddhism as a world religion, it should be understood that it has a status that is empty of clear content, even as it is presumed to be referring to something clear and real.

2 Hayashi devotes even less attention to monastic education. Spiro (1970, 306–307) also refers to the "core of the monastic curriculum," but this is largely limited to a list of texts for memorization, as well as complaints about Burmese monks' low level of intellectual engagement. There are counterexamples, including Blackburn (2001), Samuels (2004), McDaniel (2008), and Kawanami (2013), some of which are discussed in the pages that follow.

3 On Laos, see Kourilsky (2010); for Cambodia, see Hansen (2007).

4 I have sought to complicate the narrative of "relevance" in Borchert (2008).

5 See Nietupski (1999, 96) for Labrang.

6 Here, I am following the lead of Martin Reisebrodt (2010), who elucidates a similar argument in developing a "content-based" theory of religion.

7 There is no perfect translation for the Chinese term *shaoshu minzu*. *Minzu* is a neologism, probably from the Japanese *minzoku,* and might be translated as "people," "nationality," or even "ethnicity," but these do not really capture both the sense of belonging and the Marxist/Stalinist heritage or the degree that it is contained by the Chinese nation-state, which understands itself to be a "multi-*minzu* state." While some scholars such as Charlene Makeley (2008) have chosen not to translate the term, for ease of communication, I will generally refer to *shaoshu minzu* as "minorities."

8 Although I will continue to use "Theravāda" in this book, it is a problematic term, as is well known by most scholars. It is not a neologism of the modern period, but its widespread usage only began in the middle of the twentieth century. It was adopted first by Buddhists and later by scholars to refer to those forms of Buddhism that were based in some way on Pāli texts and were primarily located in Sri Lanka and mainland Southeast Asia. It was adopted so that it would be possible to speak of this form of Buddhism in relation to Mahāyāna Buddhism, without using the term "Hīnayāna," which is normally understood in negative sectarian terms. See Skilling et al. (2012) for recent discussion of the history and use of the term.

9 Generally speaking, within Theravāda communities, there are two different ordinations, *pabbajjā* and *upasampadā*. The first, "leaving home," is also referred to as the novice ordination and is usually undertaken by boys who accept ten precepts. The second, the "higher" ordination, has men over the age of twenty take

on 227 precepts. Fully ordained nuns have a different number of precepts, as do the monks and nuns of Mahāyāna and Tibetan Buddhism. These follow different disciplinary codes (though there is significant overlap between them).

10 This problem of a generation gap with implications for the transmission of knowledge, as well as the administration of Buddhist temples, is not unique to the Dai-lue of Sipsongpannā; indeed, it is common throughout China. See Birnbaum (2003) for a discussion of this problem within contemporary Mahāyāna temples in China.

11 My landlord in Jing Hong, herself a cadre in the local government, once said to me after a dinner that it was really good that I was studying Buddhists rather than Muslims, because the latter were "troublesome." That this conversation took place just prior to September 11, 2001, indicates the widespread nature of this attitude.

12 The Buddhist Association is a quasi-governmental association, part of the "United Front" group of mass organizations that are responsible for acting as the representatives of the people to the state as well as for implementing state regulations among the people. There are similar associations for all religions in China. It is worth highlighting that the Chinese state is a diverse and complex bureaucratic apparatus, with national, provincial, and local forms, and many different agencies and bureaus. While it is highly centralized, it is not monolithic, and these diverse entities do not always work together. In other words, different state entities are often in competition with one another, and nonstate actors can exploit this to mobilize one state entity against another to foster their agendas.

13 There is a large ethnographic literature on minorities in China. Among the most relevant for my work here are Gladney (1994, 1998), McCarthy (2000), and Schein (2000).

14 In the same way, while notions of the Han as a people go back many centuries, "the Han" were reimagined and constituted as a modern nationality in the late nineteenth and early twentieth centuries as a part of the effort to develop a successful Chinese nationalism, which was dedicated to overthrowing the Qing and fending off colonialism.

15 Mullaney (2011) provides the most extensive treatment of this process.

16 I understand that there is a certain danger here in describing the nature of Buddhism as reflective of how I understand the conditions of Buddhism in Sipsongpannā, that is, I risk universalizing from a single case, which is a widespread problem within the study of China as a whole. However, I hope to show below that the Dai-lue are reflective of certain aspects of Buddhism, rather than a unique or singular case.

17 Without denying the importance of Aśoka for understanding Buddhist, and particularly Therāvada, visions of politics, I suspect that Aśoka has been overemphasized within scholarship such as Tambiah's because this was a period when the entire Buddhist world may have been unified under his aegis, providing the possibility of a Buddhist corollary to Christendom.

18 This may seem an obvious point, but the study of Buddhism and Buddhist societies, regardless of discipline, remains strongly, though often implicitly, constrained by the logic of nation-state. Specialties within the study of Buddhism are almost always organized around national communities; they rarely venture beyond the boundaries of the nation. Sometimes this is a function of the practicalities of linguistic competence or visas. However, the monks and nuns who comprise our subject matter are not always constrained by borders in the ways that scholars are.

19 This is also a narrative beyond the scope of this introduction and this book. The European part of this story is told in Almond (1988) and Masuzawa (2005). King (1999) and Hallisey (1995) emphasize (in different ways) the degree to which the

development of the idea of Buddhism as a single entity was a part of discussions, arguments, and negotiations between Europeans (scholars and colonialists) and Buddhists (laypeople and monastics). Jaffe (2004), Tuttle (2005), and Blackburn (2010) provide important discussions of some of the ways that Buddhists reached across borders in the late nineteenth and early twentieth centuries.

20   My ability to stay in Jing Hong for an extended period of time was important, and I should acknowledge here several other factors, in addition to my status as a teacher. First, Sipsongpannā is a tourist location, and white foreigners are not uncommon there. Second, I had significant support from Professor Yang Hui of Yunnan University, and her sponsorship had already enabled Sara Davis to conduct long-term research in Jing Hong in the 1990s. Perhaps most important, my landlord, a mid-level government official, served as a significant connection and patron. When I registered with the Jing Hong PSB, she brought me to the office, chatted with the officers there, and explained what I was going to be doing. Her vouching for me made it less likely that I would come under scrutiny.

21   In addition to the fifteen months of fieldwork in 2001–2002, I took shorter trips to Sipsongpannā in September 1998 and August 1999; a brief follow-up trip in December 2002; and four trips there as an assistant professor in June 2007, November 2007, June 2009, and June 2011. These trips ranged from one to four weeks. I also interviewed Dai-lue monks in Bangkok in December 2002, Chicago in February 2005, Chiang Mai in July 2006, Singapore in 2010, and Chiang Mai in 2014.

22   Most of these conversations took place in Chinese. I spoke intermediate Thai when I came to Sipsongpannā in 2001, and used that as a bridge to learning Dai-lue. Most of the monks of Sipsongpannā understand Thai, and almost everyone under the age of sixty understands Mandarin Chinese. When I taught English to the novices at Wat Pājie, for example, I normally used Chinese to explain things. Over the course of my research, I used increasing amounts of Dai-lue in conversations, especially when interviewing people in villages.

CHAPTER ONE: LOCAL MONKS IN SIPSONGPANNĀ

1   Names have been changed to protect the anonymity of the people I worked with, with the exception of public statements by public figures.

2   Monastic education is also normally described in national terms, though often without reflection on how the imagination of Buddhism or governance might shape it.

3   It should be noted, though, that modern forms of Buddhism look different in Sipsongpannā than scholars have generally described. See Borchert (2008).

4   This is different from the problem of "localization," such as Lozada's (2002) discussion of Catholicism in a Chinese city. Rather, I am concerned with the local as a frame of reference or level of conceptualization.

5   Theut (2000, 42) makes this same observation about several *wat*s in Sipsongpannā.

6   The role of the tourism industry is important within Sipsongpannā. It is largely directed at Chinese tourists who come to visit a minority area and uses gendered images of the Dai-lue to exoticize and attract these tourists. See, for example, Gladney (1994) and Davis (2005).

7   No one knows when Buddhism arrived in the region. Local claims (among the people and on reconstructed temple dedication pillars) refer to Buddhism having had a history in the region of "more than a thousand years," but it is unclear whether this is much more than a trope that naturalizes Buddhism to the region. Chinese scholars are more likely to refer to Buddhism having come in the fourteenth or fifteenth centuries. The *Chronicle of Sipsongpannā* refers to a *cao*

phaendin having built a Buddhist temple in the 1430s (Liew-Herres, Grabowsky, and Wichasin 2012, 137). The first and second rulers of the region (Phaya Coeng, r. 1180–1192 CE, and Tao Khai Noeng, r. 1192–1211 CE) are referred to as "Buddhist," but this is a Buddhism unmarked by sectarian titles, and it is not clear what kind of Buddhism it might be referring to (ibid., 2012, 113, 117). Because of the intensive relations with "Theravāda" city-states of mainland Southeast Asia, it stands to reason that Buddhism was in Sipsongpannā not long after it was present in these places, but there is little reliable evidence attesting to the fact.

8   See Borchert (2006), Davis (2005), Hansen (1999), and Tan (1995).

9   It is interesting to note that much of the Chinese scholarship (Li 1983; Yang 1994; Zhao and Wu 1997; Wang 2001) does not report how the situation has changed. Primarily relying on research from the 1950s, this scholarship does not discuss the shifts that have taken place in the post-Liberation sangha. One can only speculate, but perhaps it is due to a desire to emphasize the feudal or semi-feudal nature of the "traditional" religious system.

10 Several of these medical professionals also argued that a number of poorer Dai-lue resented it when village wealth was poured into rebuilding *wat* buildings, but did not feel like they could do anything about it.

11 In some *wat* communities, there are also fortnightly temple sleepers. These are older villagers who spend the new or full moon at the *wat,* possibly actively taking eight precepts. This does not seem particularly common in the Reform Era, however.

12 By an economy of merit, I am referring to the interaction patterns that develop around merit-making practices. While the gift to an individual monk or the sangha is formally without reciprocity (i.e., the monk does not owe the donor anything), following Bunnag's discussion of the sangha in central Thailand, I am suggesting that there are patterns of obligation and patronage (i.e., economies) that emerge around and behind these "free" gifts.

13 Song kān is a central reason for the fame of Sipsongpannā in China more broadly. Zhou Enlai took part in the festival in the 1960s (Blum 2001, 109), and the rac-iness of the event—young people splashing each other with water with reckless abandon—has encouraged significant numbers of Chinese tourists to come to participate each April. See Davis (2005) and Borchert (2005b); on Thailand, see Tambiah (1970, 152–154); and on Southeast Asia more broadly, Swearer (1995, 36–40).

14 Education in the Chinese public schools is officially compulsory through ninth grade, but many children, especially boys, in Sipsongpannā do not attend school after elementary school.

15 The Vinaya tradition is that a boy is supposed to be fifteen years old, or "capable of chasing crows" (*Mahavagga* I.50.1, I.51.1); Thannissaro (2001, 2:423). In Thailand, the novice ordination is supposed to take place only after boys have finished the fourth grade (Tambiah 1970, 121), but anecdotally at least, boys in poor rural areas are ordained at a younger age (Pannapadipo 2001).

16 See Yang (1994, 91). Zheng Xiaoyun (1997, 132) says that before the 1950s, boys in Man Feilong, a village to the south of Jing Hong, ordained when they were five or six years old. This is not impossible, and happens (or has happened) else-where in Southeast Asia (Lester 1973, 94). Nonetheless, it seems to be uncommon in contemporary Sipsongpannā. Only a handful of novices I interviewed had ordained before the age of ten. Of the thirty-five at Wat Pājie whom I taught, only five ordained under the age of ten. The majority of these novice-students (twenty-four) ordained between the ages of ten and twelve.

17 The situation in Tibet is comparable, as can be seen in Goldstein (1998). Note, however, that in Tibet, underage novices seemed to provide the pretext the local government needed to disperse monastics who were beginning to make them

nervous. This has not happened in Sipsongpannā, though the monks in the Buddhist Association expressed anxiety to me about this possibility.

18 Prior to his formal installation as *khūbā meuang,* this monk was referred to in Dai-lue as *dubi long* (chief monk), reflecting his status as the abbot of Wat Pājie. Since the mid-1990s, he has also been the head of the Buddhist Association in the region.

CHAPTER TWO: FORTUNE-TELLING AND FALSE MONKS

1 See Sullivan (2007). Gottschalk rightly challenges Smith's emphasis on the notion that religion is a "non-native category . . . imposed from the outside on some aspect of native culture," thus highlighting the degree to which the category is adopted and adapted by local actors, even as "Western imperialists had a disproportionate role in its global naturalization" (Gottschalk 2013, 32, citing Smith 2004, 193–194). Both the imposition and indigenization of *zongjiao* is part of a much larger narrative on the development of "secular modernity" within China, which is beyond the scope of the current chapter. For a fuller discussion of the "religion question" in the development of "modern China," see Goosseart and Palmer (2011) and van der Veer (2014).

2 van der Veer (2014, 9) refers to these as a "syntagmatic chain" of concepts that are related but cannot be reduced to one another, and includes "secularism" as well. "Evil cults" is how *xiejiao* is commonly translated within China. In imperial China, *xiejiao* was a term used to refer to sects or cults that were not a part of the imperial system or patronized by the imperial sacrificial bureaucratic apparatus. Scholars have normally translated the use of *xie* for imperial China as "heterodox" rather than "evil." Palmer (2008) discusses how the CCP revived this imperial category after 1999 to address the crisis posed by Falun Gong and recalibrated it as "evil cults."

3 Document 19 is the common way of referring to "On the Fundamental Perspective and Policies of the Religion Problem in Our Country's Socialist Period" (Guanyu woguo shehuizhuyi shiqi zongjiao wenti de jiben guandian he jiben zhengce), which was first released in 1982 and available in translation in MacInnis (1989, 10–26); see Potter 2003 for a useful reading of Document 19. "Religion and Feudal Superstition" (Zongjiao yu fengjian mixin) was published in March 1979 and is available in Lancashire (1981, 277–280).

4 See, for example, "Religion and Feudal Superstition" from 1979 (Lancashire 1981); "Document 19" from 1981 (MacInnis 1989); and "White Paper: Freedom of Religious Belief in China" (1997), as well as Department of Rules and Policies for the Religious Affairs Bureau (2000), discussed below.

5 This discussion about defining religion and its related categories in the "educational handbooks" discussed above only points out some of the issues that defining religion has within governance. One issue that is important within contemporary China (but less relevant to the discussion in Sipsongpannā) are the relatively recent efforts to conceptualize the broad mass of popular traditions. These have generally been subject to being labeled as superstition, but given their widespread practice (Yang 2006) and their relatively benign place in culture (as long as they do not bleed into politics or crime), there have been efforts to consider "folk beliefs" (*minjian xinyang*) as distinct from superstition, though the institutionalization of this shift remains incomplete. See Goosseart and Palmer (2011, 346–350).

6 See Chau (2009). Xiang and Tao (2001, 6) argue that regulating "superstition" is extremely difficult for the government. Yang (2006) describes these kinds of ambiguous activities as part of a "gray market" of religion in China, as determined in part by the degree of regulatory intervention.

7 The name of the national RAB was changed to the State Agency for Religious Affairs in 1998. Most provincial-level offices have continued to be referred to as RABs throughout the first decade of this century, however, so I will refer to them as such.

8 The founding of the BA in 1953, the successor to Republican Era institutions that had fled to Taiwan, was part of a much longer effort to found a national organization to mobilize Buddhists to modernize and help build the nation. For a discussion of the early days of the Buddhist Association, and its emergence out of Taixu's reform efforts, see Welch (1972) or Chen and Deng (2000, 55–59). For a broader discussion of the management of religious communities, see Goosseart and Palmer (2011, 152–155).

9 Nichols (2011, 376). See also the example of Venerable Jing Hui and his development of a "marketable" form of Buddhism, with summer camps for young Chinese professionals that attracted the positive attention of Jiang Zemin (Yang and Hui 2005). Koesel (2014, chap. 2 [but see especially the chart on p. 16]) has argued for the importance of understanding when and how the interests of religious actors and local regimes intersect.

10 Wank (2009) notes that monks will take on overlapping titles as a strategy for consolidating power or authority, or both.

11 There are other offices with which they occasionally interact. Wat Pājie held conferences in 1998–1999 on HIV-AIDS and environmental degradation at the *wat* with the participation of the public health and environmental offices of the government. Building projects at the temple also require permits, and the monks also interact with the officials at Chunhuan Park, even if these are not always cordial interactions.

12 The Hui are the most prominent of the Muslim nationality groups in China. Unlike the other predominately Muslim *minzu* (such as the Uighurs), who live principally on China's borderlands, the Hui live throughout China. On the Hui, see Gladney (1998).

13 On several occasions in 2002, I spoke with educational officials and vice-principals of public schools. On every occasion, they told me that the educational offices of the local government had nothing to do with the education of monks.

14 The Buddhist Association is technically responsible for all Buddhists. Because the Dai-lue are considered to be Theravāda Buddhist as a part of their "natural" condition as members of the Daizu, this could mean that in some way the BA could be held responsible for the Dai-lue en masse. In practice, however, the BA seems to be largely responsible for monks and novices alone.

15 In saying "attractive," the rules are making explicit the link between disciplinary standards and aesthetics ones. For some discussion on this, see Samuels 2010.

16 On Khūbā Bunchum and his efforts to foster a Tai identity, see Cohen (2001).

17 An officer of the Yunnan Buddhist Association reported this to me in October 2001.

18 International censure is obviously not something that China has been completely successful in avoiding, particularly with regard to Christians and Tibetan Buddhists. However, while there is nothing resembling perfect religious freedom in China right now, the difference between 1980 and 2016 is quite significant and should not be minimized.

CHAPTER THREE: MONKS ON THE MOVE

1 By "national networks," I mean those with structures that are generally contained within the geo-body of the PRC; their spokes are generally at least partly defined by laws and policies of the nation-state.

2   In July 2013, I visited the *wat* in Chiang Mai where I had taught English and lived in 1994. The abbot of the *wat* was visiting with a colleague of his from Phrae Province. He was very excited to see me because his friend was, he told me, accompanied by a monk from Sipsongpannā who had lived in Phrae for a number of years. When I spoke with this monk (in Chinese), it turned out that he was not Dai-lue, but Dai-neua. This difference was completely invisible to my Thai monastic friend.

3   There is a fourth spoke: there are Dai-lue who have emigrated to other parts of China who sometimes invite Dai-lue monks to come and serve as fields of merit for several weeks in the Chinese cities in which they are living. In effect, these are nationalizations of local networks.

4   This was not a long-term effort, but at least two Han monks became naturalized enough to Sipsongpannā that they began to wear saffron robes rather than the gray coats more common among Chinese Mahāyāna Buddhist monks and nuns.

5   There is a valuable counterexample from the late eighteenth century, when some men teaching Mahāyāna Buddhism came to the general Sipsongpannā area and were roundly rejected by the local *cao,* who did not like seeing "Han monks" missionize the local hill dwellers, so they sought to eject them violently from the region. See Giersch (2006, 113n63).

6   A comment is in order about Dai-lue monastic perspectives on Tibetans. It would seem that Tibetans' status as subaltern ethnic minority Buddhists might encourage a certain amount of sympathy between them and the Dai. In general, this did not seem to be the case. The Dai-lue monks whom I asked directly about Tibetans tended to be somewhat critical of the other nationality. They said that Tibetans tended to get whatever they asked the local government for, and that the Tibetans also complained a lot.

7   The first time I met Khūbā Siang Lā was in September 2001 when he visited Wat Pājie and my English classes were canceled so the novices could celebrate his arrival and listen to a Dhamma talk that he gave. When I talked with him afterwards, he told me about visiting the United States, and how much he had enjoyed eating at McDonalds.

8   See, for example, Theut (2000), Phairot (2001), and Princess Galyani (1986).

9   Personal communication, Chiang Mai, Gasai District, Jing Hong (1999).

10 At least this has been the perspective of the officers of the BA. It should also be acknowledged, however, that there is a certain lack of visibility of the novices who might have traveled on their own to Thailand.

11 This is perhaps one of the reasons why Wat Pājie has solidified a role as a central node in educational networks with Southeast Asia: as a result of their connections, the BA can ensure an invitation to study.

12 The Buddhist and Pali College in Singapore is itself an example of transnational Buddhist education. Its program was developed by the Sri Lankan Buddhist and Pali University, and it was founded by a Sinhala monk, though its students are primarily Chinese Singaporeans.

CHAPTER FOUR: LEARNING TO READ IN VILLAGE TEMPLES

1   Keyes stresses that these are processes that have taken place over the course of the last century, and that the educational role of the *wat* remains, even if it is severely attenuated (1991, 124n9; 13). This attenuation has accelerated since Keyes' work was published, particularly with a decline in monastic high schools in Thailand.

2   This is not the case with Dai-lue girls. As noted in chapter 1, because there is no female ordination in Sipsongpannā, there has been no effort to (re)develop a Buddhist education system for Dai-lue girls.

3 Having conducted research more recently and in a different area of Sipsongpannā, Diana (2009) makes a very different argument about young Dai-lue and
   their identity vis-à-vis China. She sees them as much more integrated into the
   Chinese political-economy (regardless of their education) than towards ethnic
   (and in particular, transnational ethnic) identity.

4 This does not even account for smartphones. In the first years of the 2000s, it
   was increasingly common for monks to have cell phones, and many novices had
   them as well. By the end of the decade, most monks I encountered in Sipsongpannā increasingly had smartphones as well.

5 Comment from questionnaire answered by novices at Wat Pājie, May 2002;
   student 34.

6 Wat Pājie questionnaire, student 31. While most monks take their responsibilities seriously, it is almost certainly the case that abuse, whether physical or sexual, is present in some *wats,* though there has been little if any research done on
   these kinds of issues. Stories surface occasionally about monks in Thailand who
   have been arrested (Rarinthorn 2015), or the abuse of Tibetan Buddhist novices,
   but these are often anecdotal and the scope of the problem remains unknown.

7 On the ordination of novices in Theravāda Buddhism, see Tambiah (1970, 103–
   108), Sao (1986), and Swearer (1995, 49–51).

8 At the time of this ordination in 2002, one yuan was roughly $0.12. Most of the
   bills on the money tree would have been two or five jiao. There are ten jiao in a
   yuan. While boys who were ordaining did not receive a great deal of money, it
   was not inconsequential. To put it in perspective, for ten yuan ($1.20), we were
   able to buy a month's worth of rice and a day's worth of vegetables.

9 Novice-apprentices differ in some ways from the wood-carvers that Cooper discusses. For example, they can leave the relationship easily by disrobing with few
   consequences. In addition, novices in Sipsongpannā usually remain embedded
   within their village and thus have not really left home. See chapter 1 for more
   discussion of both of these points.

10 I not only observed this, but I experienced it when I was learning the Dai-lue letters. I was probably not a particularly good apprentice, since I kept interrupting
   my monk-teachers to ask them questions. Monks have told me that they use the
   same pedagogical practices with outsiders (be they non-Chinese like myself or
   Han who want to study Dai-lue) as they do with Dai-lue novices.

11 Blackboards are not the only tools used. I have seen at least two different alphabet textbooks used in the autonomous region (one of which is discussed in chapter 5), and also a CD-ROM that played and sounded out the letters in vaguely
   psychedelic graphics. This latter was on sale at Wat Pājie, but I never saw it in use.

12 Monks or novices will also prostrate themselves when formally greeting a monk
   senior to themselves. The twice-daily ritual of paying respect to the Buddha, saying a morning service, and sitting for a short period in meditation is widespread
   throughout Southeast Asia.

13 These texts are in a book printed at Wat Pājie, *Bap Tham-sūt Paritta Mangala* (Wat Pājie, 2001). In the morning, the novices chant pp. 2–16; in the evening, they chant pp. 22–34; on *wan sin* (the full and new moons), they chant
   pp. 35–42.

14 Southwold (1983, 38–39) provides a different argument for why the Vinaya rule
   is not always the most relevant way to determine whether a monk is considered
   to be good by his fellow villagers.

15 This is according to the *sekhiya* rules of the *pāṭimokkha,* the list of 227 rules.
   These rules of conduct are grouped into several sections, depending on the sever-
   ity of the consequences of breaking the rule. The 75 *sekhiya* rules have to do with
   conduct. They do not actually say that running is forbidden, but that a monk is to
   be well restrained in inhabited areas. See Nānamoli Thera (1966, 74–75).

16   Some Thai monks have told me that they think the issue of smoking is simply a
     health insurance issue; they think that the Thai government does not want to pay
     for the treatment of monks. I would suggest that part of the disagreement arises
     from these monks' more restricted notion of disciplinary formation. Informa-
     tion about Theravāda monks and smoking can be found, among other places, on
     the Internet at news-bbc.co.uk/2/low/asia-pacific/1905371.stm or at www.prn2
     .usm.my/mainsite/tobacco/cambodia.html.

17   See Samuels (2004, 964n12). One teacher comments to Samuels: "The most
     important aspect of their training is not my advice. . . . The thing I do here is
     put them into a group. . . . If you want to catch an elephant, you have to go to the
     jungle with two tamed elephants. The tamed elephants hit the wild elephant, and
     through that, control him. They do it themselves. . . . My advice is secondary."

18   In the same way, the *cao ao wat* or *dubi long* also reproduces teachers in his
     image. *Pha long* (senior novices) often conduct the rudimentary training of nov-
     ices; they learn to do this by having learned from the abbot themselves.

19   I have heard monastic action referred to as "unattractive" in Chinese (*bu haokan*),
     Dai-lue (*bao ngām*), and Thai (*may suay*).

20   This can also help explain variation between Theravāda polities. For example, in
     Sipsongpannā, no one cares if a novice rides a bicycle or plays soccer. In Thai-
     land, however, such behavior would be seen as inappropriate in most parts of the
     country. Thai monks sometimes suggest that this is because the Dai-lue in Sip-
     songpannā have lower disciplinary standards, principally as a result of the Cul-
     tural Revolution. While it may be true that the disciplinary standards of Dai-lue
     Buddhism were damaged by the experience of the Cultural Revolution, the Thai
     monks who make this claim are assuming (indeed asserting) that comportment
     standards for Theravāda should be seen as universal across the Theravāda world
     and also unchanging over time. Rather, Theravāda societies have differed in what
     rules they want to enforce. In making this argument, I am echoing one made ear-
     lier by Southwold (1983, 5–6), who asserted that we need to see what he calls
     "village Buddhism" as real Buddhism and not a corruption of "true Buddhism."
     In this, he is responding particularly to Spiro (1970), and to a lesser extent, Gom-
     brich (1971) and Tambiah (1970). I differ from Southwold in concentrating on
     how discourse about modernity and policies aimed at modernizing or civilizing
     people reach down into the villages. I think that in defending the legitimacy of
     village Buddhism, Southwold does not adequately address the modernity of villa-
     gers. I would suggest that we need to see Dai-lue villagers as modern subjects, and
     consequently, part of the academic problem is how to think about the modernity
     of subjects such as villagers, who have been represented as "traditional."

21   Despite the fact that the Vinaya clearly states that monks are not to ingest alco-
     hol (see Nānamoli Thera 1966, 58, *pācittiya* rule no. 51: "In drinking liquor and
     spirits, there is to be expiation" [*surāmerayapane pācittayam*]"), monks in Sip-
     songpannā often drink spirits. Alcohol was also forbidden in the rules and regu-
     lations I discussed in chapter 2 (rule no. 22). Two rationales for allowing it were
     regularly used by monks and laypeople. The first was that it is okay "if it's just
     one cup" or "if they don't get drunk." The other was that if a layperson gives a
     monk some alcohol, he must drink it because it is *dān* and must therefore be
     accepted. The drinking of alcohol by monks happens more frequently than we
     generally suspect in other parts of Southeast Asia, but it is not something that
     scholars have paid much attention to.

22   Li (1983, 3:101) says that the time that novices have to study *suttas* on any given
     day is not great, and that as a consequence, literacy among the Dai-lue is quite
     low. This is interesting because the essays in this volume were first published in
     the late 1950s. In part because of this, it is not clear what "literacy" means in this
     context. For the Dai-lue, like other Theravāda communities, reading texts has

been as much about their performance in ritual as an intellectual understanding of them.

23 Wat Man Ting, interview, May 1, 2002.

24 Interview at Jing Hong Board of Education, March 19, 2002. Shih (2002, 193) makes the case that the economics of many rural Daizu reduce the educational imperative, and Hansen (1999, 124) quotes a cadre whose perspective was echoed by the official I interviewed.

CHAPTER FIVE: THE FRAGILITY OF AUTONOMY

1 There have been several different institutions that we can describe as schools within Sipsongpannā over the last twenty years. The first school was opened in Meng Hun, Meng Hai County, by a colleague of Khūbā Meuang Jom's. It closed in the early 2000s because of the illness of the abbot who was also the head teacher. The school at Wat Pājie was the second. It was relocated to Wat Long Meuang Lue in spring 2009, though this seems to simply have been a change of venue, rather than a change in the nature of the institution. There was a third school in the late 1990s based at Wat Manchuanman in Meng Kham. It graduated one *nak-tham* class in 2002, but then did not take on a second class. An additional school based at the same temple was in the works for several years, which would be focused solely on a Buddhist curriculum. Similarly, there has been much talk by monks over the years about opening a Dhamma school in Meng Long. These seem to have remained largely at the level of discussion, however.

2 Since the development of Wat Long Meuang Lue, Wat Pājie has seen a decrease in the presence of tourists. There has also been significant development in Manting Park since the construction of the *wihān* in 2012. Conditions are always in flux.

3 At Wat Long Meuang Lue, the Dhamma school is very much out of the way of the tourist route at the *wat*. Tourists can walk there, but guided tours, which most tourists at Wat Long take, do not go to that part of the grounds, and so the likelihood of this kind of disruption is greatly diminished.

4 This statement and much of the demographic data came from a questionnaire that the students filled out in May 2002.

5 Because of the publishing projects, Davis (2003, 195) refers to Wat Pājie as a "Tai Kinko's."

6 These exams, moreover, take place at a set time each year. In other words, there is a rhythm to the schedule of the academic year at Dhamma schools that is not present in apprentice education.

7 The Dhamma school has had female teachers of Chinese, and monastic high schools in Thailand often have female teachers. Because of the constrained nature of male–female interactions in Theravāda Buddhism, these relationships are different than one would find in the public school setting.

8 Another question to consider is whether curricular education is a modern phenomenon. Standardized forms of monastic education are at least several centuries old (Blackburn 2001; Dreyfus 2003), and may in fact date back to the monastic "universities" of India in the first millennium CE (Dutt 1962). Local states, moreover, were involved in supporting these early forms of curricular education. However, I suspect that curricular education as a mode of educating monks and novices has become more prevalent over the last several centuries. This is partly a consequence of the development of standardized systems of education in the era of the modern nation-state. Monastic education, then, is one aspect of modern state efforts to shape and control its citizens, and the modern form of curricular education is one of the technologies that fosters these efforts.

9 See Borchert (2009) and Casas (2007, 2010) for discussion of the politics and dynamics of Wat Long Meuang Lue.

10   The question that elicited this response was specifically about the *nak-tham* exams (see below) that students take every fall to show they have mastered the required Buddhist knowledge.

11   Thai and Dai-lue share very similar grammar and many of the same words, though they are not quite the same. To render a Thai book comprehensible to a reader of Dai-lue, it would not be sufficient to simply put it into Dai-lue letters. On the other hand, they are not so far apart that everything is different.

12   *Gū Meu Wināy Baññatti* (Handbook for Knowledge of the Vinaya; n.d., foreword). While this particular book is directed solely at novices, two others, *Wichā Wināy-mukh* (Knowledge of Entrance to the Vinaya) and *Wichā Dhamma-wiphāk* (Knowledge of the Dhamma), both suggest that they are not only for the benefit of monks and novices, but laymen and laywomen who might also be interested in learning the truth.

13   *Yuwen*, chapter 19, "You yi ge meili de difang" (91–92), and chapter 26, "Nanwang de Poshuijie" (168–169). The song has a particularly interesting set of circumstances behind it. It has become a de facto anthem of the tourist industry in Xishuangbanna, and is often played over the airplane speakers when planes land in Jing Hong. Ironically, I have been told that it was not originally written for Xishuangbanna, but instead for Dehong, the home of the other major Dai group in western Yunnan (Professor Yang Hui, personal communication, May 2001). Davis (2005, 88) discusses an incident at a music festival at Wat Pajie during Song kān when a famous Dai-lue singer tries to sing this Chinese song to her Dai-lue compatriots instead of a Dai language song. She was booed off the stage, having ruined her authenticity with the locals.

14   Also worthy of note here is that the word for language in Thai, *phasā*, in both Dai-lue and northern Thai, also bears the meaning of "group of people" or "nation," in a loose sense. In the Dai-Chinese dictionary discussed above, *phasā* is glossed as *minzu*, or nationality. There might therefore be a more explicit incorporation of Buddhism to "Dai-ness" involved. If it is, however, it is not one that is being specifically articulated by the people at the Dhamma school.

15   The Dai-lue word here is *hung-heuang,* which the Dai-Han Dictionary glosses as *fanrong* (flourishing or prosperous). The Thai of the same word, *rung-reuang,* means the same thing, but it adds "civilized" and "thriving" to the mix. "Civilized" (*wenming de*) was the gloss given by the monk who explained it to me.

16   This alphabet book was brought to Wat Pājie from Meng Yong in the Shan States, and it contains some words that are not in use in Sipsongpannā. In addition, there are Pāli words that the student-novices only learn after they have already worked through the lessons of *Bap heyn akkhara.*

CHAPTER SIX: TRANSNATIONAL BUDDHIST EDUCATION

1   This relic, said to be one of the Buddha's teeth, is one of two such major relics, the other being in Sri Lanka. There is also a temple of the tooth relic in Singapore that was built in the last decade. The Chinese tooth relic is sometimes a part of the Chinese foreign policy engagement with Southeast Asia. See Schober (1997).

2   There are other intra-Asian Buddhist networks that are beyond the scope of this book to address, including ones based around pilgrimage routes, international conferences such as the one organized by Mahā-Chulālongkorn Buddhist University in Thailand every year for the celebration of Vesak, transnational organizations dedicated to fostering the rights of *bhikkhunīs* (nuns), and merit-making networks such as the ones I described in chapter 3. These networks are not completely divorced from educational networks, and in some ways, facilitate educational travel.

3   The monk I met at the BCS in Singapore studied at Wat Pājie, and then had been sent to study at a Mahāyāna Buddhist institute. It was when he was there that he saw the application for the BCS. He was not sent to Singapore by the Sipsongpannā BA.

4   Many of these schools are members of the International Association of Buddhist Universities. IABU is "an international forum for institutes of Buddhist higher education to network, understand, and benefit from the richness and variety of the multinational Buddhist tradition" (http://iabu.org/About; accessed May 2015).

5   Despite official neutrality, the Singaporean government strongly and clearly articulates what it holds to be proper forms of religion within a rubric of racial and religious harmony. This can be seen on the website for the BCS, which notes that the mission of the BCS is "to specialize in Chinese Buddhism, respect other lineages and promote inter-religious harmony" (http://www.bcs.edu.sg/index .php/Grouplist/group_en/; accessed May 2015). Eng (2003) discusses the role that the Singaporean government's concern for religious and racial harmony plays in the development of modern forms of Buddhism.

6   Personal communication, dean of Academic Affairs, BCS, March 2010.

7   Thailand has had two primary *nikāyas* (monastic fraternities) since the late nineteenth century, the Dhammayut and the Mahānikai. Mahā-Chulā is the university for Mahānikai monks and Mahā-Makut is the university of Dhammayut monks. While still important in some ways, the distinctions between the two fraternities have been much more important in the past than it seems to be currently. For example, many of the teachers at Mahā-Makut are Mahānikai monks.

8   It is worth a moment to consider the validity of thinking about study in Chinese *foxueyuan* as "transnational," since the Dai-lue and the Mahāyāna monks with whom and under whom they study are all Chinese citizens. I see this as an example of TME for several reasons. While the Dai-lue and the Mahāyāna monks share citizenship, they do not share "nationality" (*minzu*). Moreover, the Dai-lue monastic students have to cross cultural, linguistic, sectarian, and geographic borders when they study in eastern China (through the mid-2000s at least, there was a checkpoint at the border of Sipsongpannā where border guards checked passports and *shenfen zheng* of bus passengers). Indeed, in some ways, the journey to Shanghai is a more profound journey than the journey to Chiang Mai or Bangkok, because the Dai-lue monastics fit in more easily in Thailand, as this section makes clear. Moreover, while the journey is different, since the mid- to late 1990s, the process by which they have gone to both types of schools—sent by the BA after finishing up at the Dhamma school—has been the same.

9   This monk had studied in Thailand in the 1990s and successfully passed the third-grade Pāli exams. This meant that he could use the title "*mahā.*" In other words, he did not have a personal problem with the Thai monastic education experience. However, from 2002 to 2006, the BA sent very few students to study in Thailand, though the numbers have grown again since 2006.

10 See Long (2002, 194–195). As discussed in chapter 2, Chinese citizens are not allowed to enter into religious education, unless they are minorities for whom underage ordination is part of their cultural history, like the Daizu or the Tibetans.

11 Material from the previous two paragraphs is drawn from Borchert (2005a, 243).

12 I base this on observations at the two meals I shared with the students and asking them if they tended to eat separately. They told me they liked the food in general, but wanted more chili. I do not think this separation was an official decision, but I also noticed that the Dai-lue students tended to talk more at meals than the Han monks.

13 Dao Shuren is from the former ruling family of Meng Ce.

14 I thank Kang Nanshan of the Yunnan Buddhist Association for providing me with a copy of this speech.

Glossary

Key: Ch. = Chinese; D. = Dai-lue; P. = Pāli; Th. = Thai

There are a number of words that are the same in both Dai-lue and Thai; where these overlap, I have identified the word as Dai-lue. There are also a number of words whose respective Pāli and Thai/Dai-lue forms are very similar, such as *dān* (Dai-lue)/*dāna* (Pāli), meaning "meritorious gift." In these cases, I provide the Dai-lue pronunciation of the term.

akkhara (D.)	letters; alphabet
arhat (P.)	fully enlightened disciple of the Buddha
Auk wasā (D.); Kaimenjie (Ch.)	End of the Rains Retreat
bān (D.)	village
bao dip (D.)	not raw (i.e., cooked)
bāp (P.)	wickedness
bosot (D.)	ordination hall
bun (D.)	merit
cao (D.)	lord
cao ao wat (Th.)	abbot
cao phaendin (D.)	"lord of the earth"; title of the traditional ruler of Sipsongpannā
chalong (D.)	celebration
chao puttha (D.)	Buddhists
chujia zheng (Ch.)	ordination card
chuzhongxue (Ch.)	junior middle school/junior high school
Dacheng Fojiao (Ch.)	Mahāyāna Buddhism
dān (D.); *dāna* (P.)	meritorious offerings
Dhamma (P.)	the teachings of the Buddha
dip (D.)	raw, uncooked
du/dubi (D.)	monk
du/dubi long (D.)	abbot
Fojiao Xiehui (Ch.)	Buddhist Association
foxueyuan (Ch.)	Buddhist institute
Gongan ju (Ch.)	Public Security Bureau (PSB)
guanxi (Ch.)	relationship
Hanzu Fojiao (Ch.)	Han Buddhism
hongheyn pha-pariyatti-tham (D.); *rongrian phra-pariyatti-tham* (Th.)	Dhamma school

kexue (Ch.)	science
khanān (D.)	former monk
Khao wasā (D.); Guanmenjie (Ch.)	Beginning of the Rains Retreat
khūbā	"venerated teacher;" a monk who is deemed to be wise or spiritually advanced
kilesa (P.)	defilements
kuti (D./P.)	monastic dormitory
lokiya (P.)	worldly
lokkuttara (P.)	supernatural, beyond this world
lūk kaew (D.)	precious child, boy preparing for ordination as a novice
luohou (Ch.)	backward
meuang (D.) (Ch.: *meng*; Th.: *müang*)	polity, usually with a *cao*
minjian xinyang (Ch.)	folk beliefs
minzu (Ch.)	nationality
minzu shibie (Ch.)	"division of nationalities"; ethnic classification by the state
minzu zongjiao (Ch.)	minority (or nationality) religion
Minzu Zongjiao Bu (Ch.)	Minority and Religious Affairs Bureau
mixin, fengjian mixin (Ch.)	superstition, feudal superstition
nak-tham (D.)	Dhamma student
Nanchuan Fojiao (Ch.)	Southern Buddhism
pabbajjā (P.)	novice
paritta (P.)	protective chant/spell
pāṭimokkha (P.)	fortnightly recitation of the *vinaya*
pha long (D.)	senior novice
pha noy (D.)	junior novice
phi (D.)	ghosts, spirits
phi-nawng (D.; Th.)	siblings
pindabāt (Th.)	alms round
pirivena	monastery school in Sri Lanka
Poshuijie (Ch.)	"Water-Splashing Festival"; Dai-lue New Year
pu cān (D.)	lay ritual leader of a *wat*
Putonghua (Ch.)	Mandarin Chinese
sāla (D.)	pavilion
salāt soy (D.)	lottery-style merit-making ceremony
sangha-nayok (D.)	head of the sangha
sangha-rāt (D.); *sangha-rāja* (P.)	king of the sangha
sāsanā, Phra Puttha Sāsanā (D./Th.)	religion, Buddhism (P *sāsana*)
Shangzuobu Fojiao (Ch.)	Theravāda Buddhism
shaoshu minzu (Ch.)	minority
shenfen zheng (Ch.)	national identity card
Song kān (D.)	Dai-lue New Year (Ch.: Poshui jie)
suzhi (Ch.)	quality
upasampadā (P.)	higher ordination
wat (D.)	monastery/temple
wat long (D.)	major/central temple
wihān (D.)	worship hall (Pāli: *vihāra*)
Xiaocheng Fojiao (Ch.)	Hīnayāna Buddhism
xiejiao (Ch.)	evil cult

xin daiwen (Ch.)	new Dai-lue script
yat nām (D.)	pouring out water at end of ritual to transfer merit
yuanshi zongjiao (Ch.)	primitive religions
zhengchang zongjiao (Ch.)	normal religion
zizhi zhou (Ch.)	autonomous prefecture
zhou zhang (Ch.)	governor of the prefecture
zong fosi (Ch.)	general temple
zongjiao (Ch.)	religion
zongjiao re (Ch.)	religion fever

References

DAI-LUE TEXTBOOKS

All books published by either Wat Pājie or by the Dhamma school at Wat Pha-Thāt Sāy Meuang (Thākhīlek) in Dai-lue.

Bap heyn akkhara (Letter Study Book). 1998. Wat Pājie.

Bap Tham-sūt Paritta Mangala (Blessings of the Mangala Sutta). 2001. Wat Pājie.

Gū Meu Wināy Baññatti (Handbook for Knowledge of the Vinaya). n.d.

Wichā Dhamma-wiphāk (Knowledge of the Dhamma). n.d.

Wichā Puttha-bawatti (Knowledge of the Buddhist Life). 2004. First year. Wat Pājie.

Wichā Wināy-mukh (Knowledge of the Entrance to the Vinaya). 2004. First year. Wat Pājie.

SECONDARY SOURCES (ENGLISH, THAI, CHINESE)

Alexander, L. G., and He Qishen, eds. (1997) 2001. New Concept English [New Edition]: First Things First. Students' book. Reprint, Hong Kong: Longman Asia.

Almond, Philip. 1988. The British Discovery of Buddhism. Cambridge: Cambridge University Press.

Appadurai, Arjun. 1996. Modernity at Large: Cultural Dimensions of Globalization. Minneapolis: University of Minnesota Press.

Asad, Talal. 1993. Genealogies of Religion: Discipline and Reasons of Power in Christianity and Islam. Baltimore, MD: Johns Hopkins University Press.

Ashiwa, Yoshiko, and David L. Wank. 2006. "The Politics of a Reviving Buddhist Temple: State, Association and Religion in Southeast China." Journal of Asian Studies 65 (2): 337–360.

———, eds. 2009. Making Religion, Making the State: The Politics of Religion in Modern China. Stanford, CA: Stanford University Press.

Birnbaum, Raul. 2003. "Buddhist China at the Century's Turn." In Religion in China Today, edited by Daniel Overmyer, 122–143. New York: Cambridge University Press.

Blackburn, Anne. 2001. Buddhist Learning and Textual Practice in Eighteenth-Century Lankan Monastic Culture. Princeton, NJ: Princeton University Press.

———. 2010. Locations of Buddhism. Chicago: University of Chicago Press.

Blum, Susan D. 2001. Portraits of "Primitives": Ordering Human Kinds in the Chinese Nation. Lanham, MD: Rowman and Littlefield.

Borchert, Thomas. 2005a. "Training Monks or Men: Theravāda Monastic Education, Subnationalism and the National Sangha of China." Journal of the International Association of Buddhist Studies 28 (2): 241–272.

———. 2005b. "Of Temples and Tourists: The Effects of the Tourist Political Economy on a Minority Buddhist Community in Southwest China." In *State, Market and Religion in Chinese Societies,* edited by Joseph Tamney and Fenggang Yang, 87–112. Leiden: Brill.

———. 2006. "Educating Monks: Buddhism, Politics and Freedom of Religion on China's Southwest Border." PhD diss., University of Chicago.

———. 2008. "Worry for the Dai Nation: Sispongpanna, Chinese Modernity and the Problems of Buddhist Modernism." *Journal of Asian Studies* 67 (1): 107–142.

———. 2009. "Relocating the Center of a Sangha: Minority Buddhists, Local Politics and the Construction of a New Temple in Southwest China." Paper presented at "Place/No Place: Spatial Aspects of Urban Asian Religiosity," Syracuse University, October.

———. 2010. "The Abbot's New House: Thinking about How Religion Works among Buddhists and Minorities in Contemporary China." *Journal of Church and State* 52 (1): 112–137.

———. 2011. "Monastic Labor: Thinking about the Work of Monks in Contemporary Theravada Communities." *Journal of the American Academy of Religion* 79 (1): 162–192.

Bourdieu, Pierre. 1984. *Distinctions: The Social Judgment of Taste.* Cambridge, MA: Harvard University Press.

Bunchuay Srisawat. (1955 [2498]) 2004 [2547]. *Thai Sipsongpannā.* 3rd ed. Reprint, Bangkok: Rongphim Rapphim.

Bunnag, Jane. 1973. *Buddhist Monk, Buddhist Layman: A Study of Urban Monastic Organization in Central Thailand.* Cambridge: Cambridge University Press.

Casas, Roger. 2007. "Wat Luang Sipsongpanna." In *New Mandala.* http://asiapacific .anu.edu.au/newmandala/2007/12/31/wat-luang-sipsongpanna/. Accessed March 23, 2015.

———. 2010. "Wat Luang Sipsongpanna: The Monks Strike Back." In *New Mandala.* http://asiapacific.anu.edu.au/newmandala/2010/08/03/wat-luang -sipsongpanna-the-monks-strike-back/. Accessed March 23, 2015.

Chakrabarty, Dipesh. 2000. *Provincializing Europe: Postcolonial Thought and Historical Difference.* Princeton, NJ: Princeton University Press.

Chau, Adam. 2009. "Expanding the Space of Popular Religion: Local Temple Activism and the Politics of Legitimation in Contemporary Rural China." In *Making Religion, Making the State: The Politics of Religion in Modern China,* edited by Yoshiko Ashiwa and David L. Wank, 211–220. Stanford, CA: Stanford University Press.

Chen Bing and Deng Zimei. 2000. *Ershi shiji Zhongguo Fojiao* (Chinese Buddhism in the Twentieth Century). Beijing: Minzu chubanshe.

Chen Jiankun. 2000. *Zongjiao, xiejiao, mixin* (Religion, Evil Cults, Superstition). Jinan: Jinan chubanshe.

Cohen, Paul. 2001. "Buddhism Unshackled: The Yuan 'Holy Man' Tradition and the Nation-State in the Tai World." *Journal of Southeast Asian Studies* 32 (2): 227–248.

Collins, Steven. 1998. *Nirvana and Other Buddhist Felicities.* Cambridge: Cambridge University Press.

Cooke, Miriam, and Bruce Lawrence. 2005. Introduction to *Muslim Networks from Hajj to Hip Hop,* edited by Miriam Cooke and Bruce B. Lawrence, 1–28. Chapel Hill: University of North Carolina Press.

Cooper, Eugene. 1980. *Woodcarvers of Hong Kong: Production in the World Capitalist Periphery.* Cambridge: Cambridge University Press.

Crosby, Kate. 2103. *Traditional Theravada Meditation and Its Modern Era Suppression.* Hong Kong: Buddha Dharma Centre of Hong Kong.

Dao Shixun, Cao Cunxin, and Dao Guolian, eds. 2002. *Dai-Han cidian* (Dai-Han Dictionary). Kunming, Yunnan: Renmin chubanshe.

Davis, Sara L. M. 2003. "Premodern Flows in Postmodern China: Globalization and the Sipsongpanna Tais." *Modern China* 29 (2): 176–203.

——. 2005. *Song and Silence: Ethnic Revival on China's Southwest Border*. New York: Columbia University Press.

de Certeau, Michel. (1975) 1988. *The Writing of History*. Translated by Tom Conley. New York: Columbia University Press.

Department of Rules and Policies for the Religious Affairs Bureau. 2000. "Yunnan sheng zongjiao shiwu guanli guiding" (Regulations for the Administration of Religious Work in Yunnan Province). In *Quan guojia zongjiao xingzheng fagui guizhang huibian* (Compilation of Rules and Regulations on Religion for the Entire Nation). Beijing: Zongjiao wenhua chubanshe.

Dhammasami, Ven. Khammai. 2007. "Idealism and Pragmatism: A Dilemma in the Current Monastic Education Systems of Burma and Thailand." In *Buddhism, Power and the Political Order*, edited by Ian Harris, 10–25. London: Routledge.

Diana, Antonella. 2009. "Re-Configuring Belonging in Post-Socialist Xishuangbanna, China." In *Tai Lands and Thailand: Community and State in Southeast Asia*, edited by Andrew Walker, 192–213. Honolulu: University of Hawai'i Press/Asian Studies Association of Australia.

"Document 19: The Basic Viewpoint and Policy on the Religious Question during Our Country's Socialist Period." 1989. Reprinted in *Religion in China Today: Policy and Practice*, edited by Donald E. MacInnis, 10–26. Maryknoll, NY: Orbis Books.

Dreyfus, Georges. 2003. *The Sound of Two Hands Clapping: The Education of a Tibetan Buddhist Monk*. Berkeley: University of California Press.

Duara, Prasenjit. 1995. *Rescuing History from the Nation*. Chicago: University of Chicago Press.

Dutt, Sukumar. 1962. *Buddhist Monks and Monasteries of India*. London: G. Allen and Unwin.

Edwards, Penny. 2007. *Cambodge: The Cultivation of a Nation, 1860–1945*. Honolulu: University of Hawai'i Press.

Eng, Kuah-Pearce Khun. 2003. *State, Society and Religious Engineering: Towards a Reformist Buddhism in Singapore*. Singapore: ISEAS.

Evans, Grant. 2000. "Transformation of Jing Hong, Xishuangbanna, PRC." In *Where China Meets Southeast Asia*, edited by Grant Evans, Christopher Hutton, and Kuah Khun Eng, 162–182. Singapore: ISEAS.

Falk, Monica Lindbergh. 2008. *Making Fields of Merit*. Seattle: University of Washington Press.

Finnucane, Juliana. 2009. "Cosmopolitanism, Conversion and Place-Making among Members of the Singapore Soka Association." Paper presented at "Place/No Place: Spatial Aspects of Urban Asian Religiosity," Syracuse University, October.

Fisher, Gareth. 2008. "The Spiritual Land Rush: Merit and Morality in New Chinese Buddhist Temple Construction." *Journal of Asian Studies* 67 (1): 143–170.

Galyani Vadhana, Princess (Somdet Phracao Phīnāngthoe Caofā Kanlayāwatthanā). 1986 [2529]. *Yunnān*. Bangkok: Bangkok Watthanāphānit.

George, Cherian. 2005. "Calibrated Coercion and the Maintenance of Hegemony in Singapore." ARI Working Paper, no. 48. www.ari.nus.edu.sg/showfile.asp?pubid =514&type=2. Accessed May 28, 2015.

Gethin, Rupert. 1998. *The Foundations of Buddhism*. Oxford: Oxford University Press.

Giersch, C. Patterson. 2006. *Asian Borderlands: The Transformation of Qing China's Yunnan Frontier*. Cambridge, MA: Harvard University Press.

Gladney, Dru. 1991. *Muslim Chinese: Ethnic Nationalism in the People's Republic*. Cambridge, MA: Council on East Asian Studies, Harvard University.

———. 1994. "Representing Nationality in China: Refiguring Majority/Minority Identities." *Journal of Asian Studies* 53 (1): 92–123.

———. 1998. "Clashed Civilizations? Muslim and Chinese Identities in the PRC." In *Making Majorities: Constituting the Nation in Japan, Korea, China, Malaysia, Fiji, Turkey, and the United States,* edited by Dru Gladney, 106–131. Stanford, CA: Stanford University Press.

Goldstein, Melvyn C. 1998. "The Revival of Monastic Life in Drepung Monastery." In *Buddhism in Contemporary Tibet,* edited by Melvyn C. Goldstein and Matthew T. Kapstein, 15–52. Berkeley: University of California Press.

Gombrich, Richard F. 1971. *Precept and Practice: Traditional Buddhism in the Rural Highlands of Ceylon.* Oxford: Oxford University Press.

Goossaert, Vincent, and David A. Palmer. 2011. *The Religious Question in Modern China.* Chicago: University of Chicago Press.

Gottschalk, Peter. 2013. *Religion, Science and Empire: Classifying Hinduism and Islam in British India.* Oxford: Oxford University Press.

Guarnizo, Luis Eduardo, and Michael Peter Smith. 1998. "The Locations of Transnationalism." In *Transnationalism from Below,* edited by Michael Peter Smith and Luis Eduardo Guarnizo, 3–34. New Brunswick, NJ: Transaction.

Gu Yumei, ed. 2009. *Essays of "Seminar on Buddhist Studies in Foreign Languages 2008".* Beijing: Zongjiao wenhua chubanshe.

Hallisey, Charles. 1995. "Roads Taken and Not Taken in the Study of Theravada Buddhism." In *Curators of the Buddha,* edited by Donald S. Lopez, 31–62. Chicago: University of Chicago Press.

Hansen, Anne. 2007. *How to Behave: Buddhism and Modernity in Colonial Cambodia, 1860–1930.* Honolulu: University of Hawai'i Press.

Hansen, Mette Halskov. 1999. *Lessons in Being Chinese: Minority Education and Ethnic Identity in Southwest China.* Seattle: University of Washington Press.

———. 2001. "Ethnic Minority Girls on Chinese School Benches: Gender Perspectives on Minority Education." In *Education, Culture and Identity in Twentieth-Century China,* edited by Glen Peterson, Ruth Hayhoe, and Yongling Lu, 403–429. Ann Arbor: University of Michigan Press.

Harrell, Stevan. 1995a. "Languages Defining Ethnicity in Southwest China." In *Ethnic Identity: Creation, Conflict and Accommodation,* edited by Lola Romanucci-Ross and George A. De Vos. Walnut Creek, CA: AltaMira Press/Sage.

———. 1995b. "Introduction: Civilizing Projects and the Reactions to Them." In *Cultural Encounters on China's Ethnic Frontier,* edited by Stevan Harrell, 3–35. Seattle: University of Washington Press.

Hayashi Yukio. 2003. *Practical Buddhism among the Thai-Lao: Religion in the Making of a Region.* Kyoto: Kyoto University Press.

Heberer, Thomas. 1989. *China and Its National Minorities: Autonomy or Assimilation?* Armonk, NY: M.E. Sharpe.

Hill, Ann Maxwell. 1998. *Merchants and Migrants: Ethnicity and Trade among Yunnanese Chinese in Southeast Asia.* Monograph no. 47. New Haven, CT: Yale Southeast Asia Studies.

Hill, Michael. 1999. "The Macho-Management of Religious Diversity in Singapore." *Australian Religion Studies Review* 12 (2): 70–93.

Holt, John C. 2009. *Spirits of the Place: Buddhism and Lao Religious Culture.* Honolulu: University of Hawai'i Press.

Hsieh Shih-Chung. 1995. "On the Dynamics of Tai/Dailue Ethnicity: An Ethnohistorical Analysis." In *Cultural Encounters on China's Ethnic Frontier,* edited by Stevan Harrell, 301–328. Seattle: University of Washington Press.

Hyde, Sandra. 2007. *Eating Spring Rice: The Cultural Politics of AIDS in Southwest China.* Berkeley: University of California Press.

Ishii, Yoneo. 1986. *Sangha, State and Society: Thai Buddhism in History*. Honolulu: University of Hawai'i Press/Center for Southeast Asian Studies, Kyoto University.

Jaffe, Richard M. 2004. "Seeking Sakyamuni: Travel and the Reconstruction of Japanese Buddhism." *Journal of Japanese Studies* 30 (1): 65–96.

Ji Zhe. 2008. "Secularization as Religious Restructuring: Statist Institutionalization of Buddhism and Its Paradoxes." In *Chinese Religiosities: Afflictions of Modernity and State Formation*, edited by Mayfair Yang, 233–260. Berkeley: University of California Press.

Jory, Patrick. 2002. "Thai and Western Scholarship in the Age of Colonialism." *Journal of Asian Studies* 61 (3): 891–918.

Kamala Tiyavanich. 1997. *Forest Recollections: Wandering Monks in Twentieth-Century Thailand*. Honolulu: University of Hawai'i Press.

Kawanami, Hiroko. 2013. *Renunciation and Empowerment of Buddhist Nuns in Myanmar-Burma*. Leiden: Brill.

Kemper, Steven. 2005. "Dharmapala's *Dharmaduta* and the Buddhist Ethnoscape." In *Buddhist Missionaries in the Era of Globalization*, edited by Linda Learman, 22–50. Honolulu: University of Hawai'i Press.

Keyes, Charles F. 1991. "The Proposed World of the School: Thai Villagers' Entry into a Bureaucratic State System." In *Reshaping Local Worlds: Formal Education and Rural Cultural Change in Southeast Asia*, edited by Charles E. Keyes, E. Jane Keyes, and Nancy Donnelly, 1–18. New Haven, CT: Yale University Southeast Asia Studies.

———. 1992. "Who Are the Lue Revisited? Ethnic Identity in Laos, Thailand and China." Working Paper, Center for International Studies. Cambridge, MA: MIT.

———. 2002. "Presidential Address: 'The Peoples of Asia': Science and Politics in the Classification of Ethnic Groups in Thailand, China and Vietnam." *Journal of Asian Studies* 61 (4): 1163–1203.

Kindrop, Jason, and Carol Lee Hamrin, eds. 2004. *God and Caesar in China: Policy Implications of Church-State Tensions*. Washington, DC: Brookings Institution Press.

King, Richard. 1999. *Orientalism and Religion: Postcolonial Theory, India and the "Mystic East"*. London: Routledge.

Kingshill, Konrad. 1960. *Ku Daeng, the Red Tomb: A Village Study in Northern Thailand*. Chiang Mai, Thailand: Prince Royal's College. Distributed by the Siam Society, Bangkok.

Kipnis, Andrew. 1997. *Producing Guanxi: Sentiment, Self, and Subculture in a North China Village*. Durham, NC: Duke University Press.

Koesel, Karrie J. 2014. *Religion and Authoritarianism: Cooperation, Conflict and the Consequences*. New York: Cambridge University Press.

Kourilsky, Gregory. 2010. "The *Institut Bouddhique* in Laos: Ambivalent Dynamics of a Colonial Project." Paper presented at "Theravada Buddhism under Colonialism," ISEAS, Singapore, May.

Krämer, Hans Martin. 2015. *Shimaji Mokurai and the Reconception of Religion and the Secular in Modern Japan*. Honolulu: University of Hawai'i Press.

Kurtzman, Charles. 2005. "The Network Metaphor and the Mosque Network in Iran 1978–1979." In *Muslim Networks from Hajj to Hip Hop*, edited by Miriam Cooke and Bruce B. Lawrence, 69–83. Chapel Hill: University of North Carolina Press.

Lancashire, Douglas, trans. and ed. 1981. *Chinese Essays on Religion and Faith*. San Francisco: Chinese Materials Center.

LeMoines, Jaques. 1997. "Féodalité Taï les Lü des Sipsong Panna et les Taï Blancs, Noirs et Rouges du Nord Ouest du Viet Nam." *Peninsule: Etude interdisciplinaires sur l'Asie du Sud-Est Péninsulaire* 35: 171–218.

Lester, Robert C. 1973. *Theravada Buddhism in Southeast Asia.* Ann Arbor: University of Michigan Press.

Liew-Herres, Foon Ming, Volker Grabowsky, and Renoo Wichasin. 2012. *Chronicle of Sipsòng Panna: History and Society of a Tai Lü Kingdom, Twelfth to Twentieth Century.* Chiang Mai: Mekong Press.

Li Zhaolun, ed. 1983. *Daizu shehui lishi diaocha, Xishuangbanna* (Research on the Society and History of the Dai Nationality of Sipsongpanna). Vols. 2 and 3. Kunming: Yunnan minzu chubanshe.

Long Darui. 2002. "Buddhist Education in Sichuan." *Educational Philosophy and Theory* 34 (2): 185–206.

Lozada, Eriberto, Jr. 2002. *God Aboveground: Catholic Church, Postsocialist State, and Transnational Processes in a Chinese Village.* Stanford, CA: Stanford University Press.

MacInnis, Donald E., ed. 1989. *Religion in China Today: Policy and Practice.* Maryknoll, NY: Orbis Books.

Makeley, Charlene. 2008. *The Violence of Liberation: Gender and Tibetan Buddhist Revival of Religion in Post-Mao China.* Berkeley: University of California Press.

Masuzawa, Tomoko. 2005. *The Invention of World Religions; or, How European Universalism Was Preserved in the Language of Pluralism.* Chicago: University of Chicago Press.

Ma Yao. 1988. "The Religion Which Protected the System of Feudal Leadership." In *Yunnan Project Newsletter,* no. 2: 16–21. Translated by Irene Bain. Reprinted from *Daizu shehui lishi diaocha: Xishuang Banna* (A Survey of the Social History of the Daizu: Sipsongpannā) (Kunming: Yunnan minzu chubanshe) 2: 46–50.

McCargo, Duncan. 1999. "The Politics of Buddhism in Southeast Asia." In *Religion, Globalization and the Political Culture in the Third World,* edited by Jeff Haynes, 213–239. Basingstoke, UK: MacMillan.

McCarthy, Susan Kathleen. 2000. "Ethnoreligious Mobilisation and Citizenship Discourse in the People's Republic of China." *Asian Ethnicity* 1 (2): 107–116.

——. 2001. "Whose Autonomy Is It Anyway? Minority Cultural Politics and National Identity in the PRC." PhD diss., University of California, Berkeley.

——. 2009. *Communist Multiculturalism.* Seattle: University of Washington Press.

McDaniel, Justin. 2008. *Gathering Leaves and Lifting Words: Histories of Buddhist Monastic Education in Laos and Thailand.* Seattle: University of Washington Press.

——. 2011. *The Lovelorn Ghost and the Magical Monk: Practicing Buddhism in Modern Thailand.* New York: Columbia University Press.

McKhann, Chaz. 1995. "Naxi and the Nationalities Problem." *Cultural Encounters on China's Ethnic Frontier,* edited by Stevan Harrell, 39–62. Seattle: University of Washington Press.

Mendelson, E. Michael. 1975. *Sangha and State in Burma: A Study in Monastic Sectarianism and Leadership.* Edited by John P. Ferguson. Ithaca, NY: Cornell University Press.

Mueggler, Erik. 2001. *The Age of Wild Ghosts: Memory, Violence, and Place in Southwest China.* Berkeley: University of California Press.

Mullaney, Thomas. 2011. *Coming to Terms with the Nation: Ethnic Classification in China.* Berkeley: University of California Press.

Murphy, Rachel. 2004. "Turning Peasants into Modern Chinese Citizens: 'Population Quality' Discourse, Demographic Transition and Primary Education." *The China Quarterly* 177: 1–20.

Nānamoli Thera, trans. 1966. *Patimokkha: 227 Fundamental Rules of a Bhikkhu.* Bangkok: The Social Science Association Press of Thailand.

Natchā Laohasirinadh. 1998 [2541]. *Sipsongphanna: Rāt-cārit* (Sipsongpannā: A Traditional State). Bangkok: The Thailand Research Fund/Foundation for the Promotion of Social Sciences and Humanities Textbook Project.

National Religious Affairs Bureau. 2001. *Zhongguo zongjiao* (Religions in China). March 3. Beijing: National Religious Affairs Bureau.

Nedostup, Rececca. 2009. *Superstitious Regimes: Religion and the Politics of Chinese Modernity*. Cambridge, MA: Harvard University Asia Center.

Nichols, Brian. 2011. "History, Material Culture and Auspicious Events at the Purple Cloud: Buddhist Monasticism at Quanzhou Kaiyuan." PhD diss., Rice University.

Nietupski, Paul Kocot. 1999. *Labrang: A Tibetan Buddhist Monastery at the Crossroads of Four Civilizations*. Ithaca, NY: Snow Lion.

Ohnuma, Reiko. 2005. "Gift." In *Critical Terms for the Study of Buddhism*, edited by Donald S. Lopez, Jr., 103–123. Chicago: University of Chicago Press.

Ong, Aihwa. 1999. *Flexible Citizenship: The Cultural Logics of Transnationality*. Durham, NC: Duke University Press.

———. 2006. *Neoliberalism as Exception: Mutations in Citizenship and Sovereignty*. Durham, NC: Duke University Press.

Overmyer, Daniel, ed. 2003. *Religion in China Today*. Cambridge: Cambridge University Press/China Quarterly.

Palanee Dhitiwatana. 1982. "Buddhism and Thai Education." *South East Asian Review* 7 (1/2): 75–86.

Palmer, David. 2008. "Heretical Doctrines, Reactionary Secret Societies, Evil Cults: Labeling Heterodoxy in Twentieth-Century China." In *Chinese Religiosities: Afflictions of Modernity and State Formation*, edited by Mayfair Yang, 113–134. Berkeley: University of California Press.

Pannapadipo, Phra Peter. 2001. *Little Angels: The Real Life Stories of Thai Novice Monks*. Bangkok: Post Books.

Pattana Kitiarsa. 2010. "Missionary Intent and Monastic Networks: Thai Buddhism as a Transnational Religion." *Sojourn* 25 (1): 109–132.

Phairot Bunphuk. 2001. *Yeuan khwaen daen Tai nay Sipsongpanna* (Visiting the Land of the Tai in Sipsongpannā). Bangkok: Thān Akson.

Pittman, Don A. 2001. *Towards a Modern Chinese Buddhism: Taixu's Reforms*. Honolulu: University of Hawai'i Press.

Potter, Pitman. 2003. "Belief in Control: Regulation of Religion in China." In *Religion in China Today*, edited by Daniel Overmyer, 11–31. New York: Cambridge University Press.

Qin Wenjie. 2000. "The Buddhist Revival in Post-Mao China: Women Reconstruct Buddhism on Mt. Emei." PhD diss., Harvard University.

Rarinthorn Petcharoen. 2015. "Two Monks Arrested for Child Sexual Abuse." *Bangkok Post*, March 5. www.bangkokpost.com/news/crime/489630/two-monks-arrested -for-child-sexual-abuse. Accessed May 30, 2015.

Ratanaporn Sethakul. 2000. "Tai Lue of Sipsongpanna and Müang Nan in the Nineteenth-Century." In *Civility and Savagery: Social Identity in Tai States*, edited by Andrew Turton, 319–329. Richmond, Surrey: Curzon.

———. 2010. "Lan Na Buddhism and Bangkok Centralization in Late 19th and early 20th Century: Changes and Reactions of the Sangha." Paper presented at "Theravada Buddhism under Colonialism," ISEAS, Singapore, May.

Reid, Anthony. 1998. "National and Ethnic Identities in a Democratic Age: Some Thoughts of a Southeast Asian Historian." In *Religion, Ethnicity and Modernity in Southeast Asia*, edited by Oh Myung-Seok and Kim Hyung-Jun, 11–42. Seoul: Seoul National University Press.

"Religion and Feudal Superstition." (1979) 1981. Translated by Christopher Morris. Reprinted in *Chinese Essays on Religion and Faith*, edited by Douglas Lancashire, 277–280. Hong Kong: Chinese Materials Center.

Reynolds, Craig. 1972. "The Buddhist Monkhood in Nineteenth Century Thailand." PhD diss., Cornell University.

Riesebrodt, Martin. 2010. *The Promise of Salvation*. Chicago: University of Chicago Press.

Samuels, Jeffrey. 2004. "Toward an Action-Oriented Pedagogy: Buddhist Texts and Monastic Education in Contemporary Sri Lanka." *Journal of the American Academy of Religion* 72 (4): 955–971.

———. 2010. *Attracting the Heart: Social Relations and the Aesthetics of Emotion in Sri Lankan Monastic Culture.* Honolulu: University of Hawai'i Press.

Sao Htun Hmat Win. 1986. *The Initiation of Novicehood and the Ordination of Monkhood in the Burmese Buddhist Culture.* Rangoon, Burma: Department of Religious Affairs.

Schein, Louisa. 2000. *Minority Rules: The Miao and the Feminine in China's Cultural Politics.* Durham, NC: Duke University Press.

Schober, Juliane. 1995. "The Theravāda Buddhist Engagement with Modernity in Southeast Asia: Whither the Social Paradigm of the Galactic Polity?" *Journal of Southeast Asian Studies* 26 (2): 307–325.

———. 1997. "Buddhist Just Rule and Burmese National Culture: State Patronage of the Chinese Tooth Relic in Myanma." *History of Religions* 36 (3): 218–243.

———. 2007. "Colonial Knowledge and Buddhist Education in Burma." In *Buddhism, Power and Political Order,* edited by Ian Harris, 52–70. London: Routledge.

Scott, James. 1992. *Domination and the Arts of Resistance: Hidden Transcripts.* New Haven, CT: Yale University Press.

———. 1998. *Seeing Like a State.* New Haven, CT: Yale University Press.

———. 2010. *The Art of Not Being Governed.* New Haven, CT: Yale University Press.

Seneviratne, H. L. 1999. *The Work of Kings: The New Buddhism in Sri Lanka.* Chicago: University of Chicago Press.

Shih, Chih-Yu. 2002. *Negotiating Ethnicity in China: Citizenship as a Response to the State.* London: Routledge.

Skilling, Peter, Jason A. Carbine, Claudio Cicuzza, and Santi Pakdeekham, eds. 2012. *How Theravāda is Theravāda: Exploring Buddhist Identities.* Chiang Mai, Thailand: Silkworm Books.

Smith, J. Z. 2004. *Relating Religion: Essays in the Study of Religion.* Chicago: University of Chicago Press.

Southwold, M. 1983. *Buddhism in Life: The Anthropological Study of Religion and the Sinhalese Practice of Buddhism.* Manchester: Manchester University Press.

Sovanratana, Venerable Khy. 2008. "Buddhist Education Today: Progress and Challenges." In *People of Virtue: Reconfiguring Religion, Power and Moral Order in Cambodia Today,* edited by Alexandra Kent and David Chandler, 257–271. Copenhagen: Nordic Institute of Asian Studies.

Spiro, Melford. 1970. *Buddhism and Society: a Great Tradition and Its Burmese Vicissitudes.* Berkeley: University of California Press.

Sullivan, Winnifred. 2007. *The Impossibility of Religious Freedom.* Princeton, NJ: Princeton University Press.

Swearer, Donald K. 1976. *Wat Haripunjaya: A Study of the Royal Temple of the Buddha's Relic, Lamphun, Thailand.* Missoula, MT: Scholars Press for the American Academy of Religion.

———. 1995. *The Buddhist World of Southeast Asia.* Albany: State University of New York Press.

Tambiah, Stanley. 1970. *Buddhism and the Spirit Cults in Northeast Thailand.* Cambridge: Cambridge University Press.

———. 1976. *World Conqueror, World Renouncer: A Study of Buddhism and Polity in Thailand against an Historical Background.* Cambridge: Cambridge University Press.

Tanabe Shigeharu. 1988. "Spirits and Ideological Discourse: The Tai Lü Guardian Cults in Yunnan." *Sojourn: Social Issues in Southeast Asia* 3 (1): 1–25.

Tan Leshan. 1995. "Theravada Buddhism and Village Economy: A Comparative Study in Sipsongpanna of Southwest China." PhD diss., Cornell University.

——. 1999–2000. "Autonomy Is Not What It Was." *Chinabrief* 2 (4): 1–6.

Tannenbaum, Niccola. 1995. *Who Can Compete against the Word? Power-Protection and Buddhism in Shan Worldview.* Monograph and Occasional Paper Series, no. 51. Ann Arbor, MI: Association of Asian Studies.

Thanissaro Bhikkhu (Geoffrey DeGraff). 2001. *The Buddhist Monastic Code: The Patimokkha Training Rules Translated and Explained.* Valley Center, CA: Metta Forest Monastery.

Theut Kianphumi. 2000. *Peut lok Sipsong panna* (Opening the World of Sipsongpannā). Bangkok: Thān Akson.

Thongchai Winichakul. 1994. *Siam Mapped: A History of the Geo-Body of a Nation.* Honolulu: University of Hawaiʻi Press.

——. 2008. "Nationalism and the Radical Intelligentsia in Thailand." *Third World Quarterly* 29 (3): 575–591.

Tsing, Anna Lowenhaupt. 2005. *Friction: An Ethnography of Global Connection.* Princeton, NJ: Princeton University Press.

Tuttle, Gray. 2005. *Tibetan Buddhism in the Making of Modern China.* New York: Columbia University Press.

Tweed, Thomas. 2006. *Crossing and Dwelling: A Theory of Religion.* Cambridge, MA: Harvard University Press.

——. 2011. "Theory and Method in the Study of Buddhism: Toward 'Translocative' Analysis." *Journal of Global Buddhism* 12: 17–32.

Vala, Carsten. 2009. "Pathways to the Pulpit: Leadership Training in 'Patriotic' and Unregistered Chinese Protestant Churches." In *Making Religion, Making the State: The Politics of Religion in Modern China,* 96–125. Stanford, CA: Stanford University Press.

Veer, Peter van der. 2014. *The Modern Spirit of Asia: The Spiritual and the Secular in China and India.* Princeton, NJ: Princeton University Press.

Wachirayān Warorot, Somdet Phra Mahā Samana Chao-krom-phraya. 1973. *Entrance to the Vinaya.* Bangkok: Mahāmakut Rājavidyalaya Press.

Wang Haitao. 2001. *Yunnan Fojiao shi* (The History of Buddhism in Yunnan). Kunming: Yunnan meishu chubanshe.

Wank, David. 2009. "Institutionalizing 'Religion' in China's Buddhism: Political Phases of Local Revival." In *Making Religion, Making the State: The Politics of Religion in Modern China,* 126–150. Stanford, CA: Stanford University Press.

Wasan Panyagaew. 2010. "Cross-Border Journeys and Minority Monks: The Making of Buddhist Places in Southwest China." *Asian Ethnicity* 11 (1): 43–59.

Welch, Holmes. 1968. *The Buddhist Revival in China: 1900–1950.* Cambridge, MA: Harvard University Press.

——. 1972. *Buddhism under Mao.* Cambridge, MA: Harvard University Press.

"White Paper: Freedom of Religious Belief in China." 1997. People's Republic of China. http://www.china-embassy.org/eng/zt/zjxy/t36492.htm. Accessed April 2010.

Wilson, Constance. 1983. *Thailand: A Handbook of Historical Statistics.* Boston, MA: G.K. Hall.

Wu Guirong, ed. 2006. *Xue kexue, po mixin* (Study Science, Break Superstition). Kunming: Yunnan keji chubanshe.

Wyatt, David. 1994. *Studies in Thai History.* Chiang Mai, Thailand: Silkworm Books.

Xiang Xiang and Tao Guoxiang, eds. 2001. *Fan mixin, fan xiejiao: Jiaoyu duben* (Oppose Superstition, Oppose Evil Cults: An Educational Handbook). Kunming: Yunnan keji chubanshe.

Yang, Fenggang. 2006. "The Red, Black and Grey Markets of Religion in China." *Sociological Quarterly* 47: 93–122.

Yang, Fenggang, and Dedong Hui. 2005. "The Bailin Buddhist Temple: Thriving under Communism." In *State, Market and Religion in Chinese Societies,* edited by Joseph Tamney and Fenggang Yang, 63–86. Leiden: Brill.

Yang Xuezheng, ed. 1994. *Yunnan zongjiao zhishi bai wen* (One Hundred Questions on Religious Knowledge in Yunnan). Kunming: Yunnan renmin chubanshe.

Yi Kang. 2006. *Xishuangbanna Daizu shenghuo xisu yu chuantong wenhua* (Traditional Culture and Life Practices of the Dai People of Xishuangbanna). Kunming: Yunnan renmin chubanshe.

Yu, Anthony C. 2005. *State and Religion in China: Historical and Textual Perspectives.* Chicago: Open Court.

Yunnan Buddhist Association. 2006. *Cai yun fa yu* (Enjoying the Favor of Buddha over Rosy Clouds) 7 (3).

Zack, Stephen J. 1977. "Buddhist Education under Prince Wachirayān Warōrot." PhD diss., Cornell University.

Zhao Shilin and Wu Jinghua. 1997. *Daizu wenhua zhi* (A Cultural History of the Dai Nationality). Kunming: Yunnan minzu chubanshe.

Zheng Xiaoyun. 1997. "Shehui bianqian zhong de daizu wenhua" (Dai Culture in the Midst of Social Change). *Zhongguo shehui kexue* (Chinese Social Science), May, 126–141.

Zheng Xiaoyun and Yu Tao. 1995. *Muyu shengshui de nuxing* (Women Bathed in Holy Water: The Dais). Kunming: Yunnan jiaoyu chubanshe.

Index

Abbots, 40–41, 84, 85, 185n. 18;
   acting *in loco parentis,* 109;
   promotion, 47; on public
   schools, 121
Accreditation, 145, 147, 157–158
Action-oriented pedagogy, 116
Aesthetics and discipline, 115, 185n. 19
Ajahn Brahm, 4
Akkhara, 134, 149, 187n. 16
Alcohol, 185n. 21
Alphabet, Dai-lue, 45, 71, 72, 106, 112,
   117–118, 127, 134, 142, 149, 170,
   184n. 11
Appadurai, Arjun, 17
Apprentice education, 8, 108, 109,
   110, 119, 124; and curricular
   education, 137; Dai-lue identity,
   118; laity and, 117; local forms of
   Buddhism, 126; teacher-student
   relationship, 138; variety within,
   112; and village temples, 125
Asad, Talal, 30, 34
Ashiwa, Yoshiko and David Wank,
   12, 54
Authority, 41, 49, 50, 76, 78, 171
Autonomous prefecture, 15, 32, 86, 119
Autonomy, 75, 139–141, 147, 151

Behavior, 21, 108, 110, 114, 117, 185n.
   20; in temples, 31–32
Blackburn, Anne, 8, 16, 90
Borders, and Buddhist communities,
   20, 158; Buddhists crossing, 8,
   92; of China and Southeast Asia,
   16, 33; transnational, 97
Bourdieu, Pierre, 92
Buddha, the Life of the, 5, 7, 142, 143–144
Buddhism: and belonging, 23; crossing
   sectarian boundaries, 158; Dai-
   lue identity, 35, 38; Daizu, 34;
   and Dai-lue culture, 133, 150;
   and economic development,
   65; and English language
   propagation, 157, 158; and Falun
   Gong, 56; and flexibility, 154;
   intra-Buddhist competition, 172;
   legitimacy of, 19–20; marketable
   forms, 182n. 9; minority form
   of, 174; modern forms of,
   179n. 3; and national laws, 74;
   and nation-state, 17; between
   national and transnational, 21;
   nature of, 18, 157–158, 169, 173;
   network spoke, 154, 157; original
   forms of, 29; and patriotism,
   164; and politics, 75–77; post-
   Mao, 41; scholarship about, 178n.
   16, 178–179n. 19; "smokeless
   factory," 70; Southeast Asian
   forms, 6, 29; and the state, 5;
   state governance, 55; trans-
   sectarian, 169; threefold
   division, 4, 168; and tourism,
   65; translocal, 29, 143; Yunnan
   forms of, 168
Buddhism of Sipsongpannā and
   Chinese discourses, 31
Buddhist and Pali College, 99, 183n. 12
Buddhist Association of China, 56,
   64–65, 76, 80, 87, 92, 99, 157,
   168, 178n. 12; as network spoke,
   171
Buddhist Association of Shanghai, 163
Buddhist Association of Sipsongpannā,
   37, 49, 53, 66–71, 72, 182n. 14;
   discipline, 75; networks, 75,
   87, 156; networks spoke, 161;
   publishing projects, 133; support
   for public education, 120;
   Yunnan Buddhist Institute, 167

Buddhist Association of Yunnan, 13,
    80, 156, 167
Buddhist College of Singapore, 1, 3, 8,
    16, 99, 157–158, 175, 183n. 12,
    188n. 3
Buddhist conferences, 164, 187n. 2
Buddhist education as international
    project, 168
Buddhist ethnoscape, 17–18, 80, 81, 91,
    153, 159, 167
Buddhist Institute of Sipsongpannā.
    See Dhamma school of
    Sipsongpannā
Buddhist institutes, 6, 7, 8, 168
Buddhist knowledge, variance in, 112,
    114
Buddhist networks and politics, 100
Bulang, 10, 53, 90, 132, 172
Bunchuay Sisawath, 41, 42
Bunnag, Jane, 180n. 12

Calibrated coercion, 63
Cao phaendin, 36, 42, 179–180n. 7
Casas, Roger, 39
Chakrabarty, Dipesh, 175
Chau, Adam, 63
"China" moments, 14, 55, 108, 122,
    125–126, 129, 151, 154
Chinese academics: on Daizu, 99; on
    ordination, 45, 180n. 16; on
    Sangha, 75; on Sipsongpannā,
    33, 34
Chinese Buddhism, 1, 2, 64, 164
Chinese Buddhist ethnoscape, 87
Chinese minorities, 14
Chinese monks, 10, 88, 91; attitudes to
    Dai-lue novices, 166
Chinese state, 4, 10, 174–175, 178n. 12;
    attitudes to Buddhism, 150;
    defining religion and religion,
    12, 54, 62; governing religion,
    100; and legibility of networks,
    100; and regulating religion, 63,
    128; and Sangha hierarchy, 45
Christians/Christianity, 38, 68
Citizens/citizenship, 18, 61, 81,
    89, 82, 100, 108, 126, 162;
    Buddhist institutes, 167, 188n.
    8; and development, 61; and
    minorities, 11; monks as, 15, 21,
    154, 176; and networks, 167; and
    religion, 57
Civilization, discourses and status, 38,
    91, 108, 124, 187n. 15

Communist Party of China, 57, 64, 147
Cooke, Miriam and Bruce Lawrence, 81
Crosby, Kate, 4
Cultural nationalism (Dai-lue), 71
Cultural Revolution, 2, 37, 47, 94, 113,
    134; Dai-lue Buddhism, 11
Curricula, 8, 137; bilingual, 121;
    Buddhist, 142–144; and Dai-lue
    identity, 143; and government
    regulation, 15; in Mahāyāna
    Buddhist institutes, 165;
    secular, 145–147; Yunnan
    Buddhist Institute, 168
Curricular education, 8, 9, 136–139;
    and comportment, 137; goals,
    147; modernity of, 186n. 8;
    standardized knowledge, 137;
    and the state, 138; time and
    space, 136–137

Dai-Han Dictionary, 71, 72, 127, 134,
    135, 187n. 15
Dai-lue: as Chinese citizens, 89; culture
    and gender, 125; cultural
    curriculum, 148; and Dai-neau,
    91; ethnoneme, 15; history, 33;
    identity and governance, 154;
    language practices, 34, 151;
    minority of China, 19
Dai-lue Buddhism: Chinese names
    for, 35; Chinese state, 17; and
    disciplinary practices, 115;
    and gender, 36, 183n. 2; and
    governance, 126; and identity,
    118, 129; languages, 32; local
    and transnational, 108; land
    networks, 95; political power,
    37; and public schools, 123;
    preservation of, 133; rebuilding,
    37, 45; relation to ethnicity,
    35; relations to other Chinese
    Buddhists, 88–89; tourism
    and development, 49; and Wat
    Pājie, 72
Dai-lue culture and Buddhism, 133, 173
Dai-lue culture and civilizational
    status, 123
Dai-lue monks, 2, 10, 80, 172
Dai-lue script. *See* Alphabet
Dai-neua, 13–14, 21, 80, 87, 90, 132, 170
Daizu, 1, 2, 10, 34, 87, 89, 124, 170, 172
Dān/dāna. See Meritorious offerings
Dao Shuren, 167, 168, 188n. 13
Davis, Sara, 140

Dhamma course. See *Nak tham*
Dhammasami, Ven. Khammai, 7
Dhamma school of Sipsongpannā, 69,
    85, 128–129, 139, 169, 186n. 1;
    arts education, 148; computers
    at, 128; curricula, 142, 147; and
    Dai-lue culture, 142; Dai-lue
    cultural curriculum, 148–150;
    Dai-lue history, 148; and Jing
    Hong Technical College, 147;
    and public schools, 121, 128;
    secular subjects, 146; teaching
    Mandarin, 129, 145; teachers,
    146; textbooks, 143; time, 146;
    tourists, 150; transnational
    resources, 150; and Wat Long
    Meuang Lue, 130; and Wat
    Pājie, 130
Dhamma school of Thailand, 19,
    159–161; and international
    students, 160
Dhamma text, 29
Disciplinary codes, 41, 73–74, 177–178n.
    9, 185n. 21
Discipline, 16, 32, 75, 109, 111, 114–117,
    137, 142, 182n. 15, 185n. 20. *See
    also* Vinaya
Disrobing, 12, 36, 37, 113, 119, 148, 175,
    184n. 9
"Document 19," 58, 60, 164, 181n. 3

Economy of merit, 41, 42, 48, 82, 83,
    99, 180n. 12
Education: and Dai-lue identity, 124;
    Dai-lue parents, 107, 122; and
    gender, 36, 123–124, 125; as
    international project, 168;
    and national ideology, 107;
    and networks, 84–85, 88–89;
    practices of , 112; in Thailand,
    106–107, 160; and time, 112,
    136–137; and village temples,
    106. *See also* Apprentice
    education; Curricular
    education; Transnational
    monastic education
Elephants, wild, 185n. 17
Ethnicity and religion, 89–90, 125, 166
Ethnicity and tourism, 70
Ethnic minorities. *See* Minorities
Ethnoscape, 17, 81, 89, 91, 100, 176
Evil cults, 53, 55, 58–62, 76, 181n. 2
Exams, monastic, 7, 128, 186n. 6,
    187n. 10; Buddhist curriculum,

144–145; entrance exams, 121,
    169; in Thailand, 8, 138; and
    MRAB, 69, 145

False monks, 52–53, 65, 75–76
Falun Gong, 53, 55, 58, 181n. 2
Festivals: as node, 83; and official
    participation, 13; and
    rituals (*salāt soy*), 27; stupa
    dedications, 93; village
    Buddhism, 42; Wat Long
    dedication, 32; Wannasiri Kuti,
    79–80
Five religions, 56, 58
Flexibility, 80–81, 92, 97, 153, 167, 171
Flexible citizenship, 19–20, 101
Folk beliefs, 38, 181n. 5
Foreign monks, 7, 98, 113, 114, 152
Freedom of religious belief, 58, 63, 77,
    182n. 18
Friction, 20, 81, 83, 97, 100, 167, 170

Galactic polity, 36, 77
Galyani Vadhana, Princess, 98
Gethin, Rupert, 116
Giersch, C. Patterson, 15
Gladney, Dru, 140
Globalization, 3, 19–20, 153
Gombrich, Richard, 29
Gottschalk, Peter, 181n. 1
Governing Buddhism, 16
Governing minorities, 14
Governing monks, 21, 22
Guanxi and Buddhist monks, 64–65, 70

Han monks, 22, 80, 89, 92, 165–167,
    169, 183n. 4, 188n. 12
Hansen, Mette Halskov, 107, 122, 123,
    129
Hanzu, 10
Hayashi Yukio, 177n. 2
Hīnayāna, 35, 177n. 8
History, Dai-lue, 124, 148; Chinese, 166
History of Buddhism in Yunnan, 99
Hsieh Shih-chung, 15
Huizu, 39, 182n. 12

Identity, Dai-lue, 69, 90, 118, 124, 125,
    184n. 3, 187n. 13
Identity cards (*shenfen zheng*), 4, 9,
    160, 188n. 8
Imagined communities, 7, 17
Institutional field of religion, 12, 17, 54,
    64, 65–66, 82

Interactions with monks, 27
International Association of Buddhist
    Universities (IABU), 168, 188n. 4
Islam, 38–39, 53, 56, 68, 81, 178n. 11,
    182n. 12

Jasper and monks, 21–22
Jātaka, 30
Jing Hong, 15, 85
Ji Zhe, 65, 76
Jory, Patrick, 30

Kemper, Steven, 17–18, 81
Keyes, Charles, 106–107, 136, 183n. 1
Khanān (former monks), 47, 109, 117,
    124
Khūbā, 36–37, 45–46
Khūbā Bunchum, 68–69, 74, 86, 100,
    133
Khūbā Siang Lā, 80, 133, 142, 183n. 7
Kingshill, Konrad, 6
Kurtzman, Charles, 81–82

Labor in *wats,* 116, 133, 148
Laity, 9, 10, 45; pedagogical role of, 117
Language, 31–32; new Dai-lue
    and culture, 151; and local
    government, 134; and nation,
    187n. 14; and politics, 71,
    127, 135; and power, 33;
    standardized Dai-lue, 113; study
    of in Dhamma school, 149
Languages of ethnicity, 14
Lay leader, 28, 40, 43, 47, 75, 117
Lay-monastic relations, 74
"Lessons in being Chinese," 123, 124
Life cycle of monks, 22
"Local, the," 30, 31, 50, 179n. 4
Local Buddhism, 3, 32, 108, 126
Local government, 32, 54; and Buddhist
    Association, 72; and language,
    134
Local networks, 83–86
Local temples, 8
Long Darui, 163
Lovelorn Ghost and the Magical Monk,
    30

Magic, 29, 30
Mahā-Chulālongkorn University, 96,
    157, 158, 169, 187n. 2, 188n. 7
Mahāyāna Buddhism, 35, 167
Mahāyāna Buddhist Institutes, 19, 163,
    167, 169

Mahāyāna monks, 4, 80, 166, 169,
    183n. 5
McCarthy, Susan, 71, 107, 121, 122, 140
McDaniel, Justin, 4, 8, 9, 30
Mendelson, E. Michael, 110
Merit, 28
Merit and networks, 84, 183n. 3
Merit making (*tham bun*), 28–29, 41,
    48, 79, 83, 93, 116, 133
Meritorious offerings (*dān*), 27–29, 42,
    74, 96, 185n. 21
Meuang, 36
Minorities, 1, 4, 10, 13–14, 176,
    177n. 6, 178n. 13; autonomy,
    140–141; in curricular education,
    146; ordination, 47, 188n.
    10; minority religions, 56;
    in Sipsongpannā, 90, 123;
    relations between minorities,
    132
Minority and Religious Affairs Bureau
    (MRAB), 13, 68–71, 75, 93, 128,
    145
Minzu, 1, 90. *See also* Minorities;
    Nationality
Minzu and national networks, 89–90
Minzu shibie, 11, 13
Mixin, 58. *See also* Superstition
Modern forms of Buddhism, 6, 7, 179n.
    3, 188n. 5
Modernity, 3, 109
Modernization, 8, 47, 51; *nak-tham*
    curriculum, 144, 148; and
    religion, 57; and science, 58, 109
Monasteries as schools, 106–107
Monastic careers, 45–46
Monastic education, 5–10; competition
    with public education, 106–
    108, 120; and exercise, 8,
    165; and foreign travel, 8;
    and governance, 14; national
    identity, 160; secular subjects,
    145–146; and social mobility,
    160; and stakeholders,
    8, 10, 108; and status, 49;
    "traditional," 109; and village
    life, 6; in village temples, 107
Monastic networks, 95, 100
Monastic promotions, 47
Monastic travel, 97, 157
Monks: careers of, 45; in college, 119;
    cooperation with government,
    71; discipline, 74; economies
    of merit, 83; educational

attainments, 82; educational travel, 157; false, 52–53, 69; festivals, 7; and government relations, 68, 70, 172; informal networks, 157; international travel, 152–153; intra-Buddhist interactions, 165–166, 169–170; liminal status, 167; and merit making, 29; as network node, 82; performing rituals, 28; and politics, 175; protecting Buddhism, 150; relationship with novices, 109, 138; residency rules, 98; responsibilities of, 110, 150; and smoking, 115, 185n. 16; standardization, 113; status, 49, 74, 84, 113; as teachers, 107, 184n. 10; and technology, 184n. 4; from Thailand and Shan States, 50, 80, 93, 108, 113, 119; and tourism, 92, 113, 131; travel regulations, 98, 153

Mueggler, Erik, 140
Multi-sited ethnography, 22
Muslims, 38–39, 53, 56, 68, 81, 178n. 11, 182n. 12

Nak tham, 114, 128, 134, 137, 149, 150, 186n. 1; curriculum, 7, 142–144, 168; in Thailand, 152, 153, 160
Narratives of modernization, 6
Nation, national, 5, 119, 147, 149, 187n. 14
National communities, 18
National ideology, 107, 162, 163
Nationality (minzu), 1, 13, 177n. 7, 178n. 4, 182n. 12, 183n. 6, 187n. 14; and boundaries, 155, 168; and citizenship, 100, 188n. 8; and identity, 18, 23, 90, 149, 171; and monks, 30–31; and Theravāda, 89
Nationality parks, 27
National networks, 87–92, 182n. 1
Nation-state, 8, 17, 19, 99, 178n. 18
Networks, Buddhist, 23; and Buddhist education, 95, 96; and Chinese government, 97; directed by Wat Pājie, 156; informal, 156, 157; intra-Asian, 187n. 2; local, national and transnational, 153; merit-making, 41, 49, 50; and senior monks, 96; translocal,

31, 81–83, 156; transnational monastic education, 167
Networks of reciprocity, 29
Node, network, 81–82, 183n. 11
Novices: as apprentices, 112; behavior in public school, 122; and discipline, 111, 114, 116; and family, 47, 118; high school, 119; and identity, 108, 149; and labor, 116, 148; "leaving home," 42; Mahāyāna Buddhist institutes, 163–166; ordination, 2; "passing," 160, 183n. 2; playing, 105, 185n. 20; public school, 106, 108, 119–122, 125; and public school teachers, 121–122; relationship with monks, 109, 132; responsibilities, 40, 45–46; student-novices, 8, 132, 141, 149; studying at Wat Pājie, 85; in Thailand, 98, 152, 159–161; tourism, 34; views on public school, 120; views on ordination, 124
Nuns, 6, 16, 64, 93, 155, 157, 163, 175, 178n. 9, 178n. 18, 187n. 2

Ong, Aihwa, 19
Ordination, 3, 107, 109, 177–178n. 9; age, 42, 45, 180nn. 15–16; attitudes towards, 124; Buddhist knowledge, 12; Dai-lue culture, 50; higher ordination (upasampadā), 41, 120; literacy, 36; motivations, 47, 106, 150; national policy, 46; parents views on, 122; patrons, 41, 120; and pedagogy, 110; practices of, 15; and precepts, 114; ritual, 46, 110–111; post-Cultural Revolution, 37; and social mobility, 160; temporary, 36, 93; Wat Pājie, 49
Ordination cards, 15, 98, 160, 162
Ordination hall (bosot), 42, 117

Pāli, 7, 30, 153
Pāli education, 142
Pāli imaginaire, 29
Pāli schools, 138
Palmer, David, 181n. 2
Pan-Thai discourse, 34
Passports, 4, 16, 98, 188n. 8

Pedagogy of modeling, 112
People's Liberation Army, 11, 36, 47
Politics of publishing, 71–72, 133
Politics of religion, 23, 54, 60, 64–65,
    151, 176
Poshuijie, 2. *See also* Water-Splashing
    Festival
Public school, 2, 23, 36, 85, 119, 125,
    140, 163
Public Security Bureau, 22, 52–53,
    68–69, 79, 100
Pu cān. See Lay leader
Punishment (of novices), 109–110

Qigong, 56

"Racial and religious harmony," 188n. 5
Rains retreat (*wasā*), 42
Raw and cooked, 111, 112, 154
Reading Dai-lue, 28, 36, 71, 110
Reconstruction of Buddhism, 99
Regimes of governance, 17, 167
Regulating religion, 12
Relics, 94, 153, 187n. 1
Religion: categories of, 38, 56; defining,
    54, 58, 60–62, 63, 77, 176, 177n.
    6, 181n. 1; and governance,
    58, 181n. 5; market theory of,
    181n. 6; official discourse on,
    56, 75; official recognition, 123;
    regulating, 62–63, 181n. 6; and
    superstition, 57; technology of
    control, 57, 61, 63; and Yunnan
    government, 62–63
Religion and politics in China, 77
"Religion fever," 37
Religion in China, 12, 53
Religion in Singapore, 16, 188n. 5
Religions in Sipsongpannā, 38
Religious activities, 5, 54
Religious Affairs Bureau, 39, 58, 63,
    64–65, 80
Religious education and state
    education, 107
Research methods, 22
Reynolds, Craig, 6
Ritual, 41, 42–43, 66–68, 184n. 13;
    salāt soy, 27–28

Salāt soy, 27, 41, 48, 50, 134
Samuels, Jeffrey, 116
Sangha, 2; challenges for, 124; and
    comportment, 115; developing,
    19; Dhamma school, 139;

education, 16; intra-sangha
    relations, 88; governing, 8,
    72–75; hierarchy, 36–37, 181n.
    18; legitimacy of state, 139;
    and political authority, 48; and
    political relationships, 141;
    promotion, 7, 84; reconstitution
    of, 119
Sangha-nayok, 37
Sangha organization, 36, 48
Sangha-rāt, 36, 45, 114
Schein, Louisa, 92
Schober, Juliane, 7
Scott, James C., 15, 140
Secular curricula, 7
"Seminar on Buddhist Studies in
    Foreign Languages," 164–165
Seneviratne, H. L., 115
Shaoshu minzu, 177n. 7. *See also*
    Minorities
Shih Chih-yu, 14, 107, 122
Sinhala monks: in Shanghai, 17; in
    Sipsongpannā, 93
Sipsongpannā, 10–15, 176; 1950s, 41;
    arrival of Buddhism in, 179n. 7;
    Buddha images, 120; in China,
    10; and Dehong, 13; between
    Southeast Asia and China, 33;
    Buddhism and politics in, 77;
    Cultural Revolution, 37; and
    Dai-lue culture, 80; external
    resources, 37; foreign monks,
    113; industries in, 39; "kingdom
    under two skies," 14; kinship
    networks, 84, 95–96; languages
    of, 31; the local and, 29; "middle
    ground," 15; minorities in,
    123; political organization, 48;
    religious field, 38; religious
    governance, 55; rice, 34; Thai
    homeland, 33, 96, 99; and
    Thailand, 93; tourism, 34, 92,
    179n. 20; village wats, 40
Smith, J. Z., 57, 181n. 1
Smoking, 115, 185n. 16
Song kān, 2, 42–43, 66–67, 133, 180n.
    13, 187n. 13. *See also* Water-
    Splashing Festival
Southwold, M., 185n. 20
Sovanratana, Ven. Khy, 5
Spirit cults, 29, 38, 123
Spiro, Melford, 6, 29, 30, 177n. 2,
    185n. 20

Spokes, network, 81–82, 86, 88, 90, 95, 99, 171, 183n. 3
Stalin's typology of a nation, 13
Standards, pedagogical, 112, 113
State, local, modern and premodern, 5, 7
State Agency for Religious Affairs. *See* Religious Affairs Bureau
State-sangha relations, 13, 15, 65, 77–78
Structure, network, 81–82, 86, 101
Superstition (feudal superstition), 38, 56–57, 59–62, 76, 123, 181n. 5
Swearer, Donald, 5–6, 160

Tai (Dai) unity, 71
Tai ethnicity, 10, 96
Tai Theravāda religiosity, 29
Tanabe Shigeharu, 38
Tan Leshan, 43, 139
Taixu, 7, 182n. 8
Tambiah, Stanley J., 6, 29, 178n. 17, 185n. 20
Temple reconstruction, 38, 39, 91, 92, 93, 117–118, 131, 141, 173
Textbooks, 32, 72, 134, 137, 142–145, 175, 187n. 12
Thai Buddhist schools, 15, 138
Thai monks: donations, 13; in Sipsongpannā, 96; and travel, 17
Thai Sangha, 4, 134, 161, 188n. 7
Thai State, 10
Thai views on Sipsongpannā, 34, 38, 162
Thannisaro Bhikkhu, 115
Theravāda Buddhism, 2, 4, 10, 166, 172, 177n. 8; Chinese names for, 35; and ethnic affiliation, 91; and gender, 186n. 7; pre-modern city-states, 179–180n. 7; study of, 29–30; Sipsongpannā, 5, 77, 176
Theravāda Buddhist Pāli College, 172, 174
Theravāda communities, 4, 185n. 22
Theravāda monks, 4, 136, 153, 165
Tibetan monks, 80, 169–170, 180–181n. 17, 183n. 6
Tourism, 173, 179n. 6; and nationality parks, 27; novices, 35; Song kān, 67, 76, 180n. 13, 187n. 13; transnational networks, 96
Tourists and Wat Pājie, 31, 79, 130
Tradition and modernity, 3, 4, 107

Translating textbooks, 143
Translocal and Buddhism, 30, 94, 143, 155
Translocative analysis of religion, 17, 174
Transnational Buddhist education, 17
Transnationalism from below, 156
Transnational monastic education, 99, 154, 183n. 12; accreditation, 157–158; informal networks, 156; locations of, 156; obstacles, 161; opportunities, 162–163; patterns of travel in, 155; travel issues and regulations, 161–162
Transnational monks and the rebuilding of Buddhism, 119
Transnational networks, 92–98
Tsing, Anna Lowenhaupt, 20, 83, 101
Tweed, Thomas, 17, 174

UNESCO, 39, 99, 148

Vala, Carsten, 63
Veer, Peter van der, 181n. 2
Vessantara Jātaka, 142
Village temples, 3, 40, 125
Vinaya, 7, 16, 48, 72, 110, 116, 143, 180n. 15, 184nn. 14–15. *See also* Discipline

Wat committees, 40, 41, 75
Water-Splashing Festival, 2, 43, 131, 146–147. *See also* Song kān
Wat Long Meaung Lue, 48–49, 70, 141, 186nn. 2–3; dedication, 32
Wat Manchuanman, 27, 128, 132, 186n. 1
Wat Pājie: Buddhist Association, 49; Dhamma school at, 23, 69, 141 (*see also* Dhamma school of Sipsongpannā); festival, 42, 79–80, 133; finances, 131; and local government, 128; and networks, 82, 91, 100, 156; as node, 86, 95, 183n. 11; non-Dai-lue monastics at, 90, 132, 167; organization of, 131; and Public Security Bureau, 69, 79; publishing projects, 133–134, 186n. 5; signs, 31; Song kān, 66–68, 130–131; teaching at, 21, 146; tourism, 49, 130–131, 186n. 2; and Yunnan Buddhist Institute, 168

Wat Paknām, 152, 153, 161, 167
Wat Phra-Putthabāt-takphā, 156,
    161–162
World religion, 5, 15, 18–19, 56,
    177n. 1

Xiejiao. See Evil cults
Xishuangbanna, 139, 146. *See also*
    Sipsongpannā

Yang Fenggang, 181n. 6
Yuan Ming Jiang Tang, 163–165

Yunnan Buddhist Institute, 167–170;
    interactions of monks at, 169; as
    minority Buddhist institute, 170
Yunnan Nationalities University, 127,
    134, 151, 168–169

Zhongguo Zongjiao, 55
Zhu Depu, 56, 58
Zizhi zhou. See Autonomous prefecture
Zomia, 15, 175
Zongjiao, 38, 56–57, 181n. 1. *See also*
    Religion

About the Author

Thomas A. Borchert is associate professor of religion at the University of Vermont. He has conducted research in China, Thailand, and Singapore, and his work has been published in the *Journal of Asian Studies, Journal of the American Academy of Religion,* and the *Journal of the International Association of Buddhist Studies,* among others.